International Ethics

For Miranda and Thomas

International Ethics

A Critical Introduction

Richard Shapcott

Polity

First published in 2010 by Polity Press

Polity Press
65 Bridge Street
Cambridge CB2 1UR, UK

Polity Press
350 Main Street
Malden, MA 02148, USA

ISBN-13: 978-0-7456-3142-4
ISBN-13: 978-0-7456-3143-1(pb)

A catalogue record for this book is available from the British Library.

Typeset in 10.5 on 12pt Sabon
by Servis Filmsetting Ltd, Stockport, Cheshire
Printed and bound in Great Britain by the MPG Books Group

For further information on Polity, visit our website: www.politybooks.com

Contents

Preface and Acknowledgements

Twenty years ago there were few books dealing expressly with international ethics. Moral philosophers and political theorists paid only scant attention to the ethical issues arising between communities, and the discipline of international relations remained focused on the political and strategic relations between states. However, with the advent of globalization, moral philosophers and political theorists have begun to focus their attention on the challenges of thinking ethically on a global scale. As a result the international ethics literature has grown steadily, such that there is now a need for a book that provides a critical introduction, overview and evaluation of this literature. This book has several purposes. It is intended to be explanatory, analytical, evaluative and argumentative. It aims to cover the most important aspects of international ethics in an introductory fashion. The standard terms of reference and the standard debates in the field of international ethics as an academic and policy discipline will be examined. As a critical introduction it also provides an assessment of these debates and a reflection on their strengths and weaknesses. The overall aim is to provide the reader with a set of frameworks and concepts with which he or she can situate and assess any number of ethical challenges and solutions.

One of the most important things a book of this type can do is to draw attention to the possible consequences or implications of different starting points. For this reason, the book attempts to show what conclusion can be drawn from certain assumptions and what certain positions or principles might mean in practice. It is only once we have assessed or understood these conclusions that we can reflect adequately upon our ethics and whether we think the costs of our positions are worth it, or not, or whether they are justifiable or need modification. For instance, if a person believes simultaneously in universal human rights and in some form of cultural relativism or tolerance it is important to explore how, if at all, these values can be reconciled and what that might mean in practice. It might not be easy to reconcile a commitment to the equal rights of women or children with certain cultural practices such as female circumcision. In these instances we need to be clear about the nature of our ethical judgements and their implications. Alternatively, if we advocate both a global duty to alleviate poverty as expressed in the UN Millennium goals, and at the same time wish to see the jobs of our selves or fellow countrymen protected through tariffs and so on, we might find these goals in conflict. Obviously, the most common assumption is likely to be some notion that compatriots should always take moral priority, that the well-being of our own people should take priority over those of outsiders. This does not mean we wish ill to outsiders; simply that we do not have to be too concerned with their welfare. However, it could also mean that we are willing to see them suffer, or indeed to inflict harm upon them so that our compatriots can prosper. Alternatively, if we do believe in human rights and, at the same time, want to recognize legitimate cultural differences we then have to assess how to balance those two values when they do conflict.

So the task for the reader is to use this book to aid self-examination and to think through for themselves what their starting assumptions might lead to in certain circumstances and in relation to certain issues. The book does not supply any answers to specific ethical dilemmas but should be seen as an aid to that most important of tasks, thinking for oneself.

As befits an expressly ethical book, there is no pretence about taking an 'objective' position, though it does claim to be even-handed. Thus, rather than deny the author's own moral reflections, these are incorporated into the survey and analysis. For this reason, the starting point for the ethical thinking in this book is that the argument for human equality favours some form of cosmopolitanism. (Of course, this also rests on another argument, which is that all humans ought to be treated as equal in moral terms.) In adopting a cosmopolitan starting point, this book assumes that any ethical framework that seeks to draw and enforce sharp lines between human beings is not fully moral, or, to put it more positively, is not being moral enough. However, this does not mean positions that draw boundaries between human beings can be dismissed out of hand. So, while the book is informed by the cosmopolitan position, this position itself should not be taken for granted and must be questioned, modified and defended.

In addition, the book proposes that cosmopolitanism and anti-cosmopolitanism should not be characterized as polar opposites constituting a great divide between universalism and particularism, but rather that they should be acknowledged as inhabiting positions on a spectrum of universalism.

Cosmopolitans and anti-cosmopolitans sit within a common horizon and tradition of thinking that is anchored in the twin pillars of liberty and equality. While there are significant differences between cosmopolitans and anti-cosmopolitans, both use a common vocabulary of equality and freedom, yet interpret these values differently. Significant differences appear only in relation to the extent, content and interpretation of those pillars. As David Miller (2002) has noted, agreeing that we think all people should be treated as moral equals, with equal moral concern, does not mean we can agree about how that concern is expressed or realized. Is equality best captured by formal institutional procedures and rights? Or is it best captured by a general disposition or by more abstract ideas such as Kant's categorical imperative? Does equality entail an assumption that we would not want others to suffer things that we ourselves might not wish to suffer from, such as discrimination, racism, physical violence and powerlessness? The principal distinction in contemporary debates about international ethics is disagreement of the latter sort, over what equal moral regard actually requires of us.

The second proposal is that the most important distinction between cosmopolitans and anti-cosmopolitans is between a comprehensive account of moral universalism including 'duties of justice' and anti-cosmopolitan's minimal universal obligations to 'natural duties'. This argument has not received sufficient attention in the literature and it is one of the aims of this book to evaluate its significance and consequences.

Finally, the book suggests that the appeal to natural duties is best understood as an appeal to Kantian principles and that the proper understanding of these principles leads to the recognition of significant cosmopolitan duties.

This book began as an attempt to educate myself about a number of debates of which I was inadequately knowledgeable. I also hoped to be able to contribute to these discussions by providing an analysis and some sort of reframing of the debates. In the process of writing I have achieved my goal of coming to understand this literature better than I did when I started. I hope that I have also educated the reader and helped others to navigate the complex ethical issues confronting us all. I will leave it to others to judge whether my other goals have been achieved, though of course I hope they have.

This book took much longer in the making than I either intended or planned for, but, as John Lennon said, 'life is what happens to you when you are busy making other plans'. In the years since I started the research for this book life has indeed happened to me. As a result, I have incurred a large number of debts and received a good deal of support from a number of sources. I need to acknowledge the support of the ARC Centre for Applied Philosophy and Public Ethics (CAPPE) at the University of Melbourne, where I conducted preliminary research in 2002. I also received institutional and financial support from the School of Political Science and International Studies at the University of Queensland. I would particularly like to thank Stephen Bell, former Head of School at POLSIS, for his support throughout my period at the University of Queensland and during a difficult confirmation process. Anna Lord and Helena Kaijlech both provided tremendous support as research assistants in the earlier stages of the work. I was able to provide Leah Aylward with something to do with herself in a Wyoming winter, but the debt for her proofreading and general comments on a fairly rough draft is all mine. I would also like to acknowledge my students in POLS 3502 Ethics in International Politics for their role in helping me to test-drive some of the analysis presented here. Ms Dana Ernst in particular helped me arrange my thoughts surrounding Just War thinking, and some of her research found its way into chapter 6.

Parts of the argument presented here, though in earlier forms, were presented at seminars in the University of Queensland and at the Australian National University. I would like to thank those present for their comments. Thanks to Seb Kaempf, Alex Bellamy and Anthony Burke, who all provided useful feedback on chapter 6, and Alex in particular for some very insightful discussions regarding Just War in general. Jacinta O'Hagan at the Australian National University provided some crucial advice and comments on chapter 4 and on humanitarianism in general. Robert Goodin and Andrew Linklater responded positively to an early draft of chapter 2 just when I needed the encouragement. I continue to benefit from the collegiality and intellectual stimulation of a very lively and exceptional group of scholars in the School of Political Science and International Studies.

Some of the ideas presented in this work were first developed in R. Shapcott (2008), 'International Ethics', in S. Smith, J. Baylis and P. Owens (eds), *The Globalization of World Politics* (Oxford: Oxford University Press), 4th edn. I wish to acknowledge the permission of Oxford University Press to use that material here, in particular, the paragraphs on global warming on pp. 6–7, several paragraphs of the discussion of realism on pp. 60–6, and pp. 68–70. The discussion of saturation bombing on p. 170 first appeared as a case study.

I would like to single out my father, Thomas W. Shapcott, for thanks, as he very kindly applied his professional skills to proofreading the penultimate draft. Thanks also to Helen Gray for her thorough editing. This project has taken so long that I have forgotten the names of all the editors at Polity who have stuck with me through every extension of 'just another' year, so I would like to thank them all collectively, and Emma Hutchinson in particular, for their patience and continuing, if perplexing, enthusiasm and support for the project.

Above all, my thanks goes to Louise Mills, who supported and encouraged me personally and professionally while engaged in her own major work of civilizing our daughter.

Finally, I would like to dedicate this book jointly to my father, Thomas Shapcott, and my daughter, Miranda, who have in their own ways been crucial to my own ethical development.

I

Introduction

[A]t the foundation of morals lies the principle that if morality is to be argued about at all, then the onus of justification lies upon those who propose to treat men (sic) differently. The very process of moral argument presupposes the principle that everyone is to be treated the same until reason to the contrary is shown. This principle is formal in the sense that it does not prescribe how in fact anyone is to be treated. But it has important practical consequences. For it forces into the open the justification of treating people differently because of their age, sex, intelligence or color.

MacIntyre 1966: 231

Here are a few decisions facing contemporary policymakers and citizens around the world:

- Who is responsible for ending poverty in the world's poorest countries?
- Who is responsible for ending the suffering of refugees and displaced persons languishing in refugee camps?
- Is it fair that industrialized countries agree to limit their carbon emissions while developing countries are allowed to increase theirs?
- Should we reduce our carbon emissions even if it means a loss of economic growth and a rise in unemployment?
- Should I give money for humanitarian relief in conflict zones or will it do more harm than good?
- Is it harmful to consider such aid charity? Or should we treat it as an obligation of justice or morality?
- Should I or my government end poverty at home before giving aid to the poor abroad?

- What criteria should governments use to assess refugee and migration intakes?
- Should we accept more refugees and asylum seekers and fewer skilled migrants?

The answer we and our governments give to these questions and others like them reflect the fundamental question of international ethics: how should members of 'bounded' communities, primarily nation-states, treat 'outsiders'.

Ever since human beings gathered into social groups they have been confronted by the issue of how to treat outsiders. Human beings have continually lived in more or less bounded communities that draw ethically relevant distinctions between members and non-members, or between insiders and outsiders. Most communities have drawn significant moral distinctions between insiders and outsiders, applying different standards accordingly. At the same time, many communities and individuals have not made these distinctions absolute and have offered hospitality, aid and charity to strangers. Second only to the realist assertion that there is little room for ethics in the relations between states, is the issue of the moral relevance of boundaries and borders. More specifically, do we have any duties to 'others', or should we simply be concerned with our own community's self-interest and survival?

The study of international ethics also questions whether it is right to make such a distinction between 'insiders' and 'outsiders' in the first place. The age of globalization brings the ethical significance of national boundaries into stark relief. Even though our world may be characterized by high levels of interdependence, we still tend to live morally 'constrained' or isolated ethical lives in which we take national borders as having major ethical status. Many people agree with this proposition when taken at face value, yet these same people often unknowingly contradict it by practising discrimination between members of their own community and outsiders. Many people, though by no means all, in their daily lives will not consciously discriminate against others or think that different rules apply to different people because of their race, ethnicity, gender and so on. Therefore, when we see pictures of starving people in foreign parts of the world or see victims of an earthquake, or similar disaster, whether it be in Los Angeles or Ankara we recognize the victims as people. We might think something like 'nobody ought to have to go through that', or simply 'how awful to have to live under those conditions'. We might even think that we might give some money to help them out. However, most people will also think and act out their lives with the assumption that the national community, and the people they see on a day-to-day basis, like family, are their *primary* realm of concern in a moral sense and should be their first priority. In this sense, people might consider themselves *morally* obligated to their compatriots and family, in the sense that it would be wrong not to aid them. This means that they do not consider themselves obliged to help people in distant countries; nor do they believe it is morally wrong to think this way. However, they may perceive foreigners as deserving recipients of charity and, while considering it a good thing to help outsiders, not regard such action to be a moral obligation. More commonly, this is expressed in terms of moral priority. We owe more to our own kind and less to out-siders, and then only after our domestic duties have been dispatched.

In his recent work, the Australian philosopher Peter Singer draws our attention to these everyday assumptions by making an interesting comparison of the response of charities and individuals to the ter-rorist attacks of September 11, 2001. Singer (2002: 165) points out that the American public gave 1.3 billion dollars to the victims of the attacks, residents of Manhattan and families of fire-fighters and other services. The average amount given was US $5,300 per family in lower Manhattan. Singer (2002: 165) then compares this with the figure for private donations towards foreign aid, which amounted to US $20 per family going towards the poorest families in the world. While the outpouring of emotion and support for fellow Americans on one hand shows an empathy with strangers, this empathy is qualified by the fact that these strangers were part of the same community (USA). Singer's point is not that it was wrong to give money to the victims of the attacks, but that the response was disproportionate given the eve-ryday needs of the poorest people in the world. Singer argues that this is only possible because we automatically privilege our 'own'. Singer's is a cosmopolitan sentiment because he argues there is no good reason why our sense of community or 'fellow feeling' ought to restrict our moral obligations (see chapter 1).

Three questions in particular lie at the heart of international ethics as a field of study:

1 Do we have fundamentally different moral responsibilities to out-siders from those we have to our compatriots and fellow citizens (in other words, ought outsiders to be treated as moral equals)?
2 What is the nature of the obligations or responsibilities that we owe to those beyond our borders, that is, what might those principles be? Do we have duties of mere charity, or are substantive obliga-tions owed to other human beings in distant parts of the world?
3 How can we interpret these principles and how can they be applied?

Most thinkers of international ethics ask how it is possible to treat others as equals in a world characterized by two conditions: (1) the existence of international anarchy; and (2) moral pluralism. International anarchy is often viewed as a practical challenge because anarchy makes it harder to get things done and reinforces self-interested, rather than altruistic, tendencies of individuals and states. The issue of moral pluralism presents both a practical and an ethical challenge. Not only is it harder to get things done when there is no agreement, but deciding which ethics should apply in what contexts, and whether there are any universal rules, are themselves ethical dilemmas.

According to the *Oxford English Dictionary*, the field of ethics is defined as: 'The science of morals; the department of study concerned with the principles of human duty.' International ethics is the study of the nature of human duty in relation to 'strangers'. This book examines the ethical significance of boundaries and the nature of ethical responsibilities, duties or obligations that members of national communities have to outsiders or members of political communities that are outside the boundaries of one's own national state, under contemporary conditions of globalization.

Much of recent Western ethics is fundamentally informed by the twin values of liberty and equality. The central ethical question concerns how to treat others as both free and equal individuals, and what duties arise from this recognition. This preoccupation carries over into discussion of international ethics, where in some sense the central questions concern how to apply these values across national/political and cultural borders. That is, even if we accept that liberty and equality are universal values, do we apply them in relation to outsiders and, if so, how?

The vast majority of theoretical frameworks of international ethics are underpinned by a universalist stance of some form, and incorporate ideas of human equality and freedom. In this context, the presence of the 'other' raises the question of what sort of ethical standards we should apply in our relationships with other communities. Can we cause harm to outsiders that we would consider wrong if applied to insiders? Should we treat outsiders according to our own ethical framework or their unique ethical codes? Ought we simply to tolerate them? Do any ethical standards apply between us?

International ethics as a separate field of enquiry arises because the division of humanity into separate communities makes the application of any particular community's ethical code difficult when applied to others. This is often referred to as the problem of cultural, or moral, pluralism. If there are many different moral frameworks at work in the world, and no single authority to arbitrate between them, how are we to know what is the right thing to do or, rather, whose standard of right and wrong to apply?

One way to start thinking through this thorny issue is to begin with the types, rather than the substance, of moral/ethical duties. The most common form taken by the discussion of ethical obligations or duties is in terms of either positive or negative duties. Positive duties are duties to actively do something. In contrast, negative duties are duties to not do something or to stop doing something, usually duties to do no harm or to stop harming or cause suffering to others. Thus, a state has a positive duty to protect and ensure the welfare of its citizens and a negative duty not to inflict undue suffering or deny human rights. Traditionally, ethical and normative thought in the international realm has been dominated by negative duties and, in particular, the duty of non-intervention, in part because negative duties are more likely to be acceptable from different moral frameworks. The idea of positive ethical duties underlies the recent UN Report on the international 'Responsibility to Protect', where it is argued that states have a positive duty to aid or come to the rescue of the citizens of other countries if they are suffering from grave human rights abuses and their own country cannot or will not do anything, or is the cause of the problem. This is a positive duty because states are being asked to act to do good. The doctrine of RTP is intended to replace the negative duty of non-intervention, whereby states had a responsibility to not intervene in other state's affairs. However, it is a more controversial and by no means established doctrine, in part because it is harder to get a consensus about positive duties. It is also worth noting that positive duties can give rise to negative duties and, more controversially, vice versa. Thus, Thomas Pogge argues (chapter 7) that not only do states have a negative duty to cease harming the poor through an unjust international economic order; they also have a positive duty to construct a new economic order that harms no one, or does not create poverty.

In the context of international ethics, positive and negative duties can be understood in three types of relationships:

- What 'we' do to 'them' (and vice versa).
- What 'they' do to each other.
- What 'everyone' does to 'everyone' else.

What 'we' to do 'them' refers to the transboundary relationships that occur between communities, in which 'our' community might, for instance, harm or aid another. Thus, we have both positive and negative duties in direct relation to the effects our actions, and sometimes our inactions, have on others. We also have both types of duties in relation to the actions of members of other communities in their relations with each other – for instance, when governments deny human rights to their citizens or when war causes humanitarian emergencies. In these cases we may or may not consider ourselves to have duties to intervene, or assist, or in some cases duties to cease assisting, if this would mean supporting oppressive governments. Contemporary Zimbabwe illustrates this issue well: the situation raises the question of whether the suffering of the Zimbabweans is a purely internal affair, or whether there is a duty on outsiders to intervene to stop or alleviate this suffering (which is caused largely by other Zimbabweans), and whether there is a duty to cease providing any support for the government by, for example, preventing companies from dealing with it. (A German company prints the national currency and thus literally bankrolls it, so arguably allowing the suffering to continue.) The third category of relationship refers to duties that we all have to each other as members and inhabitants of planet Earth.

The case of global warming illustrates this idea: everyone on the planet will be affected by human-induced climate change, though in different ways. Likewise, everyone on the planet has contributed in some way to the generation of greenhouse gases, though in vastly different proportions. At face value, it seems reasonably clear that there are negative duties for those countries that have contributed most to global warming, and who will likely do so in the future, to cease doing so. There is a proportionate responsibility on behalf of the advanced industrial countries to reduce their greenhouse emissions (GHE) and to take financial responsibility for the harms that their past and future emissions will cause others. There are also positive duties on behalf of the richer states to aid those with the least capacity to adjust to the costs involved in global warming. This is regardless of, but compounded by, the rich countries' role in causing the problem. That is, there are positive duties to aid the poorest states and populations, who will be disproportionately affected and who have done the least to contribute to global warming. We can think, for instance, of countries like Bangladesh, mostly at or below sea level, or Pacific island states, which are barely industrialized but which are likely to be the first to disappear. In addition, there is also a positive duty that is arguably generated by the negative duty. If we have harmed someone we ought to help them overcome the harm we have caused them, especially if they are unable to do so unassisted (retributive justice). That is, there is not only a negative duty to cease or reduce greenhouse emissions, but also a positive duty to redress the damage done. This is an issue of retributive justice; a duty to aid those most affected by one's harms. These arguments are buttressed by the capacity of rich states to pay and by the two different types of costs that are likely to be faced by all countries (distributive justice). One is the cost of reducing greenhouse emissions and the other is the cost of dealing with the likely impacts of rising sea levels and other environmental consequences. Poorer countries are at a disadvantage in both regards. The overall costs to rich states of addressing global warming are proportionally lower than for poor states. Because they are richer, they can afford more. In addition, the costs that might be incurred by the rich states are likely to be of a qualitatively different nature. For rich states, dealing with climate change might only impact upon the *luxury* or non-necessary end of their quality of life, such as whether or not they can afford to drive large cars or have air conditioning; whereas for poor states reducing emissions will more likely impact upon the basic necessities of life and *survival* (see Shue 1992).

In sum, we have positive and negative duties in relationship to things that affect everyone. We have duties to cease polluting and duties to aid those who suffer, or will suffer, as a result of our actions. We might also have positive duties to defend human rights or eradicate poverty and unnecessary suffering everywhere. The issue of moral pluralism manifests itself differently in each of these different relationships. In the first, we must ask ourselves and 'them' whether our actions are justifiable. In the second, deciding what duties we do have becomes more difficult because there may be different standards of right and wrong at work, and what may appear immoral to us may not be to 'them'. It also raises the question of whether it is possible to claim that some practices are always wrong regardless. The third relationship raises the issue of whether common standards can apply across moral frameworks in situations where everyone's interests are affected. In this context moral pluralism is an obstacle, as there is no agreement, but also arguably less relevant as the common interest, or common good, is more clearly identified.

These three relationships will be used throughout this book to interpret and evaluate different approaches and positions. The major distinction we can identify is between cosmopolitans, who tend to interpret all questions through the lens of the third category, and anti-cosmopolitans, who tend to argue that we have largely only negative duties in relation to the first category. Before proceeding further, it is necessary to briefly understand these categories.

Cosmopolitanism and anti-cosmopolitanism

Most scholars (and indeed most people), writing about international ethics can be situated somewhere on the spectrum covered by the two main categories: cosmopolitan and anti-cosmopolitanism, each of which contains a number of subcategories.

The primary issue at stake in these debates is whether human beings ought to be considered as one single moral community, or as a collection of separate communities, each with their own ethical standards. If human beings are considered as one moral community (third relationship), then one can argue that there are positive duties for the wealthy to end poverty and hunger in the poorest parts of the world. If, however, human beings are considered in terms of separate moral communities, then any such obligations are severely limited and we may have only negative duties not to contribute to destitution. Alternatively, one may argue that it is indefensible to enforce, say, human rights laws upon those who do not share the assumptions upon which they are based. One may argue that nations do not have anything other than a charitable duty to accept refugees or asylum seekers, and then only when internal economic circumstances permit.

Cosmopolitans are moral universalists. They argue that human beings ought to be considered as one single moral community, with some rules that apply to all. Cosmopolitans argue that morality itself is universal, and that a truly moral rule or code should be applicable to everyone. At its most basic level, cosmopolitanism is the ethical argument that all people should be treated as equal, regardless of their race, gender, abilities and so on. Immanuel Kant referred to this as treating people as ends in themselves (see chapter 2). Thus, they see all ethical questions as 'moral' questions in the third category, and ask what we all owe to each other. Cosmopolitans emphasize extensive positive (i.e., justice and aid), and negative (i.e., non-harming) duties across borders. Anti-cosmopolitans argue that national boundaries provide important ethical constraints. Anti-cosmopolitans argue that humanity should be understood as a collection of separate communities, each with their own standards and no substantive common morality. As a consequence of this moral starting point, anti-cosmopolitans argue that primary obligations of members of such communities are to their fellow countrymen and women, so they have only limited, largely negative, duties to those outside their own community. Anti-cosmopolitans are more likely to admit only to negative duties, such as non-intervention; when it comes to outsiders, they condone very minimal positive duties, such as temporary famine relief or humanitarian emergency aid.

These ethical frameworks are reflected in the current practices of states and other actors. For instance, since the end of the Second World War many international actors have used the universalist vocabulary of human rights to claim that cosmopolitan moral and ethical standards of treatment exist, and that all people can claim their rights to these standards and that all states must recognize them. In other words, under this universalist or cosmopolitan ethical framework, human rights should 'trump' the sovereign rights of states, and the international community has a responsibility to uphold these human rights by armed intervention if necessary. In contrast, others have claimed that threats to national security require states to carry out 'unthinkable' acts, such as torture or carpet bombing (discussed in chapter 6), and that these actions can override conventional ethics. Alternatively, it is also argued that the absence of agreement on comprehensive standards means it is indefensible to enforce human rights laws against those, such as certain Asian or African states, who do not share the cultural assumptions underpinning these laws. Within this view, it is the responsibility of individual states, and not the international community, to define and uphold human rights. Thus, while it is true that a common universal language of human rights exists, there is no clear agreement about what this entails.

Neither cosmopolitanism nor anti-cosmopolitanism is a simple category; both contain significant diversity within them, which can lead to quite different outcomes. In other words, there are many different types of cosmopolitanism and anti-cosmopolitanism. Thus, these terms refer only to family resemblances, with each category having generic and specific subcategories. For the purpose of this book, and for keeping things manageable, cosmopolitanism contains the subcategories of Kantian, liberal and, more specifically, Rawlsian liberalism. Anti-cosmopolitanism includes realism, pluralism and 'communitarianism', though this latter term is problematic as it does not give rise to a specific political expression. Realism claims that the only viable ethics that can take into account international anarchy and sovereignty are those of self-interest and survival. Pluralism, on the other hand, also takes into account international anarchy and sovereignty, but argues that anarchy does not prevent states from agreeing to a minimal core of standards for coexistence. Realism and pluralism are similar in that they both begin from the communitarian premise that morality is 'local' to particular cultures, times and places which are most often represented by the nation or the state.

In many accounts, especially Chris Brown's (1992) groundbreaking 'International Relations New Normative Approaches', communitarianism is identified as the main alternative to cosmopolitanism. However, as will be demonstrated in chapter 3, there are problems with this usage today (Brown was referring primarily to eighteenth- and nineteenth-century thought). At the root of this distinction we find two different arguments about the nature of moral knowledge – that is, the nature, possibilities and source of ethics and morality. While cosmopolitans tend to be universalists who see morality as by its nature derived from an abstract, or impartial, starting point, and anti-cosmopolitans argue from a 'communitarian' starting point that morality is by nature contextual and local or 'culturally relative', this is not an absolute distinction. Not all cosmopolitans are 'foundationalists' and not all communitarians are anti-cosmopolitan (for instance, see Shapcott 2001; Etzioni 2004). Therefore, because the focus of this book is less on these foundational arguments about moral knowledge, and primarily with the significance of boundaries, it makes more sense to classify the field according to the stance regarding boundaries. I also wish to leave open the possibility that there are communitarian paths to cosmopolitan values.

It is worth stating here that 'anti-cosmopolitan' is a descriptive not a pejorative term. There is a great deal of diversity contained within this category, as well as a deal of disagreement. However, what is common to its members, as I have allocated them, is a clearly stated opposition to the type of moral thought and practice associated with cosmopolitanism, especially in its liberal form. Not only therefore do these positions have positive claims about the nature of morality and what is owed to each other; they also, in part, couch these claims as a rebuttal of cosmopolitan universalism. I also wish to make one other point in using this terminology, and that is to highlight that, contrary to much contemporary wisdom, moral universalism has been the dominant, more correctly the starting point of Western ethical thought, of which 'anti-cosmopolitanism' is a rejection.

At first glance the anti-cosmopolitan position seems diametrically opposed to, and irreconcilable with, moral universalism as advocated by cosmopolitans. However, further investigation reveals that most anti-cosmopolitan, and especially pluralist, arguments in turn rest on and endorse a variety of forms of universalism. This universalism occurs at two levels: the level of the state, and the level of the individual and natural duties. The remainder of this book demonstrates that (1) once the exclusive identification of cosmopolitanism with Rawlsian liberalism is relaxed, and (2) once the full implications of the recognition of natural duties are realized, many of the apparently most significant differences between cosmopolitans and anti-cosmopolitans dissolve.

Chapter outline and summary

The fundamental cosmopolitan claim is that communal and national boundaries should have only secondary significance. Chapter 2 provides a general overview of cosmopolitan thinking and focuses on the defining claim that humanity should be considered as a single moral community. We should think of ourselves as both citizens and humans, with obligations to other citizens of our own nation-state and to the rest of humanity as well. This chapter sets out and discusses different versions of cosmopolitanism, and what they have in common and where they differ. How one approaches the issue of the salience of borders depends in part upon one's moral epistemology, or meta-ethics. Cosmopolitans in particular, emphasize certain universal properties of morality and moral knowledge, while anti-cosmopolitans draw upon the idea that morality is a cultural product. For this reason, chapter 2 will address several fundamental questions that might at first seem far removed from international ethics. The main focus of chapter 2 is examination of the cosmopolitan case for the universality of the cosmopolitan ethical position.

Chapter 3 addresses the anti-cosmopolitan positions of communitarianism, realism and pluralism (including nationalism). The major argument of this chapter aims to demonstrate that, while they differ in important ways, they nonetheless can be considered as amounting to a single anti-cosmopolitan tradition. The chapter demonstrates that all three stem from communitarian moral epistemologies, emphasizing the communal or social origin of moral/ethical knowledge, and consequently it emphasizes the limitation on universal accounts of justice as presented by cosmopolitans. Realism recognizes cultural and moral pluralism as contributing factors to the international state of nature. There is very little room for altruistic ethics in the international realm, as states must protect their self-interest and even harm other states in the protection of their interest, at the risk of succumbing to hostile forces. In contrast, pluralism argues that communitarian concerns for cultural differences are represented in the international realm by the existence of a society of states in which the ethical language in use is not cosmopolitan but internationalist, or statist. Ethical opportunities appear within this realm in the language of diplomacy, coexistence and statehood. Pluralists and communitarians only recognize the existence of 'natural' duties and do not recognize expansive cosmopolitan duties understood as principles of justice. Chapter 3 concludes with some reflections upon the limitations of the anti-cosmopolitan position and the natural duties arguments.

The second part of the book focuses on an ethical spectrum that runs from the local to the global. This progression from the local to the global provides a useful way of categorizing and dissembling the various contexts in which ethics have international dimensions. The common aim of each of these chapters is to chart the ramifications of cosmopolitan principles of justice and moral universalism, and of anti-cosmopolitan positions that limit duties to natural duties.

Chapter 4 discusses the ethics of 'hospitality' and membership issues surrounding refugees and migrants. This chapter begins 'at home', so to speak, by examining the claims of outsiders seeking entry to a state. While often overlooked in treatments of international ethics, migration and refugee issues are arguably the starting point of ethical relationships between political communities. Debates surrounding migration and the movement of people examine the ethical justifications of the right to sovereignty and exclusion, and attempt to establish whether and how states can have such rights. Physical exclusion is one of the defining capacities and privileges of the modern state with its emphasis on territoriality. Every time a state declares or is declared sovereign, it asserts the right to decide upon membership to its political community and to restrict entry. However, every decision by a state to refuse admission to refugees or potential migrants also impacts the international community of states because every person who is not settled becomes an issue for some other country to deal with. Having accepted foreigners into their midst, political communities are faced with two further ethical choices: (1) new arrivals can be granted full membership to the community, including permanent residency, citizenship; or (2) migrants may be granted hospitality or safe haven, but are not made full members or citizens. Therefore, in terms of international ethics, migration and refugee issues are underlined by the ethical question of entry and of membership. Chapter 4 examines the cosmopolitan and anti-cosmopolitan arguments in favour of and against a policy of 'open borders'.

Chapter 5 examines humanitarianism, which refers to issues that arise from the conviction that 'we' ought to help 'others' by providing aid and assistance to people who are suffering abroad. Humanitarianism incorporates perhaps the most basic of cosmopolitan values, the commitment to respond to the moral needs of humans wherever they may be, because nobody should be exposed to unnecessary suffering when the capacity to help is present. At the same time, humanitarianism is covered by the principle of mutual aid endorsed by anti-cosmopolitans.

Humanitarianism is a deceptively simple doctrine that raises more complex issues than is often appreciated. Chapter 5 also addresses the ethical dilemmas faced by contemporary humanitarian actors and the limits of humanitarianism as an approach to international ethics. The chapter suggests that a Kantian reading of humanitarianism provides a means of addressing how natural duties of mutual aid are to be understood in the context of the moral challenges provoked by complex emergencies and the delivery of aid.

Chapter 6 turns to violence and warfare, the traditional terrain of international ethics. This chapter provides a critical assessment of the principal claims and doctrines of the Just War tradition. The Just War tradition provides an interesting vantage point from which to examine the cosmopolitan versus natural duties arguments. This tradition stems from natural duties or natural law arguments, but also expresses certain cosmopolitan characteristics. There are both cosmopolitan and communitarian arguments within the Just War tradition that focus on the types of violence and harm that it may be legitimate to inflict upon outsiders. The tradition of Just War addresses the question of what types of violence are legitimate for 'us' to do to 'them' (and vice versa). Chapter 6 also demonstrates important differences between Rawlsian and Kantian versions of cosmopolitanism. This chapter also examines why Kantian theory provides a more morally defensible account of Just War and of humanitarian intervention.

Chapter 7 discusses the issue of severe global poverty. This area has been the focal point of the debate between liberal cosmopolitans and anti-cosmopolitans. Indeed, much of anti-cosmopolitan thinking has been influenced by its opposition to the liberal Rawlsian solutions to the problem of global poverty. The question of global poverty demonstrates the strengths and weaknesses of both liberal and pluralist accounts of international ethics. This chapter examines the debate between liberal cosmopolitanism and pluralist anti-cosmopolitanism, and argues that, despite disagreement on global egalitarianism or distributive justice per se, there is a significant area of overlap between anti-cosmopolitans and cosmopolitans in relation to global poverty. This is revealed once the implications of the appeal to 'natural duties' or mutual aid and harm avoidance are explored within the overall contexts of global poverty.

In sum, there are two main themes of this book: the debate between duties to humanity and duties to compatriots; and the arguments that any duties to humanity are either duties of 'justice' or, alternatively, 'natural' duties. The aim is to understand what difference this might make to our ethical choices under conditions of globalization.

2

Cosmopolitanism

Cosmopolitanism in the diluted sense covers almost all of the territory of international ethics and political philosophy.

David Miller 2002: 975

Introduction: what is 'cosmopolitanism'?

In common parlance, to be cosmopolitan usually refers to a characteristic of a person who is sophisticated and worldly, who shares characteristics of or has been exposed to many parts of the world, and who in a sense belongs to the world or a world culture rather than any particular national culture. Likewise, we describe a cosmopolitan city as one containing many different communities and cultures who usually live together peacefully. However, the word 'cosmopolitan' in political and moral terms refers to a similar but more specific idea. Cosmopolitanism is a very broad 'church', united by the simple idea that all humans everywhere ought to be treated with moral respect (Lu 2000). Cosmopolitans, from the Stoics through to Kant, have argued in favour of a universal moral realm. Despite the division of humanity into separate historically constituted communities, it remains possible to identify oneself with, and have a moral concern for, humanity. To have such a concern requires that no one is prima facie excluded from the realm of moral duty. A cosmopolitan framework is one in which no individual person or group of people is ruled out of moral consideration a priori or by virtue of their membership of different communities. Martha Nussbaum traces the cosmopolitan ethos back at least to the Stoics, while others have identified similar ethics in writers from a number of other traditions. At its most basic, cosmopolitanism says we ought not to ignore our duties to people beyond our borders; we ought not to be indifferent to the suffering and needs of outsiders. At its most ambitious, it claims that we cannot in fact make moral distinction between insiders and outsiders. This means that we should consider ourselves subject to the same single moral code. In between this, there is an entire spectrum of interpretation. For some cosmopolitans, we should merely seek to do no harm in our relationship with outsiders; for others, cosmopolitanism means the establishment of world government (Cabrera 2004), or a single global distributional scheme which assures that no person receives less than their fair share of the global product (see chapter 7). We can identify cosmopolitan thinkers and arguments in almost every major tradition of Western ethics, and cosmopolitanism is also present at certain times in the ethical traditions of China and India, and the Middle East.

For the purpose of this chapter, the most important aspects and variants of cosmopolitanism need to be distinguished and untangled. The chapter begins by briefly distinguishing between a number of different focuses of contemporary cosmopolitan thought before outlining the major different subcategories within it. The focus is on what, ultimately, are different forms of liberal cosmopolitanism – Kantianism, contractarian Rawlsianism, and utilitarianism. If cosmopolitanism is understood primarily as an argument for universal or a priori inclusion in the ethical realm, then these categories formulate this idea in different ways.

From a cosmopolitan position, our everyday assumptions about insiders and outsiders are morally deficient. Cosmopolitans argue that distance and difference should not affect our moral responsibilities. In other words, we should not let our sense of personal connection to some specific people prevent us from recognizing obligations to all people. Thus, when Robert Goodin (1988: 663) asks, 'What is so special about our fellow countrymen?', cosmopolitans answer that, while culturally significant, nations are morally of only derivative significance. In other words, 'to count people as moral equals is to treat nationality, ethnicity, religion, class, race and gender as 'morally irrelevant' – as irrelevant to equal standing (Nussbaum 1996: 133) – because, as Nussbaum explains further:

> The accident of where one is born is just that, an accident, any human being might have been born in any nation. Recognizing this, . . . we should

not allow differences of nationality or class or ethnic members or even gender to erect barriers between us and our fellow human beings. (ibid.)

Cosmopolitans argue that physical distance, cultural difference and community belonging should not dilute our moral responsibilities. We should not let our sense of personal connection to some people prevent us from recognizing a sense of obligation and duty to all people. In this way, cosmopolitanism takes our vague background sense that we are all humans and brings it to the foreground of moral thought. In other words, to repeat, cosmopolitans begin by claiming that all international ethical questions need to be analysed in terms of the positive and negative duties that everyone owes to everyone else. In sum, cosmopolitans argue in favour of the existence of a universal moral realm. Ultimately, stated in a negative form, this means that no one should be treated as if they are less than human, inhuman, or simply not considered as worthy of respect or ethical treatment

This is, for most people, confronting and a challenge to the way they view morality. However, looked at in another light, it is simply asking us to act on and recognize something that many of us already know and believe, that we should treat all people with equal respect. As Martha Nussbaum (1996: 13) argues, 'If we really do believe that all human beings are created equal and endowed with certain inalienable rights, we are morally required to think about what that conception requires us to do with and for the rest of the world.' For most cosmopolitans, this means that we should consider outsiders as equals and that it is immoral not to do so. Accepting this belief shifts the burden of argument on to those who seek to defend exclusionary moral communities and practices and to deny human equality, not the other way round. Thus, if we think that all humans are equal, there are no good reasons for limiting our conception of equality, or moral considerability, to our own community. We must instead treat everybody in the world according to the same standard. However, of course, cosmopolitans acknowledge that the world is not politically structured according to this belief; therefore they also have to address the question of 'what we do to them' and 'what they do to each other'. Cosmopolitanism derives the answer to these questions from the viewpoint of 'what everyone owes to each other' (see Linklater 2002a).

Cosmopolitan ethics can be identified as having an impact upon contemporary international politics and as having real prescriptive value for ethical action. For instance, many activities which we increasingly take for granted in the twenty-first century are expressions of the simple cosmopolitan ethical position. The work of many non-governmental organizations (NGOs) and the developing international civil society are more often than not cosmopolitan in scope as they are concerned with the welfare of individuals as individuals and not as members of particular states or communities. International environmental organizations operate with a cosmopolitan consciousness which takes the world as a whole as its focus and which draws upon any number of nationalities united by a concern for the ecosystem. Likewise, cosmopolitan elements underlie the Universal Declaration of Human Rights (UDHR) and other international rights documents, for, while states remain the agents, human individuals, not states, are the focus, or subject, and the rights bearers. A cosmopolitan ethical position also is present in the international law of armed conflict that takes into account the rights of non-combatants. No such ethical position was present in ancient Greece when military victory meant rape, plunder and slavery (Linklater 2006). Cosmopolitan ethics are also present in debates about the rights of refugees and displaced peoples. When states declare universal jurisdiction over crimes committed in other countries, such as genocide in Rwanda, they are invoking a cosmopolitan principle. Finally, when individuals identify others in foreign and distant countries as in need of assistance or aid they are acting on a cosmopolitan impulse that is more commonly called humanitarianism.

However, while all these are evidence of the presence of a bare minimum of cosmopolitan values in international decision-making, many cosmopolitan thinkers argue that they represent nothing more than a spirit of charity. Cosmopolitans emphasize that there is an important difference between charity and morality as the proper range of obligations that are not voluntary in nature. States, individuals and non-state actors should consider themselves bound by cosmopolitan duties, which it is wrong to ignore or fail to fulfil. The cosmopolitan emphasis on positive duties recognizes not only duties of charity but much more substantial duties of justice in terms of equality. Therefore the logical conclusion for many is an account not just of global humanitarianism but also of global justice. In other words, cosmopolitanism is not a doctrine of universal charity but of obligation. As we shall see in the next chapter, this is one of the key aspects that distinguishes cosmopolitans from anti-cosmopolitans.

However, this is not to say that cosmopolitanism is exclusively concerned with 'justice', either in its legal or distributive sense. As we will see in chapters 3 and 8, many anti-cosmopolitans and critics make this assumption. However, cosmopolitanism is best understood as having a number of different foci, which identify different agents, or actors, responsible for carrying out cosmopolitan duties. In the first instance, we can distinguish between cosmopolitanism as the single simple idea that we ought to treat all others with respect, the idea of a common human community, and the more substantive position that this requires extensive rules about right and wrong practices that apply to everyone. We might think of this as a distinction between cosmopolitan ethics, or *ethos*, and cosmopolitan justice (in a strict, formal sense). Ethical cosmopolitanism denotes an ethical disposition that includes all human beings, or sentient agents, and sees no good reasons for ruling any person out of ethical consideration a priori. In other words, a cosmopolitan ethos argues that there is a presumption of inclusion when making ethical decisions. More abstractly, it refers to the ideal 'that all persons stand in certain moral relations to one another. We are required to respect one another's status as ultimate units of moral concern' (Pogge 1994: 90). As Charvet (2001: 9) states, 'A cosmopolitan ethical theory . . . holds that there is an ideal moral order that applies universally and in which individual human beings are immediately members. As such they have rights and duties in relation to all other human beings.' However, it does not necessarily identify any specific account of what treating another with respect requires. In this sense ethical cosmopolitan is often formulated at a very high level of generality.

Thomas Pogge (2004: 90) makes a useful distinction between institutional and ethical, or interactional, cosmopolitanism. Interactional moral cosmopolitanism refers to individual conduct and 'postulates certain fundamental principles of ethics, these principles . . . are first order in that they apply directly to the conduct of persons and groups' (Pogge 2004: 91). The interactional approach sees cosmopolitan obligations carried out by a variety of agents within the society, such as by individuals, NGOs or government bureaucracies. The ethical dimension addresses the issue of how to enact, apply or conceive of cosmopolitan principles in a world that is not yet fully cosmopolitan and in which sovereignty reigns.

Institutional cosmopolitanism postulates 'certain fundamental principles of justice' which apply to institutional schemes. Institutional cosmopolitanism argues that universal moral constraints apply to institutional designs. Institutional cosmopolitanism provides criteria for assessing the justice of institutions such as the World Trade Organisation (WTO) or the United Nations (UN) (see chapter 7). Institutional cosmopolitanism sees the 'agent' responsible for realizing cosmopolitan principles as large-scale institutional schemes, that is, as the basic principles of society. Is the society itself just in terms of how it distributes duties and rights and does it embody the principles of equality? The institutional dimension attempts to identify the moral universal law and to bring the constitution of the world into line with it. It envisions a fundamental transformation of the rules governing international life, without necessarily leading to the replacement of states with a world state. The difference between the two forms of cosmopolitanism is between those who see cosmopolitanism as morality that should govern the actions of individuals and groups, and those who argue that cosmopolitanism ought to be embodied in institutions or in the fundamental rules of society, and in the fundamental rules of world order.

While both are deontological approaches, they identify different agents who are to be governed by these rules. The most important impact of this distinction between interactional and institutional forms of cosmopolitanism is that, for institutional cosmopolitans, justice is the primary criteria used for deciding practices and conduct. Institutional approaches argue that the first task of cosmopolitanism is to provide an account of institutional justice from which individual and shared practices can be judged.

In contrast, ethical or interactional approaches ask whether conduct is consistent with the basic moral core of cosmopolitanism in terms of the relationship between individuals. Putting it simply, the question is whether ethics should be derived from or reduced to (institutional) justice or whether ethical conduct and practices should be derived from more general individual justice. While liberalism is not necessarily identical with cosmopolitanism (Beitz: 1999), the most important cosmopolitan accounts are liberal, understood in a broad sense. In particular, they all accept the liberal premise that morality should be focused on the individual, it should be applicable to all and it should be impartial between different claims.

This chapter will demonstrate why this premise leads to a focus on cosmopolitan justice rather than interactions, charity or humanitarianism. This aspect of cosmopolitan thought will be discussed in the second half of the chapter, followed by discussion of some comments on the standard criticisms of liberal cosmopolitanism, before looking at the inadequacies of the cosmopolitan focus on rationality and the need to reincorporate other aspects that contribute to human moral unity, in particular the capacity for pain and suffering. The emphasis of this chapter is on how cosmopolitans defend the idea of a universally inclusive moral realm, rather than on any substantive account of cosmopolitan morality or the cosmopolitan position on any specific ethical issue. The latter will be discussed in following chapters.

Cosmopolitan individualism, universalism and impartiality

What reasons do cosmopolitans give for the universality of cosmopolitan morality? On what basis are these claims made and are they sustainable or acceptable? Most accounts of ethics attempt to anchor their account of the moral life in a conception of human agency, or of human moral capacity, that is, an account of what it is about people that deserves moral respect. Following this, they then identify who has these qualities and, consequently, the scope of moral concern – that is, to whom it applies, and why those features are in reality shared by everyone. Generally, cosmopolitans identify the possession of reason or the capacity to suffer as the morally significant qualities held by all human beings, and claim that therefore morality applies to all human beings. Following from this, we can characterize liberal cosmopolitanism as: universalistic, impartial and individualistic.[1] Thomas Pogge argues that all varieties share the following elements:

> First, individualism, ultimate units are human beings, or persons . . .
> Second, universality: the status of ultimate unit of concern attaches to every living human being equally, not merely to some subset . . . Third, generality . . . persons are ultimate unit of concern for everyone – not only for their compatriots, fellow religionists, or such like. (1994: 89)

At its simplest, cosmopolitanism embodies the idea that individual human beings are the primary concern of morality. Individuals should be the measure of all accounts of rights, justice and ethics. Cosmopolitanism is ultimately a claim that individuals, no matter where they are or who they are, deserve equal moral respect because they all share morally significant qualities.

These three characteristics are interpreted differently by the different sub-traditions of cosmopolitanism. Kantian approaches focus on the possession of reason as the characteristic that distinguishes us from animals and that allows us to develop ethical rules. Utilitarians argue that the individual capacity for pleasure and pain creates the moral worth of the individual. Individuals, and only individuals (not corporations), can feel pleasure and pain, and therefore only individuals can provide the moral measure necessary. Similarly to Kantian approaches, individual human beings are counted as equal within utilitarian approaches, and all rules must be premised on this and seek to serve the interests of individuals rather than specific groups of individuals or states.

This, of course, leads to the next stage of the argument, which is universalism, or the claim that all human beings possessing the requisite characteristics should be treated the same, and subject to the same universal moral rules. Universalism means that the same rules ought to apply to everyone in the same way. Pogge characterizes this more formal, or liberal sense of universalism as applying to any moral code which:

> (A) subjects all persons to the same system of fundamental moral principles, (B) these principles assign the same fundamental moral benefits (for example claims, liberties, powers and immunities) and burdens (for example duties and liabilities) to all, and (C) these fundamental moral benefits and burdens are formulated in general terms so as not to privilege or disadvantage certain persons or groups arbitrarily. (1994: 30)

Therefore, he argues, we ought to treat everybody, including both insiders and outsiders, according to the same principles. This understanding distinguishes cosmopolitan universalism from, say, an imperial or hierarchical form of universalism, which would be a system of laws applying to everyone on the planet while also discriminating between different people, giving certain rights to some individuals or groups but not others, as occurred in ancient Rome, for instance. Universal principles must not only apply to everyone, such as the requirement that everyone must pay tax, but should apply equally, without arbitrary discrimination. A rule which says everyone must pay tax, but blonde people pay less tax, is an arbitrary rule because blonde people are rewarded for a quality that has no bearing on their capacity for paying taxes. The criteria concerning how much you pay must be fair to everyone. Cosmopolitans identify national identity as an arbitrary quality that has no bearing on your right to be treated equality.

Simon Caney (2005: 27) argues that universalism itself has two qualities in cosmopolitan thought. Following Larmore, he distinguishes between universalism of scope and universalism of justification. Universalism of scope refers to 'values that apply to everyone in the world' and universalism of justification 'refers to rules that can be justified to everyone in the world in terms they would accept'. So imperialism could be universalism of scope, but not justification, because it applies to everyone but not necessarily on terms they would agree to. All cosmopolitans are universalists of the first type but not necessarily of the second type. Universalists of the second type are usually found in the Kantian tradition and include O'Neill, Habermas and Linklater. The distinction is important for understanding some of the different defences of cosmopolitanism and the claims that are made on its behalf. The problem facing scope arguments is that they are vulnerable to criticisms from those who simply reject their substantive content, and who deny that particular universal rules are in fact universal. This is often the fate of human rights claims in non-Western countries such as Singapore or Malaysia, where the government simply rejects the emphasis on individual rights in favour of communal responsibilities (Bauer and Bell: 1999). Indeed, much of the opposition to cosmopolitan thought that will be discussed in chapter 3 is an argument that equates cosmopolitanism with imperialism.

However, this sort of objection is less of a problem for cosmopolitans who also employ justification arguments because they are also claiming that certain values can be universalized, not by imposition, but by processes of argument and agreement. Truly universal laws or principles must be acceptable to all reasonable agents who are going to be affected by them. This form of universalism cannot be rejected out of hand because of substantive content. This is not to deny there are problems with justification arguments, but rather to point out that they are less vulnerable to prima facie rejection (Shapcott: 2001).

More fundamentally, according to Caney, cosmopolitan moral universalism involves the following three claims:

> P1 The assumption that there are valid moral principles;
> P2 The claim that the moral principles that apply to some persons apply to all persons who share some common morally relevant characteristics;
> P3 Persons throughout the world share some morally relevant similarities. (2005: 36)

If these three principles hold, Caney (ibid.) argues, it follows that '(c) there are some moral principles with universal form (the same principles apply) and universal scope (these principles apply to all)'.

If individuals are understood as the focus of moral thought and they are to be treated equally, then this also means that cosmopolitanism is necessarily impartial. An impartial position does not privilege one group or set of values over others, but seeks to see things in their entirety, from a disinterested position. According to Charles Beitz:

> a cosmopolitan view seeks to see each part of the whole in its true relative size . . . the proportions of things are accurately presented so that they can be faithfully compared. If local viewpoints can be said to be partial, then a cosmopolitan viewpoint is impartial. (1994: 124)

To be impartial towards all particular affiliations, associations and contexts, to take account of the good of the whole, means, in Beitz's formulation, to view people only as individuals, and not as nationals or fellow nationals.

An impartial perspective asks us to see past national differences and disregard them for the purposes of making moral judgements. If assessed from an impartial perspective, national boundaries appear secondary rather than primary in terms of moral importance. For some liberals, impartiality extends directly from the premise of individual equality. If humans are to be considered equals, then we need 'impartial consideration of the claims of each person who would be affected by our choices' (Beitz 1991: 25). If skin colour were used to decide, say, suitability for welfare entitlements, then we would think this to be unjust because it is partial to the interests of some people over others. Cosmopolitans see the use of national identity as a basis for selection as being equivalent to such arbitrary facts as skin colour or height, as opposed to essential factors. However, the point is not that national communities are irrelevant generally, but rather that such facts should not play a primary role in deciding what we owe *morally*. We cannot use nationality as an excuse to treat people differently when it comes to basic moral issues. Thus, according to Singer:

> when subjected to the test of impartial assessment, there are few strong grounds for giving preference to the interests of one's fellow citizens, and none that can override the obligation that arises whenever we can, at little cost to ourselves, make an absolutely crucial difference to the wellbeing of another person in real need. (2002: 197)

Singer (2002) uses the position of the first Bush administration in relation to the drafting of the Kyoto Protocol to highlight this point. In this instance, the Bush administration deemed the values and interests of one group of humanity (or the citizens of the USA) more important than the values and interests of humanity as a whole. In response to the Bush administration's refusal to sign the Kyoto Protocol, claiming the American lifestyle is 'not up for negotiation', Singer (2002: 3) comments, 'It was not negotiable, apparently even if maintaining this lifestyle will lead to the deaths of millions of people subject to increasingly unpredictable weather, and the loss of land used by tens of millions more people because of rising ocean levels and local flooding.' President Bush's refusal was perceived by many to imply that his administration was willing to sacrifice the lives of outsiders to preserve the interests of Americans. A cosmopolitan viewpoint criticizes the partiality of such a standpoint because a special status is claimed for one segment of humanity. To condemn the rest of the world to suffer in order to preserve one's own standard of living (especially when that lifestyle is luxurious) can only be defended by a position of partiality rather than impartiality.

For most liberal cosmopolitans, it is very clear that it is impartiality that generates the cosmopolitan critique of national borders. However, for others, it appears that impartiality is a consequence of moral universalism. But it is fair to say that, for the most part, impartiality is an interpretation of the meaning of universality and equality.

Individualism, universalism and impartiality combine to form an argument for universal moral obligations which depicts national boundaries as, at best, of secondary significance. The three characteristics are not secondary effects or by-products of the liberal position, but serve to define the grounds from which this cosmopolitanism springs. For this reason, they are essential to understanding the argument provided by liberal cosmopolitans in the realms of ethics and distributive justice. It is therefore necessary to understand these concepts in some depth. Different traditions or variants may place different weight on each of the three characteristics and their meanings might be interpreted in radically different ways.

The next sections discuss the major subcategories of cosmopolitan thought and demonstrate how these three qualities are interpreted from such a perspective.

Deontology, Kant and cosmopolitanism

Deontological theories are concerned with the nature of ethical human duty or obligation, and about moral rules that are right in themselves regardless of the consequences. Deontology is concerned with the question of 'what everybody does to everybody else'. More specifically, deontological approaches are concerned with moral duties or commands that are justifiable for all people and for all times. Deontological theories are moral theories in the strict sense that they are concerned primarily with providing an account of 'the right', understood as the following of universal rules, and more specifically the possibility of adopting a view of morality that is capable of determining (Habermas 1990) 'rules about what everybody ought to do', no matter what their specific context or cultural or national setting.

Deontological approaches typically prioritize questions of the 'right' over those of the 'good', focusing on rules that it is always right to follow, in contrast to rules that might produce a good for me, or my society. In other words, these moral duties are right in themselves and are not dependent on their outcomes or effects for their justification.

For many philosophers. it is customary to make a distinction between moral theories and virtue theories. In contrast with deontological theories, virtue theories are theories of the 'good'. Their emphasis is not on the rules that everyone should follow, but on the qualities and characteristics of actors who contribute to their being and achieving 'good'. Moral theories differ from virtue theories, which aim to provide an account of what John Rawls called 'comprehensive' goods, that is, which try to answer substantive questions about what is good and bad and what is a good society.

Deontological approaches contrast with teleological or consequentialist views. Consequentialist accounts look at the outcome of actions, or at least the ends to which an act is directed, in order to judge its moral value. As such, if a rule or a practice is not producing a good end, say, human happiness or welfare, then that rule is not justifiable and should be changed. Utilitarians such as Peter Singer argue that consequences need to be assessed in terms of 'the greatest happiness (good) of the greatest number'. The most significant consequentialist accounts are provided by contractarians (largely Rawlsian), and utilitarians (see below).

A deontologist would claim that, regardless of its effects on an individual, or even on a majority of individuals, an ethical rule is a rule that ought to be followed because it is reasonable, acceptable to everyone or just plain right. In other words, as MacIntyre (1966: 206) explains, 'The goodness of the ultimate consequences does not guarantee the rightness of the actions which produced them. The two realms are not only distinct for the deontologist, but the right is prior to the good.' In other words: concern for what we owe each other, what we owe to everybody, and what we are owed, comes before what is good for me and my kind.

Without a doubt, the most important deontological form of cosmopolitanism is derived from the thought of Immanuel Kant. For Kant, the most important philosophical and political problem facing humankind was the eradication of war and the realization of a universal community governed by a rational cosmopolitan law. Most Kantian thought focuses on the nature of the obligations that accompany the belief in human equality and individual autonomy. While not all cosmopolitan approaches are strictly Kantian, most are consistent with his central premise of moral universality. The major task of Kantian cosmopolitanism has been to defend moral universalism, to develop an account of an alternative political order based on Kant's work, and to explore what it might mean to follow this imperative in the existing world that is divided into separate communities. The central proposition of Kantian cosmopolitanism as a moral (interactional) and *political* (institutional) doctrine is that humans *can* and *should* form a universal (that is global) moral community. That community does not have to take the form of a global state, but there should be elements of global legal order based on universal rights and duties. These rights and duties are both negative and positive in that treating people with respect requires us to refrain from doing some things, like imposing suffering, and to actively do other things, like aid those who are suffering.

Kant and the categorical imperative (CI)

The central moral idea of Kant's work is the categorical imperative (CI), which is a measure of whether an action or a principle is 'right' or moral. It is perhaps the most profound statement of the principle of human equality. The CI enjoins us to think whether we could expect anybody and everybody to act on the principle at all times. In order for a rational being to act morally, he or she must always ask first whether they are conforming, not with a national or local law, but a universal, or universalizable, law, one that everybody could follow without making exceptions or creating special rules.

According to Kant, a rational moral stance meant that one should:

> CI 1 Act only on laws which are universalizable, or which any and all reasonable beings could also act on at the same time;

This observation generates the following conclusion, that to act morally one must:

> CI 2 Act only in such a way that you treat all others as ends in themselves and not as a means to your own end. (Kant 1785/2002)

Kant argues that certain rules are universalizable, but that to be so they must be justifiable to all reasonable beings. In other words, 'the point of this formulation is to stress that not only must I be able to will that the precept in question should be recognized as a law universally, but you must also be able to will that it should be acted on universally – in the appropriate circumstances' (MacIntyre 1966:

193). This means that 'if a person acts on a principle, which he could not wish another person to employ in his action towards him, that principle is not a moral one' (Linklater 1990a: 100).

The most famous example of this idea, one that Kant used, is that it is not possible to will that lying should be a universal rule. Nor is it possible to wish that only I can lie but no one else can. In the first instance, this is because if everybody thought it was okay to lie, the society would fall apart and no one would get their needs met or be recognized as equal. In the second instance, if only I was allowed to lie, then everybody would know not to trust me so lying would lose its utility for me and therefore become obsolete. As MacIntyre illustrates:

> to will that this precept (lying for me only) should be universalized is to will that promise keeping should no longer be possible . . . But to will that I should be able to act on the precept (which I must will as part of willing that the precept should be universalized) is to will that I should be able to make promises and break them, and this is to will that the practice of promise keeping should continue, so that I can take advantage of it. Hence to will that this precept should be universalized is to will both that promise keeping as a practice should continue and also that it should not. So I cannot universalize this precept consistently. (1966: 193–4)

The key idea here is the principle of reasoned consent. I should only act if I think that my actions can reasonably be consented to by all rational beings, or, in other words, become a universal law. A universal law must be acceptable to all rational beings on the premise that we are all rational beings, hence no one can be excluded from the formulation of the law, of the rules of obligation. If something I do affects others, then I should in principle be able to secure their consent before I act. That is, I must take into account their interests. In other words, no one's freedom should override the freedom of others to pursue their own interests. The recognition of the categorical imperative in this form has the political implication that the pursuit and attainment of any individual's desires or interests should not be premised upon the lack of assent by others who are likely to be affected by its achievement.

The CI directs us to act only on universalizable laws, and more clearly to rule out action guided by an injunction that cannot be universalizable. We might think of another example by imagining a society governed by rules that made most people rich and happy, but a core rule of that society was that blonde people couldn't own property. Even if that society was one in which the happiest people were blonde and they had access to all the material wealth they needed, say through wages, Kant would say that the society was immoral because the law denying property rights to blondes could not be justified as blondness is not related to the capacity for reason (despite popular stereotypes!).

Historically speaking, the obvious violation of the categorical imperative is the institution of slavery in which people have been treated as property or tools, purely as means for the ends of others. Slaves are granted no recognition of their rational capacities as human beings and are disposed of by their owners when no longer useful or needed. Their sole purpose is to make profit for their owners. Warfare between states is likewise another violation because it reduces both citizens and non-citizens alike to being purely the means of achieving the (state's) ends of victory or conquest.

Kant's philosophy is a critical one because he implores us to follow the dictates of duty, of conscience, if we seek to act morally. Kant emphasizes that proper moral motivation is central to acting morally. In this, he truly is a deontologist because a good act is to be judged not by its outcome but by its motivation. Only if an act is done from duty, rather than habit, natural inclination or blind obedience to authority, and from the conscious acceptance of the categorical imperative as an 'ought', does it qualify as moral action: 'An action done from duty derives its moral worth, not by the purpose which is to be attained by it, but the maxim from which it is determined' (Kant 1785/2002: 305). Apart from major issues, Kant might well be seeking to criticize those who see themselves as good citizens, or good Christians, because they go to church or give alms to the poor. If you do so because it is expected of you, or because you see that you will gain from it, then, Kant implies, you are not behaving from duty and your action is not moral. If you do a good deed because you are just a nice person, because it is your 'natural' disposition, it is not done from duty. Morality is to follow the commands of duty because you know it is right, and have freely recognized it to be so. This means that under certain circumstances duty commands me to go against my own inclination or well-being, the opposite of what Kant perceived the arguments of consequentialism to be.

In making this claim, it seems that Kant is pointing to something that does seem to lie at the heart of ethics and morality. His arguments about duty, reason and motivation are all directed towards a transcendent sense of the ethical – that ethics ultimately lies in selflessness. It is interesting to note that many modern deontologists seem to have rejected Kant's notion of duty. For these thinkers, ethics is concerned not with the virtues or motivations of specific people, but with the rules by which different conceptions of the good can coexist. For instance, John Rawls and other liberals, as well as critical theorists such as Jürgen Habermas, argue that we cannot describe the nature of the good life or tell individuals what sort of person they should be, but we can design rules, which should be turned into laws, about how society ought to be organized (Rawls), or about the best procedures to mediate different interests (Habermas). For these thinkers, it doesn't so much matter why you follow the law, so long as you do. (Though it would be unjust if you followed a law as a result of compulsion rather than because it is freely chosen. However, this is not a reflection on your motives but on the acceptability of the law.)

For Kantians, the categorical imperative embodies, and for some is, the source of the criteria of impartiality, individuality and universality. Treating peoples as ends in themselves means treating everyone as an individual, and this applies universally. Universalizability is also a mechanism for a type of impartiality. An impartial position is one that passes the test of universalizability. The effect of the CI is to grant every individual equal moral standing in relation to each other. It generates a system of rights and responsibilities geared towards individual human freedom.

How does Kant justify his claims? In the *Groundwork for the Metaphysics of Morals* (1785/2002), he gives some sense of a definition of morality: it consists of duty, of an imperative, "every one must admit that if a law is to have moral force . . . it must carry with it an absolute necessity" (qtd in Cooper 1998: 169). In one sense, Kant sought to place morality beyond the realm of the human experience, custom and desire. For him. the only available answer to this was reason, a pure reason 'a priori to him (man) as a rational being' (qtd in Cooper 1998). He argues that reason alone reveals the laws. They are not given by providence, or natural law; they are not derived from, or formulated, according to their perceived consequences but are derived from within reason alone. Kant wanted to ground morality. He wanted to provide it with some certainty which was independent of individual human desires and fallibility, and yet which ultimately was a morality for reasonable beings. Pure reason provides the only grounds for securing the moral realm against the vagaries of human experience, custom, habit and desire, and yet it is not a reason that exists independently of humans either.

To make a claim that someone ought to be treated morally is to make a claim that, in Kantian terms, all people should be treated as persons. Persons are capable of moral agency, or freedom; in Kant's terms, they are different from non-persons who may have a capacity to act, to do things in the world, but who do not have other capacities required to be moral. For example, severely mentally impaired people have capacities to act, to be happy or unhappy, but not many have the capacity to reflect upon their means and ends for achieving these states of being. Likewise, small children are not considered to be moral agents because they lack the full ability to reason and therefore do not have the capacity to act according to conceptions of right and wrong. Both people with mental impairment and most small children are, however, considered to be moral subjects rather than agents. That is, even while they cannot exercise agency in the full sense, they are nonetheless deserving of moral/ethical treatment by those who can. Thus, they have a moral standing but it is not fully equal because of their limited mental capacities. If someone is a rational being, they are so regardless of where they live or how far away they are. Therefore our obligations to them are not diminished by such factors. Reason is what distinguishes us from other animals and it is only to reasoning beings that we owe moral duties. Reason provides the means by which moral universals can be grasped and formulated, but it also provides the unifying quality for humanity because all human beings have the ability to use reason.

In many contemporary discussions of cosmopolitanism the direct connection to Kant is unclear (see Beitz, Moellendorf, Rawls). However, at least two thinkers stand out as exceptions here: these are Onora O'Neill and Jürgen Habermas. O'Neill argues that Kant's account of practical reason provides the best basis and justification for thinking about ethics within a cosmopolitan scope.

For O'Neill, the nature of our cosmopolitan obligations, indeed the nature of ethics, arises from a conception of practical reasoning. She argues that when we reason about action, about how to act or what to do, we have to take into consideration the fact that we live in a world occupied by other beings who are like us in the sense that they are imperfect, finite, and yet have a capacity to make decisions and to act upon them. If others have the capacity to be agents or to act, then they have ethical standing for us and we cannot deny them ethical standing without being hypocrites. Therefore, once we start dealing with others, no matter where they are 'we are committed to ascribing to them the same moral standing that we ascribe to nearby and familiar others in whom we assume like capacities' (O'Neill 2000: 197). O'Neill's underlying justification is that we have ethical relations with any and all persons that we interact with and therefore the scope of ethical action is universal. National boundaries and cultural differences matter very little in this assumption. Within this ethically bounded relationship, we must treat others as ends in themselves because they are subject to universal law.

Another interpretation of Kant's thinking has been advanced by

Jürgen Habermas. While Habermas's work has still to be widely applied in the field of international ethics, it has been one of the most important attempts to rethink Kant's ideas in the contemporary era, and it points to a possible alternative direction in thinking about international ethics (see also Linklater 1998; Shapcott 2001; Benhabib 1992). According to Habermas, Kant placed too much emphasis on abstract individual reasoning in isolation from others. Habermas developed a different interpretation of the categorical imperative. He argued it should be understood not in terms of an individual monological exercise in abstract reason and hypothetical consent, but rather as a principle of actual intersubjective dialogical consent. For Habermas (1990: 66): 'Only those norms can claim to be valid that meet (or could meet) with the approval of all affected in their capacity as participants in a practical discourse.' Thus, for Kant, universal applicability was the result of private reasoning on the part of the philosopher, while Habermas, on the other hand, envisages a process of discourse and argumentation between real people: "rather than ascribing as valid to all others any maxim that I can will to be universal law, I must submit my maxim to all others for purposes of discursively testing its claim to universality" (McCarthy, qtd in Habermas 1990: 67).

In this account, impartiality and universality can only be achieved in a universal conversation between equal people who are willing to be guided by reason alone. The conversation itself is an impartial forum for assessing different moral claims, as all participants must be treated as equal.

This form of cosmopolitanism argues that any universal rules, any rules applying to everyone, ought to be derived from a discursive procedure that includes everyone. In order to find out what rules might be agreeable to everyone we cannot just sit alone in our room and derive such rules from reason alone, as Kant sought, but rather we must seek to discursively redeem them in real conversation. The recognition of the categorical imperative in this form has the political implication that the pursuit and attainment of any individual's desires or interests should not be premised upon the lack of assent by others who are likely to be affected by its achievement. In other words, no one's freedom should override the freedom of others to pursue their own interests.

According to Linklater, what Habermas's defence of universalism emphasizes is 'the need for the destruction of all systematic forms of exclusion and the pre-eminence of the obligation to develop global arrangements that can secure nothing less than the consent of each and every member of the human race' (Linklater 1992: 92). The current political order of sovereign states rests on the consent not of citizens, but of states themselves. So, if you are affected by any one else's actions, anywhere else in the world, then you ought to be consulted and your consent obtained before that action is allowed to take place.

Kant and international politics

According to Andrew Linklater, Kant's conclusions then necessarily lead to a critique of the state system and suggest that, as long as state-sovereignty persists, it will be impossible to realize the kingdom of ends. Kantians consequently present a challenge to how we understand international politics by arguing that the current international order is morally deficient and that it is both possible and desirable to change it (Kant 1795/1983; Franceshet 2002) The nation-state institutionalizes not only a physical separation between people but also a moral separation, by limiting rights and obligations and consideration generally to insiders. Most importantly, from a cosmopolitan position, the contemporary international system, or society of states, based on the principle of mutual recognition of sovereignty is less than fully moral. As Linklater puts it:

> While men remain estranged from one other through their membership of particularistic communities they could lead neither morally unified lives nor enjoy a social and political world subject to their control or responsive to their capacity for individual and collective self determination. (1990b: 25)

States and their citizens/subjects have not been constrained by any universal law and as a consequence have been free to disregard the interests of outsiders. Because states do not act in accord with the categorical imperative of universality, but rather according to their own ends, individuals cannot be assured that their rights are guaranteed, even those rights protected by republican constitutions. Only under a cosmopolitan world order, in which states were restrained in the same way as citizens, could the principles stemming from the categorical imperative be realized. Freedom therefore can only be fully realized in a cosmopolitan world order.

However, it is important to note that Kant himself never envisioned anything other than a federation of republican (and sovereign) states who renounced violence amongst themselves (Kant 1795/1983).

Thus, his position regarding sovereignty is ambiguous at best (Franceshet 2002). Kantian thought therefore has a duel legacy in the international context which extends from the nature of Kant's moral arguments and its relationship to his political arguments. Most Kantian approaches refer to the duties and dilemmas that states face in seeking to decide, interpret and act according to these obligations, and to incorporate them into their foreign policies. These duties consist of duties not only to act in accordance with the categorical imperative (CI), but also to seek to bring about a global institutional legal order that recognizes individual equality. As noted above, Kant makes it clear that the CI applies to individuals and concerns the nature of their actions. On the other hand, it also refers to rules, which implies its applicability to more political realms such as law. In addition, Kant's famous pamphlet on *Perpetual Peace* also envisions a cosmopolitan world political order that is reconciled, as far as possible, with the CI. The Kantian legacy in international ethics therefore has at least two manifestations. The first is the attempt to formulate and act in accordance with universalizable rules and the CI, and the second is to envision and bring into being a global political realm, to look at the institutional expressions of these principles.

In the case of the former, we can see that Kantian ethics are interactional in Pogge's sense; they stipulate rules that should govern the actions of agents. It is worth noting there that the CI is a formal principle; it does not describe what treating others as an end means in every circumstance. Thus, Kantian ethics challenges us to think through what it means to apply the CI in particular circumstances, not only concerning the foreign policies of states, but also, for instance, the practices of non-governmental agencies when delivering humanitarian aid (see chapter 5).

On the other hand, the influence of Kant's thought on institutional design is also present, especially in accounts of global distributive justice, seeking to create a globally just world order in which all individuals are not only legally entitled but also practically capable of exercising their moral autonomy. This type of Kantian thought has influenced a number of different approaches to cosmopolitanism, most notably the work of David Held (1997).

Thus, in the chapters that follow, one task will be to analyse both institutional and interactional applications of cosmopolitan thought. To conclude the section on Kant, it is most important to highlight Kant's argument that reason provides the grounds for moral universalism and forms the basis of his cosmopolitan account. Reason indicates that we owe duties to other reasonable beings. Moral action can only occur between reasoning beings as only reasoning beings can abide by and recognize the dictates of morality, understood as the CI. Only fully reasonable beings can treat others as ends in themselves or will that actions should be universalized. While utilitarians do not advocate the rejection of reason, they deny that it provides the ultimate justification for cosmopolitanism. These arguments will be discussed in the next section.

Utilitarianism

The deontological reference to rules which are simply right in themselves contrasts with teleological or consequentialist views which focus on ends. Arguably, the most systematic and rigorous form of consequentialism is that of utilitarianism and, after universal human rights perhaps, the most well-known defences of cosmopolitanism come from this tradition. While consequentialism has been around in one form or another for millennia, utilitarianism is a product of the eighteenth and nineteenth centuries. The most well-known theorists and the founding fathers of utilitarianism were the British philosophers Jeremy Bentham and John Stuart Mill. In contrast to deontologists like Kant, Mill and Bentham thought it was asking too much and vaguely missing the purpose to couch moral rules in abstract terms that had no reference to what humans actually wanted.

These philosophers thought that moral law which made no reference to suffering, motivation, impact or outcome was removed from reality, and bloodless or lacking in compassion and empathy. People, they suggested, could not be moved to do good things by abstract principles of duty. Equally importantly, abstract rules which did not take into account their own consequences or impact upon people's lives were unrealistic. These philosophers asked questions such as: what use is a moral rule if it leads to widespread misery and unhappiness? In the case of the example given above where everyone, including the blondes, is happy in a society where blondes are denied property rights, utilitarians would argue that the law was justified.

Like Kant, Bentham and Mill also sought to discover rational or reasonable principles that could govern action. However, they did not seek to formulate these as categorical imperatives; nor did they derive ethical principles from the abstract presuppositions of reason. Instead, Bentham and Mill argued that humans are motivated by objective qualities possessed by all, such as the desire to avoid pain and to seek pleasure. Therefore, according to utilitarians, 'the only rational and consistent criterion available for the guidance of action is the assessment of the pleasurable and painful consequences of any particular action' (MacIntyre 1966: 233). In other words, something is good or bad to the extent that it delivers either pleasure or pain in human beings. Instead of abstract rules of duty, Mill and Bentham suggested that the proper measure of morality was how happy it made people. Human utility, or happiness, provided the only criteria for judging a society or an action or a law. More specifically:

> an action is *right* if and only if A(it) has as high a utility as any alternative action that the agent could perform instead. (Timmons 2002:106).[2]

Bentham expressed his ethical argument in terms of a now common formula. He argued that a moral code should seek to achieve 'the greatest happiness of the greatest number'. Bentham was not suggesting that comedians such as Jim Carrey are therefore moral agents because they make people laugh, and therefore happy. Instead, he proposed happiness in a more general sense of experiencing well-being and satisfaction, what today we might call welfare.

At first glance, utilitarianism appears to be a sophisticated form of hedonism; indeed, Bentham's approach is sometimes called hedonistic utilitarianism. If the greatest good of the greatest number meant that alcohol, cigarettes and hard drugs should be freely available because they make people happy, and if they were free more people would be happy, this would be a good thing. Of course, this is not what Bentham and Mill meant, because 'happiness' is one word for whatever people desire, be it good wine, or hard work. A just society was one in which both were obtainable. Universal drunkenness might also, of course, lead to great unhappiness as well, and to difficulties in realizing other desires or goals of greater importance. This sort of consideration was studied by J. S. Mill, who sought to differentiate between higher- and lower-level pleasures and pains. Not all pleasure could be considered equal: the pleasure gained from drunkenness should not be equated with the pleasure gained from good poetry.

Bentham, like Kant, also argued that his principle was grounded in human nature. For Bentham, human nature is not directed towards lofty duty and reason but towards pleasure and away from pain. And pleasure and pain can be measured (hence the felicific index). For utilitarians, the desire to seek pleasure and avoid pain also gives their theory a better grounding in human nature, and therefore a higher likelihood of success in informing people's actions. People are motivated to do good for self-interested reasons and out of empathy, not because they are 'enlightened beings'. Therefore, for the utilitarian, an act is judged as good or bad according to its results, not the actor's moral motivations or reasons. An interesting illustrative case here might be that of Oscar Schindler, the real-life character upon whom the Booker Prize-winning novel *Schindler's Ark* by Thomas Kenneally, and the subsequent film *Schindler's List*, were based. The film of Schindler's acts during the period of the Holocaust suggests that we don't really know what his motives were in seeking to save 'his' workers from the Nazis. Did he do this for profit? To make himself feel good? From instinct? Or from a conscious recognition of his duty, in a Kantian sense? While it would be hard to praise Schindler's actions as moral if they were based purely on self-interest, making money, it would also be equally hard to condemn him for acting to save lives in the way he did, no matter what his motivation. Another way to compare utilitarianism with the Kantian approach is to think of the example of lying or promise-keeping. For Kant, lying was non-universalizable and therefore immoral. However, for utilitarianism, lying is only immoral if it leads to poor results. Another example might be torture, which for Kant was wrong because it reduces an individual to another's end (getting information). However, from utilitarian principles, it might be possible to justify torture if, for instance, it prevented a terrorist act that would kill thousands because the extreme pain suffered by one would be grossly outweighed by the saving of thousands of lives.

Bentham, in developing his criteria, sought to counter the emerging doctrine, propounded in the French and American Revolutions, that people were the bearers of natural rights, what we now call human rights. For Bentham, the idea of the rights of man was nonsense and natural rights talk was 'nonsense upon stilts', in part because no agreement was possible upon which rights were central or on where they stopped. Therefore, rights talk provides no measure for evaluating action. Bentham was no conservative, however. Utilitarianism, in political terms, has been a critical and at times near revolutionary approach to conventional institutions and practices. Not only is it critical of deontology but also of tradition, religion and the status quo, because it subjects all social arrangements to the utility principle.

Until at least the middle of the twentieth century, utilitarianism was probably the most important approach to ethics, at least in English-speaking countries. However, utilitarianism has suffered a decline in popularity as an overall approach, as a result of a number of serious criticisms of its central doctrines (for instance, B. Williams 1985). Amongst these has been the widespread adoption of the language of rights. As the case of torture suggests, utilitarianism could allow the suspension of rights in the name of utility.

At the heart of utilitarianism is a commitment to impartiality and human equality. For utilitarians, impartiality is understood in the context of the ultimate principle of the greatest good of the greatest number. In other words, utilitarians attempt to come from an impartial assessment of the greatest good that does not privilege any particular perspective or interest or criteria or individual. There is no basis within the utilitarian account for limiting one's moral consideration to one's own community. An impartial account does not recognize state boundaries because it is also egalitarian. In the writing of Bentham, and of later followers like Singer, the total amount of happiness must be the measure, but in measuring happiness no individual's happiness is 'to count for more than one'. So a king's happiness is not more important than a pauper's. Similarly, a man's happiness is not more important than a woman's, and a white person's happiness is not more important than a black person's. Likewise, no 'perspective or group of perspectives should be privileged when making moral assessments' (Jones 2000: 24). Moral principles ought to be judged from an impartial perspective, that is, how it benefits everybody, with everybody counting as one.

In the twentieth century, utilitarians began to distinguish between acts and rules. Act utilitarianists characterized the classical approaches of Mill and Bentham. They focused on assessment of the impact of actions in terms of contributing to maximum satisfaction or utility. In contrast, rule utilitarianism refers to the utility maximization (degree to which it satisfies desires, interests) of a rule or set of rules.

Mark Timmons formulates the basic conceptualization of rule utilitarianism in this way:

An action (A) is *right* if and only if A is mentioned in a moral rule whose associated utility is at least as great as the utility associated with any alternative moral rule applying to the situation. (2002: 139)

Rule utilitarianism is closer to Kant in that it asks us to calculate what would happen if everybody, or most people, acted on the same principle as I do. In other words, 'Rule utilitarianism . . . has us calculate, not the utilities of individual actions, but rather the utilities of whole patterns of action' (Timmons 2002: 140). For instance, what would happen (in terms of utility) if everybody, or most people, regularly broke promises. This seems again to bring us back to something like Kant's CI, or at least to very similar conclusions: that it is wrong to break promises unless there are exceptional circumstances. Rule utilitarianism can also be used to reconcile utility with rights because following the rule of recognizing human rights leads to an overall increase in utility (for the varieties of utilitarianism, see the Stanford Encyclopaedia of Philosophy entry on consequentialism, available online). Most importantly, rule utilarianism opens the way for an institutional response to ethical issues, whereas act utilitarianism is primarily directed at individuals.

Peter Singer is probably the most well-known act utilitarian because of his provocative claims that everyone with wealth surplus to their needs should be donating that wealth to poverty relief (see chapter 7 for more detail). Singer explicitly invokes the criteria of individualism, impartiality and universality in his use of utilitarianism. It is individuals who feel pain and pleasure, not collectives (Ellis 1992: 172). Because pain and pleasure form the measure of right action and the grounding for moral motivation in the utilitarian framework, ethics must apply to those who experience these things. All humans experience these feelings as individuals and so each individual human must count as one only (universalism). This principle also prevents utilitarianism from leading to the conclusion that it is merely the total aggregate amount of happiness that is relevant – in which case it would be possible that if you have enough ecstatically happy people it would outweigh the number of only moderately happy or even depressed people. This in turns mean utilitarianism cannot provide a blanket endorsement of the happiness of one person or group of persons at the cost of another's. From here, it is a short step to seeing that the capacity to meet needs, satisfy interests and be happy in rich countries does not justify or excuse the lack of this capacity in poor countries. Indeed, it is quite the opposite. Utilitarianism suggests that the level of affluence experienced in the rich countries is only justifiable once poverty everywhere else has been eradicated. Singer's utilitarianism is primarily expressed in interactional rather than institutional form because it spells out individual responsibilities.

Some questions might be asked of utilitarianism at this point. Where does this commitment to equality come from? Why should we treat each individual as no more than one? Does it come from within utilitarianism or is it something that is presupposed by it? Classical utilitarians have not been good at answering these questions, and it might be suggested that to a certain extent they rely on a principle of equality, a justification for treating people as equals, which is better formulated, and defended, by Kant. Peter Singer, for one, seems to acknowledge this when he points to Kant's CI in defence of his approach to ethics and impartiality (Singer 2002). Likewise, Timmons (2002: 146) argues that if 'the main injunction of the utilitarianism theory . . . really amounts to the injunction to produce as much good as one can that is compatible with respect for persons (including oneself) . . . the differences between the utilitarianism theory and the theories of Kant . . . seem to evaporate.' This line of argument is also supported by Sterba (2005) and was implied in Mill's revisions to Bentham's work.

In summary, utilitarianism reminds us that people have a variety of motivations for doing good or bad. It introduces the importance of suffering and pleasure as moral motivators. In doing so, utilitarians remind us that people are not just 'rational actors' or disembodied minds but actors with feelings and the ability to suffer, which affect human actions and play a part in our understandings of ethics. Within the deontological theories, we do not identify with other humans as suffering beings. As moral theories, both deontology and utilitarianism offer universal standards by which we can judge actions, institutions, laws and procedures. So, even though they differ about the relationship between means and ends, and the importance of motivations and individual conscience, both theories nonetheless seek to provide universal moral standards or criteria that are universal and therefore apply to all human beings.

Contractarianism and Rawlsianism

Arguably, some of the most important and far-reaching arguments in favour of cosmopolitanism have come from the contractarian tradition, which posits the idea of global social contract. Contractarians understand the source of morality as extending from an imagined social contract between members of a society. Contractarians do not usually depict an actual social contract between real people. Instead, they use the social contract as a way of imagining what rules a society ought to agree to. The main point of contractarian theory is that rules are not derived from transcendental principles, intuition, natural law or divine revelation. Instead, they imagine a possible agreement between members of society, assuming that legitimate rules come from the agreements made between (hypothetical) people. Rousseau is perhaps the most famous contractarian theorist. For him, contractarianism was a means of grounding something like popular or republican sovereignty as an alternative to absolutist monarchy, because republics sought moral justification in the people rather than the Church or monarch (Rousseau 1968).

While cosmopolitanism has a long history, contemporary interest can be traced to the 1970s and the revival of thought concerning global distributive justice in a Rawlsian vein. Since Rawls, defining the nature of justice has been understood in terms of settling 'the basic structure of society' (Rawls 1972: 7), and much contemporary cosmopolitanism emerged in the context of the development of Rawlsian accounts of justice. However, cosmopolitan interpreters of Rawls applied his social contract globally. Rawlsian cosmopolitans are universalists of both scope and justification because they claim that justice is universal, but also that it must in principle be acceptable to all reasonable people.

Rawlsian accounts are also unusual because they are contractarian, consequentialist and Kantian. Rawls's theory of justice is both a procedural and a substantive account, concerned with distribution of wealth and social advantage. In order to arrive at a contract, contractarian theorists have to devise a mechanism for determining what reasonable contractors would agree to. For Rawls, justice is the first virtue of social institutions and therefore the task of a political theory of justice is to define the circumstances under which a society's institutions can be considered just or legitimate. This can only be done by considering outcomes. Rawls, therefore, is concerned with the consequences that follow from certain social rules about the distributions of duties and rights within a society. Rawls's social contract is the result of an experiment in which members of a closed society have been told they must design the basic rules of that society. The catch is that no individual can know where she or he may end up within this society. Each individual may be wealthy, poor, black, white, male, female, talented and intelligent (or not), and so on. All individuals in this society know about themselves is that they have a capacity to conceive of 'the good', to think rationally about ends and to possess certain basic physical needs. Rawls describes this as decision-making behind 'a veil of ignorance' (Rawls 1972: 12). Rawls thinks rational contractors who are constrained in this way would choose a society in which each person would have 'an equal right to the most extensive scheme of equal basic liberties compatible with a similar scheme of liberties for others' (1972: 52). He also thinks there would be equality in terms of outcome as well as opportunity. Rawls refers to this as the difference principle, where 'inequality is unjust except insofar as it is a necessary means to improving the position of the worst-off members of society' (1972: 52). For the international realm, a second contracting session takes place between the representatives of peoples. The conclusion of this round is a contract that resembles the traditional rules of international society: self-determination, Just War, mutual recognition and non-intervention. In other words: rules of coexistence, not justice. Rawls (1999) spelt this out in his later work, *The Law of Peoples* (see chapter 3 for more detailed discussion).

Cosmopolitan interpreters of Rawls reject this conclusion and the necessity of a second session (Charles Beitz 1979; Brian Barry 1989; Thomas Pogge 1989; Charles Jones 1999). Darrell Moellendorf and Simon Caney, as well as many others, disagree with Rawls's refusal to take up the cosmopolitan implications of his theory. As Simon Caney (2001a: 986) has stated, Rawls 'is vulnerable to an imminent critique, for even operating within his parameters there are cogent (Rawlsian) arguments for embracing much more egalitarian principles of global justice than the meagre ones that he countenances.' According to these authors, there is nothing within the Rawlsian framework that suggests the need to restrict its account of justice to the domestic realm. Instead, the Rawlsian account is universalizable, first, because of its account of the nature of the moral person, and, second, because of the economic interdependence of the global system.

Cosmopolitan contractarians argue that the contract should be considered as binding between members of human society as a whole, rather than just a national or domestic society as Rawls asserts. The underlying assumption of contractarians is that conditions of global interdependence have created a global society.[3] However, because Beitz understands justice in cosmopolitan terms, of individualism, impartiality and universalism, the difference principle must apply globally to individuals and not states. But one of the most problematic dimensions of this claim is that it rests cosmopolitan justice on the existence of economic interdependence alone. The crux of the issue here is that, as many have argued, it is a bit of a stretch to claim that economic interdependence can be equated automatically with 'a system of mutual advantage', which is how Rawls characterizes a society. The international realm, and especially the international economy, are, according to Rawls, the realm of *modus vivendi* – a realm of strategic bargaining, not mutual advantage. This being the case, economic cooperation is not enough to warrant Beitz's claim that a global scheme for mutual advantage exists. In the absence of such a precondition then it would follow that we have no duties of justice to those beyond our borders.

Beitz later conceded that interdependence alone does not provide sufficiently strong grounds for adopting this principle. In particular, he has accepted that it is to Rawls's Kantian conception of the person that we must turn if we wish to find grounds for the universalizability of the difference principle.

Rawls's theory implies a conception of the person that would be applicable to the whole world, and, therefore, his conception of moral agency could be globalized. As Beitz writes: 'Since human beings possess these essential powers regardless . . . the argument for construing the original position globally need not depend on any claim about the existence or intensity of international social cooperation' (1983: 595).

More recently, Darrel Moellendorf (2002) has argued similarly to Beitz – that Rawls's conception of the original contractor and of their capacities and choices is universally applicable. The qualities ascribed to contractors are discernible in human beings per se. The only issue, then, is why should there not be a single global contract and a single global original position? And would the hypothetical contractors choose the same principles for the international as Rawls did for the domestic? Both Beitz and Moellendorf argue that they would. If Rawls is right about the moral capacities of persons in a domestic original position, then he is right about these capacities in a global original position as well. As a result, his account of justice is globally applicable. Therefore, it follows that the conditions of global justice are present because, while economic interdependence is a necessary condition, the conception of the person provides the sufficient condition. In making this move Beitz is shifting to a more traditional defence of cosmopolitanism by developing universal principles directly from an account of human qualities.

However, it is arguable that in moving his defence of cosmopolitanism, and of a Rawlsian cosmopolitanism in particular, to the level of the nature of human agency Beitz is ultimately making his foundations weaker. Why? Because now he has to rely on two stages: first, an acceptance of the universalism of Rawls's conception of agency and, second, and more problematically, an acceptance of Rawlsian method in determining what such agents might choose. If the account of agency is wrong, then the whole edifice falls down. Even if it is correct, it does not necessarily follow that Rawls's principles are those that would be chosen by such agents. Thus, the Rawlsian approach is in effect universalist in scope but not in justification. Even though it employs an account of what reasonable people would agree to, it has to rely upon a universal acceptance of Rawlsian theory per se.

As we will see in the next chapter, this criticism forms the focus of the most important anti-cosmopolitan positions, and indeed much of the anti-cosmopolitanism of recent years is focused directly on this sort of Rawlsianism. The dominance of this Rawlsian approach has meant a certain neglect of Kantian cosmopolitanism. It has also meant that cosmopolitanism has appeared to be almost exclusively associated with a particular variant of liberalism and global egalitarianism. This association has certain costs as well as benefits. The benefits are that liberals have challenged liberalism itself to think in global or cosmopolitan terms and to address matters of grave moral concern, such as global poverty. On the other hand, liberal cosmopolitanism is vulnerable to a number of serious criticisms from anti-cosmopolitans. These will be discussed in the next chapter.

Finally, it is worth noting that, in contrast with this view of contractarianism, the Kantianism of Jürgen Habermas and Andrew Linklater (1998) develops an account of rules of global scope that are derived not from a hypothetical social contract, but universal processes of consent and deliberation between real people. The advantages of this approach will be discussed more fully in the conclusion.

Human rights, capabilities and cosmopolitanism

It is worth concluding this section with a few comments on the place of human rights in cosmopolitanism. Writing in 1992, R. J. Vincent claimed that 'rights talk' had become so dominant that it could appear that it is 'all that . . . ethics is about' (Vincent 1992: 250). It is certainly the case that, in the practices of international politics and diplomacy, the language of human rights has become increasingly important. In fact, many claim we live in a 'rights civilization', or a rights-based international order (Frost 2002). Universal human rights do embody the cosmopolitan ideals of impartiality, universality and individualism. They put the idea of the individual at the core of moral thinking. As Donnelly (1989: 1) explains, 'If human rights are the rights one has simply because one is a human being, as they usually are thought to be, then they are held "universally" by all human beings.' Universal human rights apply to everybody and anyone can claim these rights. Human rights are arguably distinct from civil rights because they belong to us by virtue of being a human and not a citizen (or subject). This means that whether one is a resident or citizen of a nation-state should have no bearing upon whether one's human rights are recognized or not. Because they are rights held as a human, and not as a citizen, such rights are universal and transcendent. Human rights invoke both positive and negative duties and are primarily institutional, rather than interactional, in form. While it is possible for individuals to violate another's human rights, rights claims are usually directed against states and institutional orders. As Pogge (2002b: 168) points out, 'Human rights give persons moral claims not merely on the institutional order of their own societies, which are claims against their fellow citizens, but also on the global institutional order which are claims against their fellow human beings.' Many deontological cosmopolitans argue that

rights are meaningless without a notion of corresponding obligations and, in particular, without an account of who is responsible
for making sure that rights are met (O'Neill 1986). Usually, it is the
state's negative duty to avoid violating rights, and its positive duty
to uphold or enforce these rights with respect to everyone within the
state's borders. In the contemporary international order, however, it
is not always clear whether states have to uphold the rights of people
in other countries. The emerging doctrine of the Responsibility to
Protect (R2P) is an attempt to resolve this uncertainty in favour of a
limited responsibility to intervene to protect human rights abroad.

While the human rights discourse is pervasive, it is also largely
derivative of other ethical positions, whether the result of a social
contract situation (e.g., Rawls) or an account of natural law, positive international law or Kantian deontology. Human rights can be
viewed as generated by a social contract, that is, what the contractors
agree to. They can be viewed as a way of recognizing the status of
others as ends in themselves. Without a doubt, the most important
claims in the practical arena have been made on the grounds that
states have entered into a social contract that creates universal human
rights that they must uphold. One conclusion to be drawn from these
different accounts is that the issue of rights cannot really be treated as
a single approach, but rather as a common language that is derivative
of a number of other ethical traditions. In each of these, rights rest on
some basic assumptions about what constitutes a human being, and
why people possess these rights or deserve to be treated in a certain
way.

Most recently, Nussbaum and Sen have developed an alternative
to traditional rights-based approaches in what they call the capabilities approach. This approach focuses on the minimal entitlements of
human beings and is derivate of rights-based thinking (Nussbaum
2007). Rather than the capacity to reason or to suffer, this approach
identifies certain basic shared human capabilities that are common
to everyone in providing the basis for a universal standard. The core
idea of the capabilities approach is that all human beings possess the
capacity or potential to develop certain capabilities, and, in the words
of Nussbaum (2002b: 30), the presence or absence of these capabilities 'is typically understood to be a mark of the presence of absence
of a human life'. The logic of her argument is the same as that of
other cosmopolitans and rights approaches: once we can identify
these capabilities as belonging to humans, then there is no prima facie
reason why they should not be respected or realized for everyone.

It is certainly the case that the discourse of human rights has been
one of the most successful cosmopolitan languages (Anderson-Gold

2001). However, it is not the case that cosmopolitanism can be reduced to or made synonymous with human rights. Universal human rights are best understood as one expression of cosmopolitanism rather than the final form of cosmopolitan thinking. Indeed, despite the pervasiveness of 'rights talk' in contemporary international politics, most cosmopolitan accounts are deontological in that they are concerned with obligations rather than rights.

Reason and suffering in contemporary cosmopolitanism

One important criticism of cosmopolitanism has focused on its alleged dispassionate rationalism. In particular, its account of what it is about human beings that is universal seems too abstract, missing important aspects of what it means to be a human or why we should care for others and take responsibility for our actions. In Kant's approach, we are motivated to treat others as ends in themselves through rational insight alone. In addition, we are only motivated to treat those with rational insight as ends in themselves. Moral equality is given only to those who are rational 'agents' and moral self-determining beings in the full sense.

For Kant, obedience to duty comes because people understand it rationally as the only thing they can reasonably do. This approach minimizes such elements as the emotions, which motivate people to act. The critics of Kant and Kantianism generally agree that Kant has an inadequate account of moral motivation and, more specifically, that his depiction of human beings misses key human elements by minimizing emotions or other elements that motivate people to act. This tendency is present in contemporary cosmopolitan thought. When Martha Nussbaum, for instance, claims '[w]e should recognize humanity wherever it occurs, and give its fundamental ingredients, reason and moral capacity, our first allegiance' (1996: 7), she is implying that what unites us as humans is reason alone. For the critics, however, this is far too attenuated an understanding of our humanity. Is it really true that humanity consists only in its use of reason, as the quote from Nussbaum suggests? Criticism of this aspect of cosmopolitanism has come from both communitarian and feminist approaches to ethics. In contrast to Kantian rationalism, some feminist writers have advocated the idea of an 'ethics of Care' (Held 2006; Robinson 1999, 2008), focusing on everyday motivations and relationships of care between people to provide an alternative account of morality that is essentially tied to real contexts.

To base our account of the moral life on the capacity of reason alone seems, as utilitarians and others argue, to miss something important, and also to have some potentially negative consequences. For this reason, the Kantian approach has more recently been supplemented with the emphasis on pain or suffering. Amongst the most important insights of utilitarianism is the focus on the things that cause unhappiness. The most important of these is suffering. Suffering occurs in a myriad of forms, all of which are potentially morally relevant. The fact that all human beings, and many other sentient beings, can suffer is an important part of moral motivation and also an important reason for treating others as equals in order that they do not suffer, or that they suffer less. An identification with another's suffering is a recognition that we share something with them that we would not like to experience, and that we can understand this suffering and also are motivated to do something to alleviate it.

Contemporary cosmopolitans in the Kantian tradition have begun to be more explicit about this point and to emphasize that suffering and harm take many forms. Lu (2000: 257) argues that suffering 'has diverse implications, affecting not only physical security but also human agency and autonomy'. Our capacity to extend moral concern to others comes also from seeing them as human beings, and part of what it is to be a human being is to suffer and to be able to appreciate others' suffering. For this reason, empathy and understanding are important for treating others as equal. We can treat others as equal not only because they are rational agents, but also because we recognize their equal capacity to suffer or be harmed by the actions of others.

The recognition that we are motivated by factors other than pure reason doesn't undermine the Kantian goal of finding rules that should govern how we live, or, in particular, identifying rules that all agents can agree upon. Reason is necessary for rule-making based on what everyone might be able to agree upon, but to define humanity as reasonable cannot capture important dimensions of understanding and empathy. It is still the case that human beings are not merely physical agents, or subjects, that are acted upon, but are also social agents who need reason to define rules of activity. It still stands that rules that affect everyone ought to be agreed upon by everyone who is affected by them.

This capacity to suffer (rather than, say, a capacity to experience happiness) also provides the basis for negative duties that focus on avoiding or alleviating acts that cause suffering or cruelty. The recognition of the universal capacity for suffering suggests that the first cosmopolitan principle is a positive duty directed towards the alleviation of suffering, that is, humanitarianism. As Lu notes, 'Cosmopolitanism's moral condemnation of cruelty translates at a minimum into moral obligation to uphold the principle of humanity, to do our best to 'prevent and alleviate human suffering where it may be found' (Lu 2000: 256). Importantly, she notes that to put suffering first is not to dismiss reason but to place it in a different context. It is clear that both reason and suffering are things common to human beings everywhere and therefore both ought to provide the basis for a justifiable moral universalism.

The second cosmopolitan duty that flows from this is to do no harm. According to Linklater, citing the *Oxford Dictionary of English* definition, 'harm is "evil (physical or otherwise) as done to or suffered by some person or thing: hurt, injury, damage, mischief". Its effects include "grief, sorrow, pain, trouble, distress, affliction"' (Linklater 2001: 265).

The duty to avoid harm is perhaps one of the most basic of moral principles, best understood as the idea that it is better to suffer a wrong than to commit one. According to Linklater, the universality of the harm principle extends from:

> two universal features of human existence: first, all human beings are susceptible to particular (though not identical) forms of mental and physical pain [. . .]; second, shared (though unequal) vulnerability to mental and bodily harm gives all human beings good reason to seek the protection of a harm principle. (2006: 20)

Thus, even if one disagrees with the language of more substantive universalism, such as Rawlsian global distributive justice, it is still possible to employ the universal principle of harm avoidance in a way that can be reconciled with a great variety of ethical worldviews. Incorporating a 'do no harm convention' into 'our' relationship with outsiders does not necessarily require the existence of an already fully formed global community; instead, in the simplest form, it can apply 'unilaterally' in a world of separate sovereign states.

It also follows that the more serious or fundamental the nature of the harm, the more likely it is to be identified as such by people in diverse situations. Starvation is a clearly harmful condition that is close to being both objectively identifiable (the point at which life can no longer continue) and commanding of a near universal consensus as to its harmful status. Likewise, having one's identity, or community of belonging, removed or destroyed (harmed), is also something that might well command such a consensus. Genocide is perhaps one value that states have agreed (in principle) overrides national sovereignty, thus recognizing a universal crime (or harm) against communities as well as individuals. The core of the Genocide Convention is not only the physical destruction of a community but the destruction of a group identity through a variety of means, including, but not restricted to, murder or mass killings. Therefore, because all people experience these types of harm, it follows that there is a common interest, which is provisionally universal or universalizable, in protecting oneself and one's community from harm. It also follows that this is a reasonable thing to reciprocate.

The risk accompanying the development of universal norms – of imposing a culturally specific conception of justice, or the good society, upon others – is a significant challenge for cosmopolitanism. Nonetheless, interpreted through a cosmopolitan lens, the principle 'do no harm' can provide guidance for those who are convinced by cosmopolitan values and who wish to employ them in their treatment of 'outsiders' and strangers in a way that is consistent with a world divided into nation-states. Assessment of whether a particular act is harmful and whether it ought to be subject to sanction requires both consent and communication. Dialogue is the principal means by which consent or agreement to actions can be achieved (see Shapcott 2001, 2008a).[4] In many cases, such dialogue is the only way of ascertaining whether a harm has occurred or is perceived.

Conclusion

Long before the existence of modern states and telecommunications, the Greek Stoic philosopher Diogenes, when asked what city he belonged to, is famously quoted as responding that he was a 'citizen of the world'. Diogenes' stance is cited by Nussbaum as the exemplar of cosmopolitan thinking. For Nussbaum, Diogenes rejected the conventions of his day, which assumed that the *polis* was the centre of political and moral life. According to Nussbaum (1996), he meant that he did not consider himself to be Athenian, or Spartan or even Greek, but more fundamentally a human being. Diogenes' stance was extended from a philosophy that advocated indifference and scepticism to convention and worldly concerns. Diogenes was also famous for living in a barrel as a sign of this indifference. Diogenes was also therefore a sort of outcast or exile from his own community. While he was a citizen of the world, he also had no 'home' as such (for the definitive account of Diogenes' place in Greek thought, and of his cosmopolitanism, see Baldry 1965). For the critics, it is precisely this alienation from the community that makes

Diogenes a poor example and cosmopolitanism an unappealing moral standpoint. To be a citizen of the world, a cosmopolitan, is to be in a sense lost to the real location of moral and ethical life, the *polis* or the community. Thus, the appeal to Diogenes represents all that is wrong about the cosmopolitan position for its opponents, because its appeal to a universal standpoint requires the rejection of the very things that we need in order to live a moral life, our culture and community.

These criticisms and others have made cosmopolitanism less than attractive to many. Most importantly, they have led to the association of cosmopolitanism with imperialism. For many critics, cosmopolitanism's universalism of scope dominates or overwhelms its universalism of justification. Cosmopolitanism can claim to have provided neither a successful defence of moral universalism of scope nor of justification, because it is based on assumptions which are not likely to be acceptable to all those affected by them. This claim will be examined in more detail in the following chapter.

This chapter has attempted to set out some of the basic characteristics of cosmopolitan thought, and in particular has emphasized the form of moral universals and the basis for claiming universal scope of cosmopolitanism in a number of different traditions.[5] The next chapter discusses the most important criticisms of cosmopolitan moral universalism and then seeks to demonstrate a rearticulation of the core cosmopolitan arguments that overcomes many of these criticisms while incorporating their most salient points.

3

Anti-cosmopolitanism

Introduction

This chapter examines what I call anti-cosmopolitanism in international ethical thought. From the Athenian generals of the Peloponnesian War to G. W. F. Hegel, twentieth-century realists and communitarians such as Alasdair MacIntyre, Michael Walzer and John Rawls, anti-cosmopolitans have sought to depict the moral realm as being fundamentally different from that argued for by cosmopolitanism. Anti-cosmopolitan positions share an account of morality that is sceptical towards substantive universalism and global egalitarianism. It should be noted that I am making no claim for a single anti-cosmopolitan tradition. Instead, anti-cosmopolitanism is a stance that has been present in a number of different traditions at different times. It is at best a group of arguments, all of which have been employed by a number of different perspectives. Rather than any particular ideology or common project, what unites this diverse group is rejection of cosmopolitanism and substantive moral universalism in favour of local or contextual morality. Anti-cosmopolitans make both positive claims about the nature of morality and negative claims about cosmopolitanism that are used to defend significant, but not absolute, restrictions of human loyalties and to give moral priority to less-than-universal communities. Because anti-cosmopolitans emphasize contextual origins of community and ethics they reject cosmopolitan universalism and claim that actual particularistic community, such as nationality, overrides any abstract or imagined bonds between members of the human species.

At the core of anti-cosmopolitanism is the claim that morality is always local, and therefore that cosmopolitanism is both impossible (impractical) and undesirable, in particular because of:

a the international insecurity in the international state of nature;
b the existence of profound cultural and normative pluralism which entails the lack of universal agreement about the 'good' or the 'right';
c any attempt to act in or realize universal values would be an unjustified imposition of one account of 'the good society' upon others; and
d a world state based on universalism would be a source of violence, domination and tyranny.

In addition, Simon Caney identifies six conceptual and three normative arguments against universalism:

> Universalism is (1) flawed because it is committed to the idea of a common human nature; (2) too abstract and decontextualized to have relevance; (3) unable to provide an adequate account of moral motivation; (4) false to the experience of moral reflection; (5) unattainable because moral argument can take place only within historical traditions; and (6) vitiated by the existence of profound moral disagreement. (2005: 39)

These claims will be discussed in the sections below.

This chapter focuses on the two most common and robust expressions of anti-cosmopolitanism: realism and pluralism. Realism argues that the circumstances of international life preclude the possibility of cosmopolitan ethics or a cosmopolitan transformation because, within this setting, states are morally obliged to pursue their national interest over the common (cosmopolitan) good. For pluralists, the constraints on our moral commitments result from the absence of shared global understandings comparable to the ethical consensus present in the domestic realm of the nation-state. Common to both these anti-cosmopolitan positions is what Chris Brown identifies as a communitarian understanding of the origins of the nature of morality and ethics (see Brown 1992). Both realism and pluralism draw upon the idea that moral norms are cultural rather than transcendental and therefore that morality is essentially communal rather than global in nature. For this reason, this chapter begins with a discussion of the communitarian ideas that are common to most anti-cosmopolitan arguments.

Communitarianism

At the heart of the disagreement between the cosmopolitans and anti-cosmopolitans is a distinct moral epistemology and ontology of each tradition (Cochran 1999). As we have seen, cosmopolitanism, especially liberal cosmopolitanism, has most often been grounded in certain claims about the nature of human agency and the capacity for disinterested rationality, or, in the case of Kant himself, humanity's capacity to recognize universal transcendental reason. In contrast, communitarians made claims in both ontological and epistemological realms: individuals are formed by their culture and can only come to have moral knowledge as a consequence of inhabiting a culture. According to communitarians, morality is derived from, and only has meaning in, the specific – what Michael Walzer (1994) calls 'thick' – cultures to which we belong. Moral life begins 'at home', so to speak, in the various historical, cultural and political communities that we inhabit. Communitarianism is 'contextualist' because it argues that moral standards can only belong to the specific groups from which they emerged. The anti-cosmopolitan position takes this communitarian argument and turns it into a rejection of cosmopolitanism. Contexts place limits on universalism and foreclose the possibility of a moral point of view as such.

According to Brown (1992), the origins of modern communitarian epistemology and ontology can be found in the work of the German philosophers Herder and Hegel. While few contemporary anti-cosmopolitans present even a passing resemblance to either Herder or Hegel, they have provided inspiration and influence for anti-cosmopolitanism in general. Herder was a critic of Kant's emphasis on a pre-social or even asocial individual. According to Brown, Herder provides the basis for thinking of the national community as an organic entity, and as the social source of good and of identity. Herder was the first to emphasize the way in which culture and individual identity are intertwined. Individuals' identities are formed in the context of a shared culture or by language, history and traditions. Herder argued that 'the individual was not prior to culture . . . but shaped by it' (1992: 59). Herder is significant for today's debates because of his focus on the contextual individual. Herder's emphasis on the cultural origins of individuality also flows through to the epistemological level. From Herder's position, the Kantian emphasis on a transcendent individual reason is fundamentally in error.

Herder's preferred form of political community was a plurality of de-centred communities, which he called 'anarcho-pluralist' (Brown

1992). In contrast, Hegel was a statist. Hegel argued that the state was the most perfect form of human community and that it is only in states that people can fulfil their own individuality while reconciling it with the individuality of others. For Hegel, the sovereign state was the only setting in which people could achieve their individuality and their freedom because it was the only community within which people had reflectively constructed their identity, or in which people were capable of ruling themselves according to reason.

Statists claim that 'Social tradition within the state is the framework which founds and enables ethical discourse' (Cochran 1996: 13). The implication of this is that only when everyone inhabits their own particular state can men (sic) be free. Hegel then seeks to reconcile universality and particularity in the state, which he saw as the culmination of the process of history. According to Linklater:

> For Hegel an account of the development of human powers must analyse the emergence and evolutions of societies which are based upon rational, critical thinking. The development of human freedom is exhibited in man's increasingly rational control of his self and his environment . . . The culmination of this process in modern history is the sovereign state. Within this community, within a community of rational law-makers, humans realize the triumph of thought over nature, and express those capacities . . . which are specific to human subjects. (1990a: 147)

States could do this, not because they were organic communities in the Herderian sense but because they were rational communities built upon historical, not transcendent, rationality. That is a rationality developed in and of history. For this reason, David Boucher (1998) argues that communitarianism does not adequately describe Hegelian thought, which he refers to as simply the tradition of historical reason. Nonetheless, the conclusion to be drawn from Hegel's account is that the less than universal association known as the sovereign state is and ought to be the focus of individual life and ethics. Between the two of them, Herder and Hegel seem to capture the essence of modern anti-cosmopolitanism as an argument in which cultural and communal sources of moral knowledge and individual identity are married to a belief that the state is the best representative of the community.

While contemporary anti-cosmopolitans draw on the traditions of Herder and Hegel, their more immediate influence is the debate between liberalism and communitarianism which emerged in response to John Rawls's *Theory of Justice* (see Avineri and De Shalit 1992). The essential argument here was that Rawlsian liberalism misunderstood the nature of the moral realm and moral argument, and was premised on a de-contextualized understanding of individualism.

David Miller (2002) contrasts communitarian or contextual justice with universal or cosmopolitan justice as a way of indicating the limit of universalism. For Miller, the aim of universalism 'is to discover principles of justice that can and should guide our judgment and our behaviour in all circumstances . . . the basic principles of justice are invariant . . . it tells us what justice *is*' (2002: 7). Miller argues that no universalist account has ever succeeded in convincing everyone (universal justification) or in establishing itself as the principal account of justice. As a result, communitarians assert that different cultures have their own ethics and it is impossible to claim, as cosmopolitans do, access to one single account of morality. Instead there remains a plurality of accounts of justice in the world. This is not just some accident or the fault of poor articulation, but is instead the result of the nature of justice itself. There is no single meaning of justice and therefore no single account of justice. Therefore, all justice is contextual. The communitarian claim is that moral knowledge is ultimately relative to the particular historical communities to which we belong. Morality is a cultural artefact and different standards of morality, different understandings of right and wrong, prevail in different cultures.

For anti-cosmopolitans, the presence of significant cultural diversity, and thus of significantly different accounts of the nature of justice, mean that in practice there is no consensus on the nature of justice. Because human beings only achieve moral knowledge in concrete historical circumstances we cannot speak in terms of a transcendental universal morality that is above history and culture, in the way that cosmopolitans do. Because there is no single global culture or community of all of humanity, with a shared history or culture, there is no cultural artefact that is coterminous with the entire species. Moral communities, Walzer argues:

> have members and memories, members with memories not only of their own but also of their common life. Humanity by contrast, has members but no memory, so it has no history and no culture, no customary practices, no familiar life-ways, no festival, no shared understanding of social goods. (1994: 8)

Moral duties, therefore, exist only in the context of a society that can share these cultural artefacts. We simply cannot have duties to those we have no shared 'social contract' with, and whose values we do not share and with whom we do not identify. In other words, there is no universal context for global justice, only local or particular ones. As Walzer explains, 'our common humanity will never make us members of a single universal tribe. The crucial commonality of the human race is particularism: we participate, all of us, in thick cultures that are our own' (1994: 83). The lack of these shared understandings both prevents the application of cosmopolitan moral code and at the same time indicates why people will not identify with cosmopolitanism. People identify with their own communities and this provides them with the moral motivation to do good. In contrast, we cannot identify with humanity sufficiently to motivate us to act in its name or in the cause of distant strangers (see Kymlicka 2001; Calhoun 2003). Our membership of humanity is at best attenuated, imprecise and morally secondary.

Additionally, if morality is context-dependent and can only be decided within a culture/community, then attempts to propound universal conceptions of justice come up against the barrier of cultural difference. Communitarians, according to Thompson (1992: 22), argue that 'if individuals are constituted wholly or in part by the social relations of their communities, or if their goals, their ethical judgements and their sense of justice are inextricably bound up with community life, then why should they accept the criteria or evaluations of cosmopolitans?' The communitarian critique implies that, given that knowledge is particular and contextual, there will be no way of knowing or judging between the many contextual definitions of the good and establishing which is the correct or best ethical framework. In other words, with a vast diversity of moral cosmologies it is neither possible nor desirable to decide which is the right one, or to judge between them.

This argument is sometimes accompanied by a supporting claim that contextual knowledge is necessarily incommensurable (see Brown 1992). That is, not only is it true that there is no consensus on basic values due to cultural pluralism, but such a consensus is impossible because cultures are not translatable. It is impossible, for instance, to think simultaneously as both a modern secularist and a traditional Islamic scholar. The two cosmologies are irreconcilable. This means that not only is no consensus existent today, but none is possible in the future. The only means by which it might become possible would be through the triumph or victory of one culture and the destruction or assimilation of all the others. And this is precisely the threat that communitarians identify in cosmopolitan universalism.

The critique of liberal cosmopolitanism

The most common critique of cosmopolitanism is that it is hostile to the 'local' or national community as a result of its determination to be

impartial. While there are a number of sources of this criticism, ultimately it can be traced back to a rejection of both the cosmopolitan
understanding of 'the moral point of view' and of its methodologi-
cal individualism. The most important of these criticisms is that the
individuals depicted by cosmopolitanism are not humans as such but
liberal individuals, the product of a specific liberal interpretation.
Cosmopolitan arguments rest on three assumptions:

1 That we can identify an objective account of human agency that is
   uninfected by its particular origins.
2 That it has been done.
3 Further, that such an account can generate a universal account of
   the right.

Rather than reflecting universal human qualities, liberal accounts rest
on culturally specific assumptions about certain human characteristics As a result, it is questionable whether the qualities that liberals
ascribe to all humans as universal are in fact so. If they are not, then it
would seem that the cosmopolitan project falls at the first hurdle.

The most obvious first objection here is to the Kantian appeal
to rationality. From the communitarian position, the emphasis on
rationality as the uniting feature of humanity is simply not empirically justified. Reason and rationality take many forms, depending on
the culture of the individual. In other words, humanity has little or
no capacity to be guided by a universal reason because, simply put,
there is no such reason. Reason is the product of particular cultures
and circumstances, a historical product, and not transcendent in
the Kantian sense. Hegel's account of the historical development of
reason is present in this claim.

More specifically, communitarianism argues that disembodied
abstract reason has no ethical authority because it cannot ground itself
outside a specific Western tradition of thought. Cosmopolitanism
does not sufficiently recognize that its abstract, idealized, suppos-
edly impartial, principal standpoint is, in fact, the product of a
particular history, context and culture, and not an impartial one.
Cosmopolitanism relies upon an assumption that liberal theories
of justice are determinate and final, that they are indeed universal.
However, there is good reason to think that they cannot be unproblematically universalized or that they may not be acceptable to those
outside the liberal realm. Communitarians ask '[w]here do these
"external" criteria get their authority?' (Thompson 1992: 22). The
answer, of course, is that they are authoritative only within liberalism, not globally. Ultimately, the claim is that it is not possible to

draw any substantive conclusions about universal human qualities beyond the most general, and that the type of conclusion we might draw from such an account leads to an altogether different account of justice from that portrayed by cosmopolitans (see Miller 2007).

Rawls's 'theory of justice' was the spur for the development of 'communitarianism' in its modern form. Many communitarian arguments began as a critique of Rawls's domestic liberalism, and also as a critique of his account of the nature of justice. The principal criticism levelled at Rawls was that his account relied upon too high a level of abstraction and an account of individuals that did not recognize the extent to which individual choices were the results of socialization. Rawlsian accounts are particularly prone to criticism at this level because they rely so heavily on very specific accounts of what an individual would choose in order to build their fiction of a global social contract. Much of contemporary anti-cosmopolitanism is a response to the development of Rawlsian accounts of cosmopolitanism as global justice. The issue of global distributive justice, especially when understood in terms of Rawlsian justice and constitution of 'basic institution', will almost necessarily lead to an account of a globally just society modelled on liberal if not Rawlsian principles.

Communitarians and feminists argue that liberal cosmopolitans depict the individual as some way acultural (Benhabib 1992). The feminist criticism of Rawlsianism is that the liberal model is less universalizable than liberals care to admit. Benhabib (1992: 53) argues, 'Universalistic moral theories in the Western tradition from Hobbes to Rawls are substitutionalist, [they] . . . identify the experiences of a specific group of subjects as the paradigmatic case of the human as such. These subjects are invariably white, male, adults who are propertied or at least professional.' In Rawls's case, this individual is situated behind a 'veil of ignorance'. The individual in liberal approaches is an ideally rational actor and we can model such an actor and use it as the basis for our theories, even if we can't actually find one in the real world.

For cosmopolitans, an abstracted and idealized account of the individual is used to construct and justify rules that everyone ought to be guided by. To be universally impartial, the cosmopolitan position must abstract from the particularity of agents and replace them with a generalized, and, therefore, universal, conception of the individual by reducing them to the abstract, reasoning, dispassionate (male) subject. Rawls's approach requires abstraction of the individual away from their social context and 'reduces the (actual) plurality of moral subjects to one (abstract) subjectivity' (Walzer 1983: 5). For communitarian critics of Rawls, this conception is flawed because it robs the individual of all the traits that make them individuals, or of the traits that make them identifiable as humans. The individual so modelled is not in fact universal and therefore capable of impartiality, but is rather a product of a particular culture and, usually, gender. As Walzer notes in his argument against Rawls:

> the question most likely to arise in the minds of members of a political community is not, 'What would rational individuals choose under universalizing conditions of such and such a sort?' But rather, 'What would individuals like us choose, who are situated as we are, who share a culture and are determined to go on sharing it?' (1983: 5)

In other words, the individual becomes so far removed from any real human that what that individual may or may not choose makes no sense, and therefore the edifice upon which such a concept is built collapses.

Likewise, according to Iris Marion Young (1990), the ideal of impartiality obscures the origins of the cosmopolitan account. No vantage point is completely impartial and all positions are situated in some sort of context. There is no 'non-perspectival' perspective. As Young (1990: 104) argues: '[i]t is impossible to adopt an unsituated moral point of view, and if a point is situated, then it cannot be universal, it cannot stand apart from and understand all points of view.' To be impartial, the cosmopolitan position must abstract from the specific identity of real people and replace them with a generalized conception of 'the agent'. The cosmopolitan commitment to impartiality with regard to different conceptions of the good life is itself an articulation of a particular conception of the good life. If this is the case, then it might follow that the basis for cosmopolitan universalism is less secure than it may seem.

A related claim is Rawls's own argument against the cosmopolitan interpretation of his work. The theory of justice is based upon an assumption about certain values, or the reflective equilibrium of values common to liberal, and particularly American, society. From this viewpoint, it is an account of justice for liberal societies. There is no such basic reflective equilibrium in the international realm (Rawls 1999).

The fundamental claim of anti-cosmopolitanism is that it is impossible or at least highly difficult to identify a single human nature that can form the basis of a 'thick' universal credo. Human beings differ vastly according to their cultural and historical origins. Their preferences, values and basic understandings of life and life's purposes are so vastly different that identifying any single quality to provide the basis for a substantive or robust moral universalism is impossible.

Substantive accounts of universalism, global justice or the substantive content of universal human rights are not possible or are extremely limited in scope (see Miller 2007, for instance). Therefore, we must reject the idea of a single universal morality as a cultural product with no global legitimacy. It is impossible to realize the cosmopolitan fantasy of a disembodying universal reason because both the epistemological and the ontological prerequisites are missing.

What is required is a different understanding of justice that takes different social contexts into account and does without the possibility of making statements about what everybody ought to do. Having identified the communitarian core of the anti-cosmopolitan tradition, the next task is to discuss how this translates into ethical practice and what it means for the cosmopolitan project. That is, what type of ethical options are we left with if we accept the communitarian premises, and do they indeed effectively undermine the goal of cosmopolitanism?

Anti-cosmopolitan ethics

If we reject the possibility of a universal moral realm, then compatriots must take priority, sometimes to the exclusion of outsiders. The communitarian argument about the source of morality is one which supports giving moral *priority* not to the species but to the 'community', the nation and the state, because nation or communal boundaries are of *primary* moral significance. That is to say: we owe more, and sometimes a lot more, to our fellow nationals than we do to outsiders. This means that we may have very few, if any, obligations to the human species as a whole.

As an example, communitarian reasoning favours national distributive schemes and not global ones (see chapter 7). It supports a practice of moral favouritism towards insiders (compatriots) over outsiders, limiting obligations to non-compatriots, and when universal and national values come into conflict, the universal should mostly come second (see Erskine 2002: 28). Any obligations the rich may have to the poor, or that any one person may have to anyone else, are limited by the boundaries of the political community of the nation-state. This observation provides the basis for the anti-cosmopolitan position that we should not seek to develop a world state or substantive human community because that would be an injustice to the diversity of human ways of being in the world. There is little or no obligation to construct a global order based on principles which might distribute wealth from the rich to the poor because there is no basis for a global redistribution of wealth, and such redistribution schemes can occur only within societies not across them (see Miller 2007, for a good treatment of this view; also chapter 7).

Likewise, the extent to which universal human rights can be enforced by the international community is extremely limited. If we remember the three relationships of obligations introduced at the start of the book, communitarian premises lead anti-cosmopolitans to favour minimal negative duties between political communities. What 'they' do to each other is generally beyond 'us' to judge, both because we inhabit different ethical traditions and because what everybody owes to everybody else is limited almost exclusively to rules about coexistence and non-interference.

The communitarian underpinnings of anti-cosmopolitanism find expression in two forms: (1) 'realism' (Gvosdev 2005; Erskine 2002); and (2) pluralism (Bull 1967) which itself takes several forms. Both require us to think of ethics differently from how cosmopolitanism presents it.

Realism

Realism has dominated thinking about international politics for at least half a century. Most commentaries on realism, and indeed most discussion within contemporary realism, focus on the dynamics of interstate relations, with little or no systemic thought given to ethical issues. However, at the core of the realist concern with power is a powerful ethical moral critique concerning the relationship between politics and morality, and the possibility of the transformation of political community. In the international realm, according to realists, ethics are necessarily *consequential* and *statist*. Realist ethics are a statist (and communitarian) ethics because they are directed towards maintaining and protecting the state or national community. Realist ethics are consequentialist because ethical actions are judged according to how well they serve this end and not according to how they correlate with some abstract account of 'right' or the universal community. While few contemporary or classical realists refer to or classify themselves as communitarians, their arguments nonetheless rest on some shared assumptions. Not all communitarians are realists. Most realists are communitarians in at least a sociological if not a normative sense. Realism provides strong arguments in favour of compatriot priority and against cosmopolitanism (see Linklater

1990c), including a recognition of the normative pluralism character-
izing the international realm and a scepticism towards progressivist
accounts of international life.

In its earlier forms, especially in the work of Hans Morgenthau
(1948/1960) and E. H. Carr (1939), the two dominant figures of early
twentieth-century realism, it was as much a political philosophy as a
'method' of study. As such, ethics and normative issues were central
to its definition. This is most obvious in its critique of Idealism.
According to Carr and Morgenthau, Idealists made the mistake of
putting the common good ahead of national interest by incorporating
universal values into their foreign policy goals.

Realism identifies the arena of international relations as a competi-
tion for power between separate sovereign states. States in anarchy
recognize no common good. Classical realists argued that this condition meant that human beings, being what they are, self-interested,
will seek to achieve their own advantage, sometimes to the cost of
others. States not only would but should preserve themselves, by
increasing their own welfare and security without considering the
needs of others. Realists identify this as the main obstacle to the
realization of idealist ends such as global peace.

Under these conditions, the statesman (sic) must be prepared to
follow a Machiavellian practice and do whatever it takes to win.
Incorporating universal morality into foreign policy or relations with
other states is a bad idea, because it is not applicable and is dangerous
in the international realm which is one of necessity. As Morgenthau
claimed 'a foreign policy guided by universal moral principles . . .
is under contemporary conditions . . . a policy of national suicide'
(1952: 10). Realists also claim that the lack of universal values adds
to the dynamics of anarchy, but, even if there were such values,
anarchy would prevent states from acting in accordance with them.
For instance, if all the states were liberal or Christian or Muslim,
anarchy would still overwhelm any altruistic motives they might have
towards each other.

For this reason, realists put themselves at odds with what they
see as the dominant moralist strains of US foreign policy.[1] Realism
is critical of the tendency of US foreign policy to marry ideology
with interest. States, especially great powers, too often equate their
values with universal values, and their interests with their values.
Realists believe that such statements are usually either a cynical mask
or a self-interested delusion; 'The appeal to moral principles in the
international sphere has no concrete universal meaning . . . it will be
nothing but the reflection of the moral preconceptions of a particular
nation' (Morgenthau 1952: 10). Morality in international affairs is

at best window dressing, for appearances only, or, worse, a form of hubris accompanying an over-inflated sense of a state's power. For these reasons, many people have characterized realist ethics as Machiavellian and amoral at best. However, it is possible to identify a moral/ethical core to realism that undermines or qualifies realist advocacy of realpolitik.

Ethics of responsibility

The realist tradition is united above all by pessimism about the nature of the international realm. Many observers have consequently argued that realism is dominated by moral scepticism per se. At its heart, it is sceptical about any moral dimension of politics. However, many realists often argue that underlying this toughness is a different and more pragmatic morality, the ethics of responsibility. An ethics of responsibility is an ethics that looks to the consequences of actions, and to their effects. This has usually been interpreted as meaning two things: (1) a simple means–ends pragmatism (incorrectly character-ized as prudence), in which the statesperson's responsibility is to achieve the national interest with whatever means are available; and (2) a responsibility above all to one's own state. In other words, the first duty of a statesperson is to ensure survival and security of one's own state/people in the uncertain conditions of international anarchy. Realists proclaim such self-interested ethics as virtuous (see Kennan 1986). To do otherwise would be to ignore the leader's responsibility to the lives and interests of their own community.

The most famous example of realist ethics was given by Thucydides in his history of the Peloponnesian War. The Athenians, who have delivered an ultimatum to the small island-state of Melos, along the lines of surrender or be destroyed, claim that in international politics the 'powerful do what they can and the weak do what they must'. That is, morality does not constrain powerful states or help weak ones. Powerful states will do what they can get away with and weak states must submit to this. In the case of the Peloponnesian War, the Melians did not surrender and were invaded and massacred, and the women and children were sold into slavery. The question the realists pose here is how ethical or moral was it for the Melian leaders to resist the reality they faced by appealing to principles of justice? The morally responsible decision would have been to accept their defeat and avoid the subsequent slavery and genocide carried out against their people. Thus, self-help is a moral duty and not just a practical necessity.

Realists, therefore, advise states to focus on material and strategic outcomes rather than the more conventional understanding of the morality of their actions. For instance, a realist like Henry Kissinger might advise bombing a neutral state such as Laos if it will serve the military goals of defeating the enemy of North Vietnam. Alternatively, a realist may also encourage having friendly relations with and support for governments with poor human rights records, such as Chile under the military rule of Augusto Pinochet, or arguably Pakistan under Musharraf, in order to secure an advantage against a military foe, such as the USSR or al-Qaeda. Thus, in dealing with states that practice human rights abuses, a statesperson must decide whether the human rights of foreigners outweigh the interests of even just one of their own citizens. The logic of realist thought suggests that the interests of one domestic citizen outweighs the human rights of foreigners. This means that not only do we tolerate but we also befriend 'bad' states, so long as we continue to gain from the relationship.

Only when there is no significant cost to oneself should a state be concerned with the domestic affairs of another state. John Mearsheimer, an 'offensive' realist, argues that only when there is no strategic interest at risk would it be advisable to intervene in, say, Rwanda to stop a genocide (Mearsheimer 2001). However, there is little from within realist logic to generate a policy of intervention for moral rather than strategic reasons. Strictly speaking, aid should only be given to another state when it is a strategic asset.

The logic of realism also means that we cannot be too concerned about any suffering or harm we might inflict upon other states, whether by commission or omission, as long as our own state is benefitting. If our interests outweigh the harm we do others, and they almost always do, then we must privilege our interests (see also Kennan 1986). Indeed, this is the argument of Madeleine Albright, former US Secretary of State under the Clinton administration. When asked on the US 60 *Minutes*, 'We have heard that half a million children have died (as a result of economic sanctions imposed on Iraq after the 1991 Gulf War) . . ., is the price worth it?', Albright responded, 'I think that is a very hard choice, . . . the price is worth it' (60 *Minutes* 5 December 1996). In this context, a realist might argue that the sanctions against Iraq were justified and 'worth it' as they prevented Saddam Hussein from developing and using weapons of mass destruction, kept his regime weak, and preserved international stability and the national security of Iraq's enemies. This is a good end for the US and Iraq's enemies and, according to the realist argument, the fact that it brought about huge suffering to the people of Iraq is a regrettable but necessary consequence if it serves the greater good of the US national interest. (From a Kantian perspective, Albright is clearly acting immorally because the price she refers to concerns the lives of others as a means to an end that entails punishing the Iraqi president and achieving US national interests.)

However, realists often confound expectations when it comes to their view of war as a tool of policy. While realists argue that a state must always be ready to use war, so long as other states also remain prepared to do so, they will often counsel caution in relation to specific wars. Realists advise against ideologically driven wars of conquest. Realists such as Morgenthau spoke out against the Vietnam War, because they saw it as unnecessary and imprudent, as this did not and could not strengthen the position of the US in the international realm. So, while countering and containing Soviet influence was a concern for realists during the Cold War, they argued that the threat was not ideological but geopolitical. One version of realist thinking made its way into US foreign policy under the influence of Henry Kissinger, US Secretary of State in the Nixon administration. Kissinger's policy of détente with China and the Soviet Union was premised on an understanding that China could be used to counter the USSR ('my enemy's enemy is my friend') and the recognition that the USSR could be viewed as a state with its own security interests, rather than an ideological foe bent on the destruction of the US. Likewise, in the months preceding the US invasion of Iraq in April 2003, the most consistent critics of US policy were realists such as John Mearsheimer who counselled that the strategy of containment via sanctions and the inspection regime had worked, and that Iraq presented no real threat to US vital national interests (Mearsheimer and Walt 2003). Most realists are sceptical about the Bush administration's aims of spreading democracy in the Middle East and the administration's claim that 'American values are universal values' (Lieven and Hulsman 2006). In this sense, the war was unnecessary from a realist point of view. The Iraq War was imprudent because the likely negative consequences outweighed the positives, and the war was not necessary for US survival. The point here is not that the realists are pacifist, but that they evaluate policy primarily in terms of the national interest and with an ethics of prudence.

For realists, the primary moral virtue for good statecraft is that of prudence, which involves the development of wisdom and knowledge about what is possible and what is not and, more importantly, about what are the best means for achieving one's ends. Morgenthau (1960: 10) states 'there can be no political morality without prudence, that is, without consideration of the political consequences of seemingly moral action'. Prudence involves the weighing of the consequences of alternative political action. While the ultimate purpose, to pursue national interest, may be clear, what this means in particular contexts is a matter of judgement. In substantive terms, prudence may require a statesperson to make horrible decisions or decisions which go against common-sense morality, but the decision can be justified if made for the right reasons and with the right consequences of responsibility. The most obvious example here would be the universal moral law forbidding murder. Most people see murder as wrong and yet for a statesperson murder, in the form of warfare, is an acceptable and sometimes necessary tool for achieving a state's goal of security. In this sense, realists accept what is immoral in domestic life is acceptable and sometimes laudable in political life. While the critics say this can slip into opportunism, justifying almost any actions on ethical grounds, realists maintain that statesmen have a duty to their own people first and that ignoring these realities would be a dereliction of that duty.[2]

However, contrary to common belief, prudence does not mean a purely unprincipled or purely instrumental account of judgement and action in the sense that 'what will help me meet my aims most efficiently' is prudent. Rather, according to Murray (1996) and also Lieven and Hulsman (2006), prudence for Morgenthau, at least, refers to a process whereby the moral, or universal law, is mediated through the concrete practical here and now. A prudent realist might therefore ask whether there were also not other means of 'containing' Iraq and whether the suffering of the Iraqi people was not the best means of achieving the US ends. The weapons inspections regime may have been enough to prevent or at least seriously hamper Iraqi capacities. In this case, a realist may have seen the suffering of the Iraqi people as unnecessary. Realists may also have added that there may have been negative consequences for the US as a result of resentment against this policy. That is, Morgenthau would not necessarily condone the suffering of others if he understood that suffering to be out of balance or too great a violation of the moral law. For instance, Morgenthau argued that genocide was not a tool available to states within a realist morality. Thus, any pursuit of national interest can only be responsible if it also takes humanity into account. This understanding is clear in realism's continued opposition to 'thick' moral universalism or idealism. Such idealism is irresponsible not only because it damages the national interest, but because it is harmful to others who have legitimate interests of their own. Likewise, hubris and empire are not only dangerous to the nation-state but to the stability of the system as a whole.

Nonetheless, underlying realist ethics, especially for Morgenthau, is a profound sense of not only the political realm but also the human condition as essentially tragic. Tragedy is not used in the weak or commonplace sense that the TV news refers to the loss of a life as tragic, but rather in the classical sense, as depicted in the Greek plays or the classics, and in the work of Shakespeare (Lebow 2003). A tragedy here refers to a situation in which, no matter what choice you make, a bad consequence will occur. There is a sense here that politics, despite the best efforts of people, remains beyond human control. Realism identifies the international realm as tragic because it sees human beings as imperfect and imperfectible. We cannot entirely conquer our own nature and we can never have complete knowledge of the social world and the outcomes of our actions. Sometimes there is no option of a 'moral' or good choice. Only a choice between the lesser of two evils (if you are lucky) remains. For instance, the decision to drop an atomic bomb on Japan was, from one perspective at least, a tragic one – either risk losing lots of American lives taking the Japanese mainland, or kill more than 100,000 civilians in order to bring the war to a quick end. This is tragic in the sense that both alternatives were horrible but there was no escaping the decision to choose one of the alternatives. The notion of the security dilemma indicates this sense of tragedy very well. No matter which choice is made, security is not assured – you either have an arms race or a war. This means that we are constantly placed in situations where we have to assess which is the least bad action to take. Realist ethics, then, are an attempt to think about how to act well morally under these circumstances. They are an ethics of the least bad rather than a morality which seeks to articulate an absolute conception of the good.

Conclusions

Realism can be said to be communitarian and anti-cosmopolitan because it takes the nation-state as a given and argues for the ethical primacy of the national or state community. This is both a pragmatic and principled position. This position is pragmatic because realists aim to take the world as it is. It is principled because realist ethics are the best ethics available in terms of the reality of the world. Realists are also communitarians because the effect of adopting realist principles is to give primacy to the particular rather than universal, and because realists routinely express sympathy for the plurality of communities. While it is sometimes necessary to override other states' interests, realists argue that it is generally a good thing that no state is able to do so all the time and impose its own account of universality. While never fully theorized in realist thought, this concern for diversity is almost always present. As Murray (1996: 101) notes, for Morgenthau, 'ultimately toleration and the acknowledgment of the right of the other to pursue an alternative conception of the good are asserted as fundamental moral necessities'.

Realists are vulnerable to the observation that not every choice faced by states is between survival and destruction. The realist objection that the state of nature determines the state's ethical choices only applies in instances in which state survival is at risk, or where following a particular ethical policy would place the state at real risk of dissolution, or leave a population open to real harm.

However, for many states, and in particular the wealthiest states, such conditions exist only intermittently and are often restricted to certain issues. Given that most of the time states do not face life-threatening consequences to themselves if they choose to act ethically, the realist argument against international ethics only holds under certain extreme circumstances (see Beitz 1979 and Moellendorf 2002). Though it is true that most states face choices that will have consequences that affect their interests, these consequences do not normally affect a state's ability to exist or survive. Many decisions, rather, are between advantage or disadvantage. It does not stand to reason that seeking advantage allows the statesperson to opt out of conventional morality in the same way that survival might. The context is similar for individuals and their ethical choices. Ethics is about considering individual costs and benefits, and determining at what point one's own interests should take priority over the interests of others and vice versa.

The central ethical question that emerges from realist analyses of the nature of international politics is whether it is ethically irresponsible for the realist statesperson to direct foreign policy towards transforming the logic of the international system, so that the logic of realpolitik is less or no longer pervasive. The arguments above suggest that realism directs foreign policy towards managing the status quo rather than transforming the international environment. However, it is worth noting that both Morgenthau and Carr suggested that human survival will require overcoming the logic of anarchy, and the replacement or supplementation of the idea of state sovereignty (see Morgenthau 1949; Carr 1939).

While realism is consistent with nationalism, realists themselves are often opposed to nationalism, both as an ethical stance and because of its pernicious effects, many preferring to use the term patriotism

(Lieven and Hulsman 2006). Morgenthau (1949) and Carr (1939) in particular both made statements to suggest they did not view the national state as the ultimate form of political community. Indeed, these theorists saw nationalism as a negative development which would contribute to international disorder, precisely because it exacerbated 'centrifugal' tendencies already present in anarchy. National survival may rest on the possibility of pursuing piecemeal and gradual reform of the international order in a cosmopolitan direction. Morgenthau's comments in his chapters on international morality and the concluding pages of *Politics Among Nations* (1948/1960) suggest that ultimately human well-being can only be served by the creation of a cosmopolitan world-society or world-state. A realist ethics of responsibility could be understood as aiming for the latter because pursuit of the national interest should always occur within the framework of the good of humanity. Such an argument has recently been made by Lieven and Hulsman (2006). However, it is not clear that these types of claim are either inherent in realism or simply reflect the limitations of realism as a complete political philosophy (on the latter, see Carr 1939).

In conclusion, while realism is often associated with realpolitik and the narrow pursuit of national interest, it is also concerned with the creation of a stable international order. Such an order is a prerequisite for the security and stability of the communities which make it up. As Gvosdev argues, 'realism's emphasis on making the world's nations . . . stakeholders in a stable and predictable international order intersects with the communitarian interest in constructing a viable global architecture' (2005: 1593; see also Wesley 2005). However, the ethics associated with this are perhaps more fully developed in the pluralist idea of an international society, which is addressed in the next section.

Pluralism: ethics of coexistence

Because communitarians value community and diversity, they recognize that the many ways in which individuals are formed in different cultures is a good thing in itself. Therefore, they argue that the best ethics is one which preserves diversity over homogeneity. This view lends itself to the idea of pluralism. Pluralists contrast the universalism of cosmopolitan visions with the idea of a heterogeneous world, in which each community pursues their own conceptions of the good life. Such a world is the world envisioned and defended by pluralist anti-cosmopolitans. Pluralism has a number of expressions. For our purposes, we can distinguish between nationalist, statist and non-statist pluralism. What they have in common is that they are 'oriented to the pre-existing group, and likely to ascribe to each individual a primary identity within a single community of descent . . . [and their] concern to protect and perpetuate the cultures of groups that are already established' (Hollinger 2002: 231). Communitarians claim that particular norms and cultures are to be valued and protected, and any imposition of universal standards is a denial of integrity or group autonomy.

Pluralists such as David Miller and Michael Walzer claim that 'strong' or 'thick' cosmopolitanism requires the universalization of a particular account of the good and the overriding of particular under-standings and 'shared ways of life', and this is unjust. For Walzer, justice exists precisely in the preservation of the different moral 'spheres' of human activity. Walzer (1983: 314) claims that because 'Justice is rooted in the distinct understanding of places, honours, jobs, things of all sorts that constitute a shared way of life. To over-ride those understandings is (always) to act unjustly.' To impose a single universal standard is unjustifiable, because no such standard exists, and harmful, because it forces people to conform to standards they might not share and punishes them for not conforming to those standards.

Nonetheless, the anti-cosmopolitan argument cannot function without a belief in human equality, however this value is expressed in the context of the 'thick' national communities we grow up in. For instance, the claim for national self-determination is one form of the claim that we can only be free in the context of national community. Equality needs to be understood as equality between communi-ties that in turn serve the interest of their individual members (see Kymlicka 2001). For communitarians, equality and humanity are expressed in difference and identity. To be human is to have a culture, and to belong to a community less than the species is to identify with one's community of origin or belonging. Therefore, the way to realize this goal is to preserve and recognize these cultural differences. In this context, Walzer argues that the duty to recognize different cultures as equal but different is a universal duty.

The pluralist account offers us a particular reconciliation of these two values that relies on a degree of universalism. Walzer (1994: 8) wishes to advocate 'the politics of difference and, at the same time, to describe and defend a certain sort of universalism'. He claims to be able to identify a certain minimal universalism, with the observa-tion that 'the members of all the different societies, because they are human can acknowledge each other's different ways, respond to each other's cries for help, learn from each other and march (sometimes) in each other's parades' (1994: 8).

Pluralism and nationalism

Nationalism is the belief that we all belong to nations and that this community has special claims upon our moral obligations. It is arguably the everyday understanding held by most people. It certainly underwrites the political structure of the world, as can be seen in the very ideas of national self-determination, national sovereignty and the United Nations. However, nationalism is not coterminous with communitarianism. There are as many communitarianisms as there are nationalisms, and communitarianism does not necessarily have to designate the nation as the relevant community. Religious, sub-national and other communities could be as – if not more than – influential as the nation. Nonetheless, nationalism is perhaps the most common political expression of communitarian premises.

Most accounts of nationalism which address the international realm envision a pluralist world of nation-states. This is what Miller juxtaposes to the liberal cosmopolitan view which he claims 'implies a world state with a single distributive scheme and single homogenous citizenry' (2002: 976). That is irreconcilable with 'a world of diversity in which the variety of national cultures finds expression in different sets of citizenship rights, and different schemes of social justice, in each community' (ibid.).

Defences of nationalism identity the nation as the community in which universal values such as equality and liberty and justice can be expressed. Many nationalist and anti-cosmopolitan writers today seem to operate within the spirit but not the letter of Hegelian thought, in that they interpret the state based on Herderian rather than Hegelian principles. The Herderian state is closer to a romantic view of the relationship between community, culture and tradition, rather than an Enlightenment view focused on reason, freedom and individuality. Modern communitarians tend to identify the state with the community in practice, if not in theory, and, even though they defend individuality, they defend the cultural, national sources of individuality rather than the state as guarantor of freedom and individualism.

Mervyn Frost, for example, is much more Hegelian than communitarians such as MacIntyre and Walzer (Frost 1996, 2002). David

Miller distinguishes between the nation and the state and emphasizes that national ties are what provide our cultural frameworks (Miller 1995). This makes him closer to Herder than Hegel. What they do share is a view that insofar as there are any moral universals, it is the duty of nation-states to uphold them internally, and then only in exceptional circumstance in other countries (genocide, for instance).

Nationalists vary in their views about what duties are owed between nations. While they are united in rejecting 'global egalitarianism' and 'liberal cosmopolitanism', they do not wish to reject all moral universals. Will Kymlicka and David Miller both defend the nation in liberal terms such as individual rights and freedoms, but also recognize the cultural assumptions necessary to secure commitment to those values. For liberal nationalists, basic individual rights trump community identity but they can only be realized within national communities (Miller 2000: 181). Kymlicka understands nationalism as a corrective to cosmopolitanism rather than an alternative (Kymlicka 2001). David Miller's defence of nationalism is less indebted to liberalism and therefore more hostile to liberal cosmopolitanism, though he does accept that nations have universal duties to secure the welfare of their members and to uphold basic human rights everywhere (Miller 1995, 2007; see chapter 7 for further discussion).

Nationalists identify the right of self-determination as a positive universal good, with it following, therefore, that there is some duty to support national self-determination in other countries (and not just one's own). Of course, in its most pathological forms, nationalism can lead to a hierarchical conception of the relationship between nations (e.g., Nazism), but for the most part contemporary nationalists emphasize equality between nations. The identification of the nation as the vehicle for moral universalism also finds expression in the doctrine of natural duties in the next section.

Rawls's non-statist pluralism

The most philosophically rigorous account of a non-statist pluralist ethics has been developed by John Rawls (1999) as *The Law of Peoples*, though Rawls is most famous for his *Theory of Justice* (1972). As discussed previously, many cosmopolitan theorists have adapted the theory of justice to the international setting. However, Rawls himself resisted and rejected this move. The theory of justice, he argued, must rely upon an existing reflective equilibrium amongst competing fundamental doctrines, or where there is an overlapping consensus of core values around which principles of egalitarianism can cohere. Rawls argued that a system of global justice was neither possible nor desirable because the preconditions of reflective equilibrium and overlapping consensus were absent from the international realm (Rawls 1999). Rawls further endorsed the communitarian argument that the conception of the moral person upon which his theory is based is not uncontested, and therefore moral universalism is problematic.

In the original position, the contractors are rational individuals (Rawls 1972). However, for the international realm he argues that a second contracting session ought to take place, this time with the rules being chosen by representatives of peoples who are just. In this second round of bargaining, the representatives of peoples are not given any information about where their population lives, what quantity of natural resources they have, what income or wealth they have or how they compare to other societies. The conclusion of this second round is a contract that by and large resembles the traditional rules of international society and diplomacy. These include rules of self-determination, Just War, mutual recognition, non-intervention and so forth.

In other words, on the international level, contractors come up with a set of rules of coexistence, not rules of justice, though Rawls argues they are the equivalent of the first principle – free and equal rights coextensive with the same rights for all. However, while the existence or non-existence of a shared language or culture places limits on the possibility for a universal community, these limits are not absolute. Rawls earlier identified minimal or 'natural' duties that apply to all humans as 'the duty to help another when he (*sic*) is in need or jeopardy provided that one can do so without excessive risk or loss to oneself (mutual aid); the duty not to harm or injure another . . . [and] the duty not to inflict unnecessary suffering' (1972: 114). In addition, there was a duty to 'support and to comply with just institutions that exist and apply to us . . . [and] to further just arrangements not yet established' (1972: 115). For Rawls, these natural duties exist independently of any social contract we might be party to or any moral or ethical commitments we have made as individuals, and they apply universally to us as humans (for further discussion, see Kokaz 2007).

In addition, Rawls argued that the international realm does not resemble a system for mutual advantage. Controversially, he proposed that states or societies ought to be considered to be largely self-sufficient with only minor interaction of any moral significance. Societies are to be understood in isolation, as if they have only minimal impact upon each other and are only minimally bound together by webs of interdependence. As a result, the best that can be hoped for is not a theory of justice but a theory of international legitimacy and coexistence, a 'law of peoples', which covers rules of coexistence between liberal and other decent peoples.

The rules of international coexistence that Rawls comes up with in *The Law of Peoples* (1999) are as follows:

> People are free and independent, and their freedom and independence are to be respected by other peoples.
> Peoples are to observe treaties and undertakings.
> Peoples are to observe a duty of non-intervention.
> Peoples have the right of self-defence but no right to instigate war for reasons other than self-defence.
> Peoples are to honour human rights.
> Peoples are to observe certain specified restrictions in the conduct of war.
> Peoples have a duty to assist other people living under unfavourable conditions that prevent their having a just or decent political and social regime (mutual aid).

Although he doesn't mention them in *The Law of Peoples*, natural duties inform the account of mutual aid here (Kokaz 2007). Mutual aid is provided only to enable a people to develop and enjoy a well-ordered society. It is not clear whether this is a duty because a well-ordered society is what everybody deserves, or because it allows a functioning *modus vivendi*, which is necessary for liberal societies to remain well-ordered. Kokaz claims that mutual aid is defended by Rawls as a condition of sociability: without it there can be no society, not even a society of peoples (Kokaz 2007). However, while the representatives of decent societies can agree on mutual aid, they are not capable of agreeing on principles of distributive justice or global egalitarianism; nor are they required to.

The obvious question provoked by the inclusion of natural duties is: how can even this minimal moral universalism be defended from communitarian premises? There are two possible sources that can be used to answer this question. The first is the tradition of natural law, and the second is the work of Immanuel Kant. The idea of natural duties could perhaps be derived from the idea of natural law, which David Boucher (1998) identifies as one of the main traditions of international political thought. According to Boucher, normative thought in international relations is best characterized as divided between empirical realism, universal moral order (natural law) and historical reason. Boucher's categories provide a useful addition to the cosmopolitan/anti-cosmopolitan framework because they allow us to highlight another aspect of anti-cosmopolitan thought that is not inherited directly from the presuppositions of Herder and Hegel.

According to Boucher, natural law thinking is an expression of the idea of a universal moral order. Natural law thinking attempts to identify certain universal moral principles or laws, which all humans have access to via the use of reason (see also Nardin 2002b). Martin Wight describes natural law as a 'belief in a cosmic, moral constitution, appropriate to all conscious things, a system of eternal and immutable principles radiating from a source that transcends earthly power' (Wight 1991: 14). The idea of natural law aims to identify basic moral categories that are not culturally dependent. Natural law theorists argue that cultural differences do not prevent the recognition of a universal moral order. These basic moral categories are necessarily thin, yet binding and substantive. Freedom of commerce, travel, right of private property, mutual assistance and, above all, to do no harm are fairly consistently included in the list of natural laws. In some variants, natural law thinking includes certain cosmopolitan elements and emphasizes individual duties and rights, while in others natural law develops into a statist code of coexistence. Samuel Pufendorf is generally cited as the epitome of the statist tradition (Devetak 2007), while Kant's cosmopolitanism clearly sits at the cosmopolitan end.

Walzer has offered a defence of his 'minimal moral universalism' in terms of thick and thin cosmopolitanism. This defence includes a claim that mutual aid or something like it can be identified 'in different times and places . . . even though (it is) expressed in different idioms and reflects different histories and different versions of the world' (Walzer 1994: 17). However, on other occasions, Walzer has explicitly invoked Rawls's conception of natural duties as providing 'one positive moral duty' which extends beyond frontiers (see Walzer 1981, 2003b). Miller, on the other hand, defends his more complex notion of a basic global minimum 'humanitarianism', and of basic human rights, on what he calls an 'empirical' grounding in human suffering and need (Miller 2007). It is possible that Walzer, Miller, Jackson and others might claim natural law as the source of their endorsement of mutual aid.

Rawls himself defended mutual aid as one of his natural duties and he did so on broadly Kantian grounds rather than natural law. For Rawls, the natural duty of mutual aid is consistent with the categorical imperative (CI) and indeed Rawls recognizes that in a way Kant is trying to provide a rational foundation for the earlier natural law principle. For Kant, it was defended based on human reason and not on the capacity to suffer:

as a person's true needs are those which must be met if he is to function (or continue to function) as a rational, end-setting agent. Respecting the humanity of others involves acknowledging the duty of mutual aid: one must be prepared to support the conditions of the rationality of others (their capacity to set and act for ends) when they are unable to do so without help. The duty to develop (not neglect) one's talents and the duty of mutual aid are thus duties of respect for persons. (Herman 1984: 597)

Herman argues that Rawls attempts a different grounding from Kant and derives his mutual aid principle from the method of the original position. Contractors behind the veil of ignorance would agree on this rule, including applying it to non-contractors, again from rational calculations of interests. Therefore, Rawls argues that the principle of mutual aid holds universally across borders and to all humans.

If we take Kantian premises rather than natural law as the source of Rawls's natural duties, it is clear that the idea of natural duties extends directly from Kantian arguments rather than communitarian premises. Thus, when Rawls and subsequently communitarians such as Walzer invoke natural duties, they are implicitly at least invoking Kantian moral universalism. The implications of this will be returned to in the remaining chapters of this book.

In conclusion, Rawls's inclusion of cosmopolitan elements such as human rights and natural duties contributes to the case for inclusion of cosmopolitan principles as foundations of international order, even if these principles are not fully fledged or institutionalized. This has led some critics to dismiss his *Law of Peoples* as just another version of liberal imperialism or indeed cosmopolitanism (see Jackson 2005; Mouffe 2006). However, the criticism of Rawls levelled by liberal cosmopolitans is that he is not liberal enough, and that it is possible to extend his account to the international in a way he is unwilling to do (see chapters 2 and 7).

Rawls's account in *The Law of Peoples* is consistent with his own earlier account in *Theory of Justice*. While Beitz may be correct that the international sphere is interconnected enough to count as a system of social cooperation, what the international sphere does not have in Rawls's terms is an overlapping consensus. Therefore, what Rawls attempts is an account of liberal justice that liberals can live with, without having to fully liberalize the international realm and thereby violate a liberal principle of toleration and pluralism. In this way, a decent liberal state should not try to, and has no duty to, globalize its conception of distributive justice. Thus, even though cosmopolitan elements are present, Rawls's position is anti-cosmopolitan overall because, as Wenar (2006: 3) argues, for Rawls, individuals cannot be the focus of a global theory under conditions of pluralism and anarchy. Rawls's view of justice will be returned to in chapter 7.

Pluralism and statism: the international society of states

Rawls's list of liberal duties to other states owes a lot to writers such as Terry Nardin (1983), who work in the international society tradition of statist pluralism, or the English school (see Linklater and Suganami 2006). Nationalism and the law of peoples refer to two expressions of communitarian ethics which focus on the cultural or sociological level. Statist pluralism pursues the political expression of these ideas.

As we have seen, non-statist pluralism does not necessarily equate political/cultural community with the state which is seen as an administrative apparatus which governs but does not necessarily reflect or embody the values and traditions of a political community. In this view, the state is analytically distinguished from the nation (Miller 1995) or peoples (Rawls 1999), or simply political community (Walzer 1983). There is a variety of reasons for making this sort of distinction. The most obvious one is that not every state reflects a single nation or people. However, while this may be analytically the case, when it comes to the political realm most observers argue that it makes little sense to talk of political communities in the contemporary world without reference to the state because the state has become the single model of legitimate *political* association. In its statist form, anti-cosmopolitan pluralism is expressed in the Grotian idea that states form an international society and not just an international system (see Bull 1966, 1977). Statist pluralists argue that any obligations to humanity are best mediated through states and through the society of states.

While many anti-cosmopolitans such as Walzer and Miller fit Boucher's category of historical reason (Hegelianism), these same authors are 'Grotian' or pluralist in their understanding of the morality of international life. In his discussion of Just War, for example, Walzer (1977) appears to endorse a statist understanding of international law.

For our purposes, it is the statist pluralist argument and the distinction between pluralist and solidarist accounts of international society that is of most relevance. Terry Nardin (1983) claims that the society of states is a 'practical' association of those 'who are associated with one another, if at all, only in respecting certain restrictions on how each may pursue his own purposes' (Nardin 1983: 9). This type of association covers those areas concerned with the rule of law and standards of conduct entailing 'a set of considerations to be taken into account in deciding and acting' or rules of engagement (Nardin 1983: 6).

In contrast, purposive association is concerned with pursuing common and shared goals such as a trade union might do. Nardin (1983) himself draws on the work of Michael Oakeshott for this distinction. In Nardin's pluralist ethics, 'the nature of international society is such that all-inclusive association can only be practical' (1983: 215). In such an association the objective is merely to keep the various purposive associations apart. Indeed, it was precisely because the universal moral consensus of Christendom was fracturing and the legitimacy of the Catholic Church was in doubt that the Treaty of Westphalia was instituted and the society of sovereign states brought into being. In Bull's terms, the Treaty of Westphalia was a compact of coexistence designed to overcome the breakdown in consensus regarding the legitimacy of the Church's temporal role.

In international society, pluralism is contrasted with solidarism, which is another name for what Nardin called a purposive international society. Solidarism is different from pluralism because it goes beyond an ethics of pure tolerance and raises the standards by which tolerance is accepted (see Bull 1966). Solidarism contains elements of cosmopolitan ethics because it makes sovereignty conditional upon treatment of individuals (Nardin 1983; Brown 1992). Pluralists are sceptical about the use of human rights in diplomacy as it gives some states the opportunity to deny others their sovereignty (Jackson 2000), while humanitarian intervention in emergencies which offend the 'conscience of humankind' can occasionally be defended (Walzer 1977, 2004).

The absence of centralized law enforcement in international society means that any collaborative action requires a high degree of consensus amongst the sovereign autonomous members of international society. It was only when such consensus existed that effective action was possible in relation to issues such as the sanctioning of the apartheid regime in South Africa (Bull 1983).

However, for the most part, such a consensus is lacking between states. This position essentially holds that the absence of a genuine moral consensus in international society means that the morality or legitimacy of any claim to universal morality is suspect. A lack of consensus on substantive normative or ethical questions makes it difficult for the members of international society to act in a concerted fashion.

Pluralists resist attempts to develop a more solidarist world in which principles of human rights are enforced and humanitarian intervention is institutionalized. Instead, for pluralists, what is required is a toleration of a plurality of cultures. If we have any international obligations to those beyond our borders, it is an obligation to refrain from imposing a particular conception of the good life, a particular culture, or a particular ethical morality upon others. In this view, sovereignty is an ethical principle and not just a *modus vivendi*, which allows states and the different cultures they harbour to exist alongside each other. Likewise, pluralism does not advocate universal distributive justice, either as a practical possibility or as a moral good in itself because it requires the imposition of a specific, usually liberal, account of justice upon other cultures. According to pluralists, the primary ethical responsibility of the statesperson is to maintain order and peace between states, not develop a global account of justice.

Pluralists are cautious about undoing the compact of coexistence by holding up states to scrutiny for their human rights records because there is no international consensus strong enough to justify this, and the effect of acting as if there were would be to undermine the capacity of international society to maintain order. In Bull's words, 'the rules of coexistence serve to maintain order in an international society in which a consensus does not exist in normal circumstances about much else besides these rules' (1977: 157). A solidarist international society goes beyond coexistence by adopting shared goals, such as justice, defence of human rights and practices of armed intervention in defence of these shared purposes. The ability of international society to move in a solidarist direction will depend on the degree to which they reflect a consensus amongst its members (Bull 1977; Wheeler and Dunne 1996). Bull argued that:

> the interests of order are not served . . . if in the situation in which no such consensus actually exists and the international society is divided into contending groups, one of these groups claims to represent the consensus and act as if it does . . . the result is that the traditional rules which assume a lack of consensus are undermined. (1977: 157)

Therefore, sovereignty and pluralism are the most appropriate ethical responses to cultural diversity and normative disagreement. Pluralism recognizes that states have different ethics but can agree upon a framework whereby they tolerate each other, do not impose their own views upon others and agree on certain limited harm principles. R. J. Vincent (1986) has described this as the 'egg box' conception of international society where 'The general function of international society is to separate and cushion, not to act.' In international society, states acknowledge that domestic conceptions of the good are not necessarily shared and, more importantly, can only be secured by a pact of coexistence between these competing conceptions to guarantee freedom from undue outside influence. Thus, international society is the means by which different particular cultures maintain their separateness. This allows them to feel reasonably secure and to go about their business in relative peace.

The pluralist view is that the obligations of states are those of states rather than individuals. In the pluralist view, this is a moral community in which the members make laws and develop norms to govern their actions. There is a global social contract, or covenant, between states (see Bull 1979; Frost 1996; and Jackson 2000). Obviously, the most important of these agreements is that of sovereignty. The appropriate moral realm, and ethical vocabulary, is that of state, sovereignty and international law. Sovereignty imposes moral obligations upon members of international society to respect each other's independence, to avoid war against each other and to uphold and defend the rules of international society (see chapter 6). These obligations, however, apply only to states, as they are the contractors.

Very few pluralist writers today defend a pure ethics of coexistence and most concede that human rights should form part of the norms of international society. For instance, Mervyn Frost (1996) views human rights as essential to an ethical society of states, Robert Jackson (2000) includes them in his account of a pluralist international society, and John Rawls cited human rights as a basis for the liberal 'law of peoples'. Michael Walzer endorses the 'morality of states' in some cases (Just War, see chapter 6) and initially characterizes international society as a regime of toleration (1997), but has in later work (1994: 11) argued that 'We can (and should) defend some minimal understanding of human rights and seek its universal enforcement' (though this statement contradicts his earlier argument above). Likewise, Miller provides a strong case for a global basic standard based on fulfilment of basic rights (2007; chapter 7).

Nonetheless, what ultimately unites anti-cosmopolitans is scepticism about moral progress, a normative defence of the status quo, and the division of humanity into separate political and moral communities. Anti-cosmopolitans reject efforts to transform the *political* structure of the world to bring it more into line with any universalist account. Moral universalism is both misguided and pernicious; therefore it follows that there is no duty to institutionalize cosmopolitan principles within the current international order or to transform the contemporary world order in the way envisioned by cosmopolitans. At best, with regard to international ethics, the traditions discussed in this chapter only incorporate a duty to act on principles of natural duty, minimal or basic rights, and to maintain order.

Problems with anti-cosmopolitanism

With the combination of the condition of international anarchy, practical problems of normative pluralism, and the defence of diversity, anti-cosmopolitans present a significant case for defending particularist values and arguing against cosmopolitanism. Drawing on communitarian critiques of liberalism, the anti-cosmopolitan traditions of realism and pluralism make some very important observations on the limits of universalism in the international realm. Communitarian objections indicate that many universalist accounts, especially liberalism, rely upon certain assumptions and forms of reasoning that are problematic. The liberal account of agency, which depicts a uniform and idealized account of human beings, is problematic and too substantive to be the basis of a genuine universal ethic. Likewise, some forms of universalism do appear to be 'hostile' or inconsistent with substantive moral/cultural pluralism. The universalization of a Rawlsian account of justice, as understood by Beitz or Moellendorf, does indeed appear to require overriding alternative interpretations of fairness. Insofar as the anti-cosmopolitan critique is directed towards liberal cosmopolitanism, then the charge of indifference to the plural conceptions of the good has some purchase.

Nevertheless, whether or not these observations undermine cosmopolitanism as a whole, as many particularists claim, is debatable. The most important thing about the communitarian critique of cosmopolitanism is the desire to resist homogenization and to acknowledge the diversity of moral cosmologies. The question for cosmopolitans in response is to ask whether these values are necessarily or only contingently in conflict with universalism, and whether they override universal duties to the individual or not?

Cosmopolitans point out several flaws in pluralism and anti-cosmopolitanism. Cosmopolitans, especially liberal cosmopolitans, have faith in reason as the provider of objective, or at least grounded accounts of ethics and morality. For cosmopolitans, this gives their account an authority, and ultimately justifies its universalism. In order to be coherent, communitarianism or pluralism must also be situated within a form of universalism.

Communitarians also make certain foundational claims regarding truth, the most important of which involves the provision of meaning by culture, which is also the source of ethics and identity. As a consequence of this observation, communitarians argue that different cultures ought to be preserved and defended. However, pluralists can't make this case without violating or substantially surrendering certain aspects of their case about the nature of moral knowledge, and adopting certain universalist premises such as equality, or the universal importance of defending different cultures. That is, despite the relativistic implication of the communitarian position that norms are culturally dependent, writers such as Miller, Walzer and Frost all tend to make certain foundational claims about their position's objectivity or truthfulness. Cochran argues that communitarians proceed 'as if their weak foundations yield non-contingent ethical claims' (1999: 16) or, while they claim weak foundations, they reason as if these foundations are strong. Anti-cosmopolitans operate as if their argument – that it is always wrong to override particular understandings – is non-contingent, and can be grounded and defended universally. If this is the case, then the anti-cosmopolitan argument is also culturally particular and cannot claim a universal status; it cannot claim to be true in any trans-historical or moral sense. Why, then, should cosmopolitans accept its arguments as having universal significance?

The question to ask at this stage is: what claim to truth can any ethics make? Is it possible to provide firm foundations for ethical judgements, and for judgement between judgements? The justifications provided for anti-cosmopolitan concessions to universalism are either very thin or, more seriously, fundamentally contradict other premises of their arguments. This prompts another question: if some universalism is okay, why not more? The answers to this can only be pragmatic once universalism is conceded, that is, they can rest only upon contingent and not absolute claims. If universalism is a violation of community priority, then how can communitarians accept any universalism? On what basis do communitarians accept minimal human rights or natural duties? Is it because such rights are already agreed upon? If so, then communitarians are conceding to the fact that universal agreement is possible. If that is the case, communitarians must be able to explain why we ought not move towards more agreement. If it is possible or acceptable to hold that no one ought to be denied their right to live, to housing or to basic standards of human decency, then why is it also not possible to argue that no one ought to be denied the right to speak freely or marry the person of their own choosing? (Miller 2007 is the exception in that he does provide a clear position on exactly these questions, though one in which rather a lot of ground is conceded to cosmopolitanism.) The communitarian's best defence is that there is, at present, no consensus on these issues. This only begs the question: why not develop or pursue such a consensus?[3]

Another criticism is that pluralists reify communities. Be it nations or states, communitarians or pluralists assume that communities are relatively coherent and that diversity does not exist (or is at least managed) within communities. Pluralists tend to see communities as organic beings that are in some sense natural and singular. This is ironic because one of the critiques of cosmopolitans shared by communitarians and pluralists is that cosmopolitans idealize humans and do not pay attention to particular human beings. Nevertheless, pluralists tend to ignore particularities or to dismiss the existence of disagreement within communities and the historical ways in which the so-called consensus or shared norms of political communities rely upon historical domination or assimilation. Pluralists are unable to provide reasons why intra-community disagreement is in any way substantively different from inter-community disagreement. Likewise, if domination and assimilation are bad between communities, then why ought they be acceptable 'within' communities? Pluralists can only defend their point of view if they think there is something special about the national state. However, for many other pluralists who are less Hegelian, no such argument is forthcoming. Walzer and Rawls pretend that states do not matter or even exist; they talk of people and communities. And yet it is the national state that exists today as the most powerful form of communal affiliation in history.

The pluralist idealization of the national state is compounded by a general inability and unwillingness to address the existence of interdependence between communities. There is both a normative and empirical point to be made here. The first empirical point is that communities today are intertwined with other communities in increasingly complex ways. This means it is harder for communities to be conceptualized as 'autarkic'. Yet this is precisely what theorists like Rawls insist upon (again, Miller is the exception to this; see his 2007).

Many anti-cosmopolitans treat communities as if they were self-sufficient. There are two problems with this. Communities are not coherent singular identities, and treating them as if they were self-sufficient results in a refusal to deal with the impacts that communities have upon each other. This is one of the most profound failings of pluralist accounts. Even if we accept that communities are largely singular in identity, we cannot accept that they are autarkic or that they have no impacts upon outsiders. Even the act of defining a border of a nation-state, for example, often affects those not included within the border (see chapter 4).

Thus, given that most states engage in international trade and commerce, travel and so on, communitarians must ask what obligations if any the members of these communities have to outsiders. However, as we have examined in this chapter, many pluralists limit these moral or ethical obligations to the minimum. Rawls's *Law of Peoples*, for instance, provides little or no guidance for thinking about the ethics of global warming, or even of economic growth, in situations where domestic activity has profound impacts on those outside the borders.

If pluralists are to be taken at face value, they must hold either that economics is outside the realm of the moral, or that states should seek to reduce the amount of interaction they have with each other. Communitarian ethics also imply a right of closure to outside influences. Communities have the right to maintain their identities by restricting access to these communities (see Walzer, and the next chapter on refugees). The implication is that almost any interaction with outsiders will constitute a harm done to the community. This includes actions we domestically might consider to be beneficial to our own community, resulting from the interaction with outsiders, such as trade or exposure to another's culture through literature, television or film. (This line of thought conforms to realist understandings of interdependence as a cause of conflict and not a way of overcoming it.)

From this reification of communities, it follows that pluralists emphasize states' rights, but not their responsibilities (again, Miller has done the most to redress this imbalance). It is for this reason that Buchannan (2000) referred to Rawls's *Law of Peoples* as 'rules for a vanishing Westphalian world'. Pluralists have been outstripped by reality in that the world they defend no longer exists. This causes particular problems because they claim pluralism's grounding in 'reality' contrasts with the idealism of cosmopolitanism, yet the pluralists conception of reality is contentious. In this vein, cosmopolitans and solidarists argue that a strict ethics of coexistence is simply out of date and can actually be harmful, as the scope for intercommunity harm has increased exponentially with globalization and the interconnectedness of communities (see Hurrell 2007). Most cosmopolitans argue that an 'egg box' ethics is not enough under conditions of globalization.

Perhaps most importantly, while pluralists serve individual interests through defending their membership in communities, they tend also to give power to the community over individuals. Does the human right to belong to a group mean that group rights may override individual human rights, opening the way to condoning behaviour and practices that harm individuals? Thus, for pluralists, if a community has the belief that women are second-class citizens with restricted rights and duties, then it is the overall right of their community to self-determination rather than the individual rights of women that trumps here. In this example, the community overrides the individual. In other words, there are some circumstances where it is communities per se that are the relevant or even basic subject of morality rather than individuals.

Although this assumption is not always entirely clear in

anti-cosmopolitan writing, it is a clear implication. For example, Walzer (1983) condones the moral priority of the community over the individual with regard to the cases of refugees, of non-combatant immunity and supreme emergency (see chapters 4 and 7). Pluralists find themselves caught in a contradiction when they argue that individuals are best served by the norms of their community even when that community might not recognize those individuals as bearers of equal moral worth. The position of women in many cultures provides a clear example here (for an illuminating discussion, see Nussbuam 1995). Pluralists implicitly give little hope to women everywhere who seek to challenge those practices of their own culture which harm or exclude women from equal moral consideration. If a group of women has no resources with which to argue for this, then communitarianism implies that women in those communities ought to accept their lot. Communitarians are also incapable of demonstrating how those women are best served by that community (Nussbaum 2007; Nussbaum and Glover 1995). This is, of course, the position that ultimately defines cosmopolitans differently from anti-cosmopolitans.

Cosmopolitans are not willing to make the claim that the community should in some cases come before the individual. According to cosmopolitanism, it is the individual who is the moral agent and the moral subject and who therefore ought to be the focus of moral concern. To make the claim that group rights can override individual rights, it must follow that the individual would be better off having been overridden, for the value of community can only lie in its utility for individual members. Without this premise, we could end up accepting all sorts of suffering and harm on the grounds that they are community endorsed or expressions of a right of communal self-determination. One of the advantages of cosmopolitan thought, along with the idea of impartiality, is that it protects individuals from abuse by their own culture.

Conclusion

One of the most important criticisms of nationalism is that, in the words of Voltaire, it makes its adherents 'the enemy of humankind'. For cosmopolitans, communitarianism presents this type of threat. If we are to accept their moral epistemology and ontology are we not condemned to make ourselves the enemy of humankind? The challenge for cosmopolitanism is to defend a form of moral universalism that can incorporate this recognition, and the challenge for anti-cosmopolitanism is to accommodate the legitimate needs of universalism so that we don't become enemies to each other.

Any defence of cosmopolitan ethics must address the issues arising from the attempt to enact a universal moral realm in a situation where universalism is either contested or simply lacking. The existence of ethical pluralism means that we cannot assume that everybody else will act according to the same ethical framework, either in relationship to each other or to us. In other words, we cannot assume a universal ethical and moral framework.

Additionally, if it is not possible to identify any morally meaningful qualities (such as the capacity for 'rationality') that are common to all humans, then the cosmopolitan community guided by universal rules that all agree to cannot come into being. It is worth noting, however, that anti-cosmopolitanism is not a necessary conclusion to be drawn from communitarian premises; a number of accounts of moral universalism and cosmopolitan have been derived from this starting point (see, for instance, Kung 1990; Etzioni 2004; Shapcott 2001). These accounts all argue that the contextual origins of moral thought does not prevent the emergence, development and even agreement upon some moral universals, as long as these are developed dialogically.

The point to be taken from the communitarian argument is not that universalism is impossible, but that acting ethically is difficult. While normative pluralism certainly makes the making and enforcing of laws more difficult, and also makes it harder to be confident of the morality of one's decisions, it does not render these impossible. Similarly, as individuals, many of us assume that we share some values and not others with different people. This usually means that we tolerate this diversity or that we seek to understand another's position before we act or pass judgement upon them. The most obvious example in contemporary Western societies is the difference between secular liberal values and orthodox Islamic practices, especially in relation to women. The presence of differences is not considered to relieve us of our ethical obligations, or of the idea that we should treat people ethically; it only makes these obligations and ideas more complex, and subject to reflection and modification.

In other words, within the context discussed above, what it means to treat someone ethically is problematized but not undermined, even in situations where not everyone agrees that all people (such as women, in the example above) should be treated as equals. For example, we can imagine a situation where a slave might believe that they are unequal, but we recognize them as equal and treat them as such. We would feel bad to treat them as unequal, regardless of what they believe. At the same time, we would need to be sensitive to the conditions of the slave's life; they might suffer punishment if we encouraged them to act as though they were not a slave. But this would not relieve us of the duty to view the slave as worthy of moral respect (up to and including the possibility of ending their status as a slave). The point is that, for those of us who are concerned about acting ethically, the existence of other people with different ethical frameworks does not mean that we should automatically throw up our hands and think we are no longer required to treat them well, i.e., as ends in themselves. It only means that to treat someone well is made more difficult. The same conceptual framework or idea applies to states. If we believe in human rights and incorporate them into our foreign policy goals, then the fact that others may not share the same understandings of human rights and the same foreign policy goals does not relieve us of the obligation to pursue human rights as our own ethical goals even though it requires a more sensitive handling of the issues (see, for instance, M. A. Brown 2002).

In sum, the conclusion to be drawn from this account of anti-cosmopolitanism is that it advances a legitimate concern for ethical/moral diversity and the recognition of different standards in different places. However, this criticism is best understood as a corrective to cosmopolitanism rather than a repudiation of its central ideas. Anti-cosmopolitan pluralism, we have seen, rests on universal foundations of its own and appeals to the moral universalism of natural duties.

In addition, any ethics in the contemporary era of globalization needs to draw upon more resources than are provided for by 'communitarianism' and anti-cosmopolitanism. This is implicitly acknowledged by the anti-cosmopolitan invocation of natural duties. Once this argument is advanced we are entering into a cosmopolitan domain of discourse.

Recognition of natural duties raises many questions about the extent and nature of duties to aid and not to harm, as well as the institutional structure of international ethics. Questions concerning those duties are best evaluated from a cosmopolitan framework because the anti-cosmopolitan framework has insufficient theoretical resources to address them. These considerations will be explored in more depth in the following chapters. This chapter and the previous one sketched the epistemological, ontological and moral arguments of cosmopolitanism and anti-cosmopolitanism. The remainder of the book discusses how these different perspectives are expressed in relation to some specific ethical issues.

4

Hospitality: Entry and Membership

We decide who comes into this country and the circumstances in which they come.

Campaign speech, Australian Prime Minister John Howard, 28 October 2001; cited in Gelber and McDonald 2006: 277

Admission and exclusion are at the core of communal independence. They suggest the deepest meaning of self-determination. Without them, there could not be communities of character, historically stable, ongoing associations of men and women with some special commitment to one another and some special sense of their common life.

Walzer 1983: 62

Introduction

This chapter examines the issue of moral exclusion in a very literal sense. The issues of entry and membership go directly to the heart of the tension between the rights of communities and the rights of the individual, and to the meaning of justice. Questions of entry are so important because they are foundational and yet, because they are foundational, they are often taken for granted and assumed. Once we examine the ethical foundations of our communities, then the categories we use for thinking about ethics come into question and stand the risk of seeming inadequate.

Ethical debates around migration and people movements examine the ethical justifications of the right of exclusion, and attempt to establish whether and how states can have such rights. Millions of people every day seek to gain entry to countries other than their country of origin (32.9 million refugees and 'persons of interest' to UNHCR in 2008, according to the United Nations High Commissioner for Refugees). The movement of people between communities is as old as humanity itself, and it has always been accompanied by attempts to restrict the entry of strangers into 'bounded' communities. The mass movement of peoples since the middle of the twentieth century, and again since the end of the Cold War, goes to the heart of the nation-state's claim to exist as a sovereign and exclusive political community. In the era of nation-states, the right of territorial exclusion has become a defining prerogative of sovereignty. However, a survey of books on international ethics reveals that, for most, the questions of immigration and refugees are not considered (see Amstutz 1999; Harbour 1998; Valls 2000; Dower 1998; Hayden 2005). The implication is that such questions are matters of purely domestic concern, internal to the community of the nation-state. It is a curious omission because membership and entry are arguably the first way in which states' actions have international impacts. Every time a state declares or is declared sovereign it asserts the right to decide upon membership and to restrict entry. Arguably, policies regarding access to citizenship ought not to be viewed as unilateral acts of self-determination, but rather must be seen as decisions with multilateral consequences that influence other entities in the world community (Benhabib 2004: 21). Every decision by a state to refuse admission to refugees or potential migrants impacts upon the international community, either bilaterally or multilaterally, via the offices of the United Nations High Commissioner for Refugees (UNHCR), by directing claims elsewhere.

As many cosmopolitan theorists note, ethical reflection must begin with the exclusions accompanying the domestic social contract. Therefore, it makes sense to begin with reflection upon the defence of the right of exclusion and the way in which it is exercised. The question addressed in this chapter is how members of bounded political communities ought to weigh the claims of outsiders who wish to join the social contract. More specifically, discussion of immigration, refugees, asylum seekers and the status of residents raises two questions: questions of entry and questions of membership. Immigration debates address the question of whether states have a right to restrict entry, or whether people ought to have the right to absolute free movement to settle where they choose. The fundamental issue that immigration brings to the fore is whether community rights trump individual rights and whether outsiders' interests should count as much as insiders'. This is especially so in the case of refugees and asylum seekers who attempt to flee persecution or extreme disorder or suffering. These people present the closed political communities with a moral demand to allow unconditional entry in order to relieve suffering and save lives.

The second issue which follows concerns the status that people have once they are granted entry, in terms of who is entitled to full citizenship or membership rights and the state's grounds for denying such rights to people it has admitted. For instance, guest workers, or foreigners who migrate exclusively for work purposes, raise the issue of membership because they do not have full citizenship rights and are excluded from political life, and do not have the rights enjoyed by other citizens. Having accepted foreigners into their midst, political communities are faced with two further ethical choices: (i) are the new arrivals granted full membership of the community, including permanent residency or citizenship?; or (ii) are the new arrivals granted merely hospitality or safe haven, but not made full members or citizens? The first and largest part of this chapter discusses the ethics of entry and the second part discusses the question of membership. The first part itself is divided into two sections: (i) relating to the general case of immigration; and (ii) to the specific challenges of refugees and asylum seekers.

Ethics of entry: cosmopolitanism and anti-cosmopolitanism on migration

The questions of entry and membership refer to the positive and negative duties 'we' owe to 'them', and equally raise the universal obligations of what everybody owes because there is a claim that deciding entry is not just a national problem, but also a global one. Any immigration and refugee policy takes place in the context of a global movement of people or a global refugee crisis, and is not just a national decision.

In some ways, the distinction between cosmopolitans and anti-cosmopolitans is clearest in relation to questions of entry and membership. At its most categorical, liberal cosmopolitanism argues for no restriction on movement and anti-cosmopolitan means the absolute rights of a state to restrict movement. However, cosmopolitan authors also include arguments that political communities do have some rights to decide who enters and remains and who does not, while anti-cosmopolitans also accept the claims of some outsiders to first priority. The chief difference between cosmopolitans and anti-cosmopolitans is that the latter see this issue primarily in terms of 'what we do to them', while cosmopolitans also understand this as a question of justice, i.e., what we owe to everybody and what everybody does to everybody else. That is, cosmopolitans and anti-cosmopolitans disagree over whether this is a matter of justice or of mutual aid.

The natural duties argument in the case of refugees sees entry as a question of state prerogative, that is, a matter of discretion and charity. It gives wide scope to states to decide the 'mix' and number of immigrants and refugees. In contrast, the cosmopolitan approach argues that the presumption is for inclusion, and that outsiders' interests deserve equal weight to insiders. Cosmopolitans also argue that liberal states have particular cosmopolitan duties of open borders, regardless of what other states' policies are. The real difference between cosmopolitans and anti-cosmopolitans here is between those who argue there should be a presumption of free movement, the onus being on the state to justify exclusion, and those who argue there should be a presumption of a right of exclusion with the onus being on the outsider to justify their claim to entry.

While the situation of refugees and asylum seekers is often that of desperate displaced persons, refugees and asylum seekers only become ethical problems when the right of closure exists for a political community. Logically, prior to the question and possibility of refugees, is the more general question of the right of free movement and entry. If there were absolute freedom of movement then there would be no distinction between refugees and migrants, except as might arise from their different circumstances of departure. For this reason, it is necessary to discuss migration before turning to the more fraught question of refugees.

Cosmopolitanism: Kant and universal hospitality

Many people associate cosmopolitan ethics with either the ethics of an ideal world or with the humanitarian duties we have to far-flung foreigners, which is with 'what we do to them' over there. However, cosmopolitanism, like charity, begins at home. While certain contemporary accounts of cosmopolitanism may not pay sufficient attention to the movement of peoples, they were a concern in the beginning of modern cosmopolitanism in the work of Immanuel Kant. There was, for Kant, a cosmopolitan right of freedom of movement that overrode state sovereignty. The principle of hospitality refers to the obligations we have to others or 'outsiders' who wish to access 'our' territory or community. Cosmopolitan hospitality recognizes the right of a stranger entering foreign territory to be treated as a friend 'so long as he conducts himself peaceably he must not be treated as an enemy' (Kant 1983: 137; Benhabib 2004). For Kant, universal hospitality was one of the few cosmopolitan duties required of republican states in relation to the individuals of other states.

Cosmopolitan hospitality involves an assumption not only of goodwill towards strangers, but also a recognition of their right to travel the surface of the Earth. Kant believed that as long as no considerable harm was foreseeable all people had the right to travel and engage in commerce with each other without restriction. States had a duty not to harm those who sought to enter in good conscience. Kant made no distinction between those who seek access to another territory for commercial purposes, and those who wish to simply travel or migrate. Kantian hospitality did not extend as far as a right of permanent membership, or what we would term citizenship; it was only a temporary right of sojourn, and it was also an imperfect duty of beneficence of the sovereign. In other words, sovereigns had a duty to presume in favour of free movement but had the right to exclude where necessary.

The right of sojourn represented a positive right of movement or association, to be treated as a friend not an enemy, as well as the negative right not to be harmed. Benhabib (2004) points out that Kant did not want to restrict interaction between people and peoples; he wanted to encourage civil society and relationships while also discouraging domination and imperialism. Benhabib explains Kant's reasoning as follows:

> the right of humanity in our person imposes a reciprocal obligation on us to enter into civil society and to accept that our freedom will be limited by civil legislation, such that the freedom of one can be made compatible with the freedom of each under a universal law . . . The right of humanity entitles us to become a member of civil society such that we can then be entitled to juridico-civil rights. The moral claim of the guest not to be treated with hostility upon arriving in the lands of another and his or her claim to temporary hospitality rest upon this moral injunction against violating the rights of humanity in the individual person. (2004: 59)

For David Held, universal hospitality is an expression of a principle of freedom of *communication* and interaction, and the right to engage with others in non-violent ways. Held argues that the third article of perpetual peace 'connotes a right and duty which must be accepted if people are to learn to tolerate one another's company and to coexist peacefully . . . universal hospitality is, therefore, the condition of cooperative relations and of just conduct' (1997: 228).

Behind Kant's argument lay a distinction between the territory and the political community or *polis*. The political community was a body of people who recognized each other as co-legislators, and they just happened to inhabit a particular piece of territory. For Kant, there was nothing in the nature of the political community that gave it absolute right over territory. Territory belonged to all humans in common; what mattered politically was access to a community of rights-bearing co-legislators. Because the Earth belonged exclusively to no one, Kant allowed freedom of movement, but he did not allow for membership because membership required an act of recognition and a commitment to a certain public realm. Kant's limiting of the right of hospitality to temporary sojourn is also informed by recognition of the need to prevent the Western appropriation of non-Western peoples' land and territory, and to defend them against Western expansion. It was a rejection of Lockean property rights and *res nullius* thesis, and an affirmation of an anti-cosmopolitan value that 'every community has the right to defend itself against those who seek access to its territories' (Benhabib, 2004: 28). In other words, the Kantian hospitality claim was strictly limited in order to preserve communal autonomy.

What then are the implications of Kant's hospitality principles? The first is that states have no right to a priori exclusion of well-intended outsiders. A cosmopolitan order requires freedom of movement and interaction and communication. However, the principle of free movement was not extended to a right of permanent residence or migration. This would suggest that states retain the right to control membership but not entry.

The only additional ethical criterion Kant gives refers to something like the contemporary right of asylum, which is now enshrined in international law: it is unjustifiable to deny sojourn if to do so would cause a serious harm or lead to 'destruction'. A Kantian hospitality principle involves the recognition that treating people as equals requires acknowledging that they ought to be allowed in if they will be harmed or (destroyed) by exclusion. The only condition under which this might be modified is if the presence of others would constitute a significant harm to us. Thus, a state has a duty to its own people to exclude, for instance, known terrorists or criminals. It also means that refugees and asylum seekers have an unqualified right of entry, based on the threat to their personal safety. Kant then can be understood as balancing the right of individuals with the rights of political communities to self-preservation, but he does so within the framework of the categorical imperative (CI) which places ultimate reference on the right of individual freedom (see Timmons 2002).

It is interesting to note that in practice Kant's position is now closer to such anti-cosmopolitan authors as Rawls, Walzer and Miller, than it is to contemporary liberals and cosmopolitans such as Beitz or Joseph Carens. The following sections examine these contemporary cosmopolitan accounts.

Liberal cosmopolitanism: open borders

In chapter 2, it was argued that cosmopolitanism consisted of three basic qualities: universality, individualism and impartiality. For certain liberal cosmopolitans, recognition of these requires that liberal states, and by implication others, should eradicate border control policies and any real distinction between residents and citizens. If the world is one single community from a moral perspective, and national boundaries have no deep *moral* significance, then national communities have no basic right of exclusion (in the absence of pragmatic counter-arguments).

The case for open borders has been most vigorously argued by Joseph Carens. Carens (1980) begins with the liberal cosmopolitan premise that impartiality requires a viewpoint that perceives national borders as arbitrary and contingent and therefore morally unjustifiable. From an impartial position, citizenship in Western (affluent) states is an arbitrary privilege. It is only by luck that some people have the rights and privileges associated with membership in affluent Western liberal democracies. For Carens, the implication of this reading is that 'one could not justify restrictions on the grounds that those born in a given territory or born of parents who were citizens were more entitled to the benefits of citizenship than those born elsewhere or born of alien parents' (1980: 261). In other words, members of rich countries cannot justify their right to exclude others from the privileges they accrue merely from being lucky enough to have been born into an affluent part of the world. Current state policies restricting immigration in Western democracies, therefore, 'are not justifiable. Like feudal barriers they protect unjust privileges' (Carens 1980: 261). An impartial (cosmopolitan) position requires that there be free movement across the surface of the Earth and that people from poor countries ought to be able to move into wealthy countries (and vice versa) without restrictions (other than those required for law and order).

For liberal cosmopolitans, this argument applies first and foremost to liberal states. As Phillip Cole argues, 'with its universalist commitment to the moral equality of humanity, liberal theory cannot coherently justify these practices of exclusion, which constitute "outsiders" on grounds any recognizable liberal theory would condemn as arbitrary' (2000: 2). For liberal democratic states, there is particular tension, if not outright contradiction, between their principles of individual autonomy and human rights and state autonomy and self-determination, or sovereignty.

Liberalism is first and foremost a universal doctrine premised on the universality of individual rights and freedoms. There is a particular moral burden that falls to liberal states because of this commitment. More specifically, for the liberal position to be consistent, it must recognize the universal right of free movement. Liberal states impose no internal restrictions upon movement for their own citizens and cannot justify doing so for outsiders (see also Moses 2006). According to Carens (1980: 251), individuals also possess the same right to free movement globally and 'borders should generally be open and people should normally be free to leave their country of origin and settle in another subject only to the sorts of constraints that bind current citizens in their new countries'.[1] As Dummett argues:

> The presumption of individuals is always for freedom: there must be a particular ground why any state is entitled to curtail that freedom, if indeed it is . . . The onus of proof always lies with a claim to the right to exclude would-be immigrants. (2001: 57)

Carens argues that these conclusions are consistent with and can be derived from the major varieties of liberalism – Nozickian libertarianism, utilitarianism and Rawlsian. Robert Goodin (1992) has pointed out that liberalism is inconsistent between its attitude to money and people; in practice, money has far greater freedom of movement than people do, and this is generally seen as consistent with liberalism. So it stands to reason that people ought to have at least as much freedom as money.

For utilitarians, the argument is not so clear-cut, as it depends upon a number of variables such as what sort of utilitarianism you use. It depends also on what the overall utility would be, and this may change at different times as, say, economic circumstances vary. For Rawlsians, a right of free movement could be envisioned as a reasonable conclusion. Behind the veil of ignorance, it can be imagined that most contractors would favour open borders for the following reasons: 'if one does not know which country one will reside in one does not know whether one will need to settle in another country for economic or political reasons . . . [and]; if liberty includes the right of free movement then all individuals should have equal rights to move around freely across borders' (Fabre 2007: 118), so long as this does not undermine the exercise of liberty. Rawlsians also might argue on distributive grounds that immigration could be restricted only if doing so would benefit the worst off.

Carens's argument, while logically persuasive, is also very illustrative of the limits of this sort of idealized or decontextualized thinking and the problems with liberal cosmopolitan understanding of deontology. Carens's argument rests not on the consequences of a right of free movement, but purely on its inherent qualities. As a result, he pays little heed to what the possible implications of adopting such a policy in the real world might be.[2] In the context of contemporary politics, it is quite possible that such a policy would actually work against the achievement of another cosmopolitan goal of egalitarian global justice.

Many liberals have also defended free movement as a way of achieving distributive justice, as it would facilitate a net transfer of wealth to the poor via repatriation, or because it would simply allow the poorest people to move to the wealthier parts of the world and so escape poverty (Carens 1980; Moses 2006). One way in which states can fulfil their cosmopolitan distributive responsibilities to end poverty might be to allow entry to the poor. However, the problem here with using global distributive justice as a category for immigration, as Carens and also Pogge (1997) acknowledges, is that the movement of people might not be the most effective way of discharging obligations of justice. Redistribution of resources or a more just world order, and other global economic arrangements, may deliver this result more effectively.

More importantly, there could also be good reason for thinking that the movement of people from the poor to the rich world might actually contribute to the continued poor conditions of the south due to brain drain or the departure of capital (Kapur and McHale 2006). Arguably, one of the most liberal areas of current immigration practice is in the area of skilled migrants. Many states target skilled migrants for entry as they offer the best 'value added' and the lowest adjustment costs, with the highest likelihood of adapting to new countries. However, the result of this has been a brain drain from the poorer countries to the richer, with skilled migrants seeking to improve their quality of life by taking advantage of the relative freedom of movement offered them. This in turn has meant a lack of such skills in the developing countries where they are needed more. According to one account, there are more Malawian medical practitioners in Manchester than there are in Malawi (Kapur and McHale 2006). A regime of free movement could contribute to such a drain, as the less skilled and destitute are less likely to be able to move to take advantage of opportunities. A possible Rawlsian response to this problem would be to invoke the difference principle (see chapter 7), where the movement of people might make the worst off even more worse off. So movement of people can only be justified if it will improve the position of the worse off.

However, for Carens, these types of calculation are hard to defend from a deontological liberal position which emphasizes individual rights over consequences or utility 'to say that we should actually try to keep people from emigrating (by denying them a place to go) because they represent a valuable resource to their country of origin would be dramatic departure form the liberal tradition' (1980: 261); instead, distributive duties should be discharged through means other than immigration. It is possible that such a position would be less problematic for utilitarianism because, while it is individualistic, it is also consequentialist and therefore less concerned with rights than with outcomes. Restricting entry on the grounds of stopping brain drain is therefore a plausible utilitarian response if the brain drain can be shown to have reduced overall utility (welfare)

These issues point to the problem or contradiction at the heart of the liberal project, between its universalistic assumptions and the reality of a world divided into sovereign nation-states in which 'the existence of a liberal polity made up of free and equal citizens rests upon the existence of outsiders who are refused a share of the good of the liberal community' (Cole 2000: 2). Liberal states are just that, liberal *states*, existing in a sovereign political order with other non-liberal states. This means that liberalism will always be modified by that situation. However, recognizing this political reality does not necessarily mean that open borders can be rejected out of hand or that cosmopolitanism is always inconsistent with some form of control over populations and borders. This next section examines the democratic cosmopolitan argument that a degree of exclusion is necessary in order to maintain liberal, human rights-enforcing democratic institutions.

Democratic cosmopolitanism on exclusion

The radical conclusion of 'open borders' liberals like Carens is not shared by all cosmopolitans. Cosmopolitan democrats such as Habermas, Benhabib and Linklater argue that justifications for limited practices of exclusion exist, but only if they have the consent of those excluded as well as those included. In other words, justifications of exclusion must in principle be acceptable to both insiders and outsiders. For instance, Benhabib argues:

> if you and I enter into a moral dialogue with one another, and I am a member of a state of which you are seeking membership and you are not, then I must be able to show with good grounds, with grounds that would be acceptable to each of us equally, why you can never join our association and become one of us. These must be grounds that you would accept if you were in my situation and I were in yours. Our reasons must be reciprocally acceptable; they must apply to each of us equally. (2004: 138)

States must be able to give equal weight to the legitimate interests of outsiders as well.

It is possible to develop legitimate arguments for exclusion because most people value communal autonomy and freedom from external domination. People also value the freedom to move when circumstances face them with a choice between living and dying, so it is also likely that consensus might exist regarding the free entry of people fleeing persecution, starvation or destitution. In addition, it is not unreasonable to imagine that people might also agree to a restriction on their own freedom of movement in order to preserve a valuable asset, such as restriction of access to national parks. According to this logic, immigration restrictions might be justifiable to everyone if it can be shown that open borders would lead to destruction or harm for a receiving country (see Barry: 1992).

The fundamental principle upon which both liberal and democratic cosmopolitans agree is that the onus of proof is in favour of open borders. There is a presumption in favour of inclusion; therefore the state must justify exclusion rather than inclusion. The state does not have the right to choose to restrict everyone; it must open its doors to all, in principle, unless there is good reason to believe a person might harm the community in some way. For cosmopolitan democrats, only certain forms of restrictions are compatible with such a stance and only certain forms of harm justify exclusion. As Mervyn Frost argues:

> when dealing with a civilian (member of civil society who claims basic rights for themselves and recognize them in others) the presumption is that people have a right to freedom of movement. Democratic states may only limit movement when they have good reason, such as public order, security, or the threat to liberty of all. (1998: 288)

The most important justification is a threat to democracy itself. Cosmopolitan democrats agree that while liberalism favours open borders, democracy requires some restrictions because democratic processes can be threatened by an influx of people not committed to this process. Democratic citizens therefore have a legitimate interest in the preservation of their political culture. Democratic states base their claim for self-determination upon their political culture rather than exclusively on their ethnic or historical culture (though it is never this simple). This necessarily means they invoke universal values, such as individual liberty and the right of individuals to consent to or participate in the making of laws. This is an act of both individual and communal self-determination. As Habermas argues, 'The democratic right to self determination includes the right to preserve one's own political culture, which forms a concrete context for rights of citizenship, but it does not include the right to a self-assertion of privileged cultural form of life' (Habermas 1992/2008: 307) Therefore, the preservation of democratic political communities is important because of their claim to universality and legitimacy, not just because they enshrine 'our values'.

Liberal democratic states have no right to systemically exclude, say, Muslims as a group on the grounds that Islam is claimed to be incompatible with democracy. But they do have grounds to exclude political extremists of any kind who endorse or engage in terrorist or violent action. This sort of discrimination can only be against individuals; the presumption ought to be that Muslims have as much right of entry as anyone else. The relevant point to be taken from these debates is not the generic fear of cultural incompatibility, but rather the argument that a state is justified in excluding those who are unwilling to abide by democratic laws. This sort of approach is consistent with the liberal nationalism advocated by Kymlicka (2001: 173). Thus, for cosmopolitan democrats, the right of democratic self-determination is couched in a cosmopolitan framework where individual human rights trump state or communal rights and where the interests of outsiders are equal to those of insiders.

Anti-cosmopolitanism and exclusion

In contrast to liberal cosmopolitans, 'anti-cosmopolitans' reflect the more everyday belief that states have the right to decide the terms of entry and membership for themselves. As noted in chapter 3, for the anti-cosmopolitan critics, the cosmopolitan assumption that we can decide things from an impartial view is simply a misunderstanding of the nature of the communities we live in and the moral worlds we inhabit. Therefore, according to anti-cosmopolitans, the cosmopolitan argument for open borders is premised on false assumptions about 'the moral point of view'.

The anti-cosmopolitan position on immigration and membership of political communities emphasizes the political and cultural dangers of the 'open borders' position. Ultimately, the principal difference between anti-cosmopolitans and cosmopolitans is that for anti-cosmopolitans the onus of proof for entry lies with the applicant, and not with the state to defend its exclusion. The only circumstance in which individual rights might trump community rights is when individuals are at risk of great suffering or loss of life, in which case a duty of mutual aid may override communal autonomy, or when a state has a causal responsibility in the decision to seek entry.

David Miller disputes the argument that freedom of movement is a basic right as claimed by Carens. Instead, freedom of movement is a means to achieve other more basic rights such as a right to work for a living. In this sense, freedom of movement is a secondary right at best and it is dependent upon other rights being unfulfilled: 'People may have an interest in being able to move to a new country but there is no straightforward reason why that interest leads to an absolute right to a freedom of movement . . . they do not have a basic interest of the kind that would be required to ground a human right' (2005: 196). However, if an individual is likely to be persecuted or perhaps starve due to lack of work in his or her own state, then he or she may claim a right of movement to fulfil other basic needs. Where there is a right to free movement, it applies only in cases where basic rights to security of an individual cannot be met in the country of current residence. Thus, Miller argues there might be a right of exit, to search for work or to escape persecution, but it does not follow that this right to exit creates a basic right to move to any country. People do not have a right to move to a different country because they prefer their culture or are more likely to secure a better-paid job. If a person can find work in his or her own state, there is no need for a global right of free movement. If such free movement is not a basic human right, then states possess a right to determine their own admissions policy. Miller's argument, however, is not representative of most anti-cosmopolitan positions as it works within a cosmopolitan frame of universal rights (Miller 2007).

Most arguments for a right of closure begin from the premise of communal self-determination. Walzer's account of the 'distribution' of membership indicates the basic assumptions of anti-cosmopolitanism and the resulting political outcomes and his views are largely, though not entirely, endorsed by other anti-cosmopolitans (see Meilaender 2001). According to Walzer, of all the things that communities distribute membership is the most important because it is the ultimate determinant of identity, and if a community cannot determine its own terms of membership then it has no capacity to determine its own identity:

> The primary good that we distribute to one another is membership in some human community. And what we do with regard to membership structures all our other distributive choices. It determines with whom we make those choices, from whom we require obedience and collect taxes, and to whom we allocate goods and services. (1981: 2)

For Walzer, the state, as a self-determining community, is the ideal vehicle for containing and preserving cultures. According to Walzer, states 'don't merely preside over a piece of territory and a random collection of inhabitants; they are also the political expression of a common life, and (most often) of a national "family" that is never entirely enclosed within their legal boundaries' (1981: 13).

Cosmopolitan liberals are therefore incorrect to claim that individuals come *before* community because individuals are always/already members of communities that provide our identity in any meaningful sense. The community has a right to defend and preserve this identity against outsiders or anything that may threaten it. The right to exclusion plays a central part in this defence: 'The restraint of entry serves to defend the liberty and welfare, the politics and culture of a group of people committed to one another and to their common life' (Walzer 1981: 10). Because belonging furnishes us with the relationships and meanings that make us who we are, the communal right of self-determination trumps the individual right to move freely and settle where one chooses because communities have to defend that relationship. Thus, it is ultimately by reference to internal communal values that the right to exclusion or inclusion can be negotiated and this right overrides individual or cosmopolitan human rights.

For Walzer, states are anomalous to clubs; they exist for a purpose and have a right to choose which types of people they let in and to exclude those who don't share their purposes. Thus, states have no obligation to prioritize the needs of migrants in their selection criteria. Internal criteria are the only grounds used to decide entry policies. Therefore it is perfectly justified for states to select potential immigrants with whom they have some 'fellow feeling' or cultural similarity. One illustration is the state of Israel. Israel's very identity as a Jewish homeland state rests upon the capacity to exclude non-Jews. Were Israel to abandon its capacity to set its own immigration policy it might soon end up as a non-Jewish state (hence Israel's refusal to recognize a Palestinian 'right of return'). This would fundamentally challenge the capacity of self-determination of those who identify themselves as Israeli.

Different communities can use different internal criteria for exclusion. For liberal democratic states, this could conceivably mean they allow in anyone who is committed to liberal democracy. But for some states, alternatively, it might mean only those who are culturally similar are given priority (i.e., white Christian Europeans). Many states host cultures in which discrimination on these grounds is arguably central to maintaining their identity. Excluding people who do not share these traits could be easily justified in terms of preserving their political culture. In the case of the 'White Australia' policy prior to 1972, the exclusion of Asians and Africans was justified as defending the character of Australia as a white Anglo-Saxon country.[3] Australia at this time was a liberal democracy with a largely European heritage.

These sorts of arguments are what prompt some commentators such as Seglow (2005: 321) to claim that anti-cosmopolitanism provides 'an academic rendering of the prejudice that a mass influx of immigrants would "swamp" our way of life'. The underlying premise of their view is that uncontrolled immigration may change the political culture in this way. Most anti-cosmopolitan accounts rest on some variant of the argument that open borders will lead to the destruction or 'swamping' of the community by outsiders. Seglow (2005) points out that arguments of the 'swamping' type actually consist of two components. The first component refers to the need for communal or cultural preservation, and the second component refers to the quality of a state's democracy. The first, Seglow notes, 'need not involve any special commitment to democracy'. A culture may or may not have such a commitment, but as a culture it nonetheless enjoys a right to self-determination and continued existence. (2005: 321)

David Miller (2005, 2007) and Rawls both cite protecting 'a people's political culture and its constitutional principles' (Rawls 1999: 39; Benhabib 2004: 88) as *additional* grounds for a right to exclusion. Anti-cosmopolitans such as Walzer, Miller, Rawls and Mielaender argue that 'the public culture of their country is something that people have an interest in controlling; they want to be able to shape the way that their nations develop, including the values that are contained in the public culture' (Miller 2005: 200). Like Walzer, Miller emphasizes the right to 'give precedence to people whose cultural values are closer to those of the existing population' (2005: 205). Thus, 'a political judgment needs to be made about the scale and type of immigration that will enrich rather than dislocate the existing public culture' (2005: 200; see also 2007: chapter 8).

These sorts of argument are especially evident in Western Europe today where many claim that substantial Islamic minorities are incompatible with, say, Dutch social democracy or British liberalism (rather than, say, Christianity or 'whiteness'). A similar claim is often made in relation to the social welfare policies of Western states. In particular, it is claimed that these policies rely on a degree of cultural cohesion that unlimited migration would undermine (for a good refutation of this argument, see Kymlicka 2001; Carens 2000). At this point, debate about immigration feeds into debates about multiculturalism and membership.

John Rawls's (1999) account in *The Law of Peoples* also supports, or at least implies, that states have a near absolute right of discretion when it comes to migration. At the core of Rawls's theory is a description of 'peoples' as self-sufficient, composing 'a complete and closed social system . . . entry into it is only by birth and exit from it is only by death' (Rawls 1999: 41). According to Rawls, then, the ideal decent political society provides for all the needs of its people; therefore, in ideal theory, there is no need or desire for large-scale or continuing migration (1999: 74). (He does, however, acknowledge that decent peoples and liberal peoples must allow for a limited right of emigration in relation to religious minorities.) In fact, Rawls views migration under ideal theory, as a *problem* that has been solved because people no longer need to move between political communities. The obvious limitation here is that he misunderstands the nature of mobility. Humans are restless and freedom of movement is a basic right for this reason, i.e., because people should be free to choose their destinies (see Jordan and Duvall 2003).

Rawls's account of migration is even more stark than the views of either Walzer or Miller because it implies the ultimate illegitimacy of migration. Even the non-ideal theoretical duty of mutual aid, or assistance to burdened societies, does not necessarily cover any right of movement. According to Rawls, the duty of assistance only covers a duty to help burdened societies become decent, presumably, in part, in order to prevent population movements, rather than any duty to any individuals to help them escape hardship or to achieve their own well-being.

It is worth closing this survey by referring to the realist position on immigration. Immigration as such normally falls outside the normal range of concern for realists as it does not directly relate to security issues. For realists, the only criteria to be used in assessing and deciding migration policy is that of national interest. This does not lead to a principled position in favour of or against more or less migration. Migration may serve the national interest, such as in nineteenth-century America, or not (during the great Depression). What realism shares with other anti-cosmopolitans is that it views the political community and not humankind as forming the relevant moral community (see Hendrickson 1992). Realism therefore would not renounce the state's right to make these decisions in favour of a cosmopolitan good.

Despite their emphasis on communal discretion, anti-cosmopolitans also attempt to indicate that communities have some obligations to outsiders that limit their right to determine their own entrance policy. Such rights, Miller argues, ought to be balanced by the interest of people wishing to migrate, but interests of the migrants do not confer a right of migration. In a remarkably similar vein to cosmopolitan democrats, he argues that hopeful migrants are owed a reasonable explanation for their exclusion and that racial, religious or gender grounds to discriminate against outsiders 'cannot be defended in any circumstances' (Miller 2005: 204).

The basic assumptions of anti-cosmopolitanism work against this type of argument and provide no real reasons for why the state cannot offend people by using race, religion, ethnicity and sexuality as grounds for exclusion. For Miller to argue as he does requires advocating a universal theory of human rights that states must respect in their migration policies (Miller 2007). However, to do so is to seriously qualify states' rights with cosmopolitan clauses, even if it does not grant a right of migration.

In a curious turn, Walzer has also sought to limit states' right of exclusion by claiming that the White Australia policy was unacceptable, not because of its inherent racism or denial of human rights, but because it preserved an unequal share of the Earth's surface for a small minority of people. Australia is a large country, sparsely populated, and cannot justify this under-population to the rest of the world. Walzer's appeal to the criteria of access to a fair share of the Earth's surface seems to invoke a Kantian defence of hospitality. However, Walzer's argument is contradictory. Why should one impartial criteria such as the fair share of land be acceptable, while another impartial criteria such as racial equality is not? Like Miller's, Walzer's account gives us neither criteria by which we can accept his conclusion nor any reason by which we can condemn the racial component of the white Australia policy.

According to Gibney, three questions can be asked of those who claim partiliaty for compatriots (partialism, anti-cosmopolitanism). The first is:

> What gives any particular state the right to exclusive use of the territory it occupies? This reveals partialism's unspoken and unjustifiable assumption of the legitimacy of the current territorial holdings of states. The second question is: What is shared by citizens that distinguishes them from outsiders? This illustrates the elision of the claims of states and those of nations that plague the partialist account of the state as a human community. The third question is: Are states responsible for the harm they cause? This makes clear the failure of partialists to deal with the full implications of states as agents and as actors in a globalized world. (Gibney 2004: 36)

The implication of the partialist argument is that whoever has control of the state is the legitimate decider of culture and community. Where the incorporation of large numbers of outsiders might actually lead to a significant change to host country identity, it might well be argued that their incorporation poses a harm and they ought to be excluded.

Gibney's argument is that many if not most states, including liberal democratic states, have a questionable claim to legitimacy. Australia, the US and Canada all claim a legitimate right to determine the entry to their territory, yet in all these cases that territory was acquired by questionable means, including war, genocide and forced assimilation. While this is not to claim that the current states have no legitimacy, it simply reminds us that the legitimacy of territorial occupation cannot be taken for granted, nor should it be.

Gibney's second point is that for many political communities their supposed cultural identity is actually shared with many other states. Very few if any cultural norms are shared between all countries. But many are shared across the world. The same countries might share a common language and common heritage, derived from a colonial past, similar political institutions and common festivals. For example, Australians, Americans and Canadians share Christmas and the English language (but not Thanksgiving or Anzac Day). Likewise, Malaysia, Singapore and many parts of Asia have significant Chinese populations who share territory with the native population. This means that these cultures are not necessarily separated from each other – indeed they share many common aspects from a common heritage. Not only does this suggest that these communities are not homogenous but also that they are not entirely distinct from each other.

A further point undermining the exclusivist rights of political communities is that the anti-cosmopolitan picture is one of an unchanging culture, or a culture that should be defended against any external change. In this context, the job of the state is to protect the members from outside change. While some forms of outside change are clearly worse than others (empire, colonization), not all outside influences are equally bad or harmful. The point is that cultures change, and they change because of both internal and external interactions. This weakens the claim that it is the state's job to protect culture.

In summary, immigration illustrates the anti-cosmopolitan prioritization of the needs of insiders over outsiders whose rights can be overridden by communal rights. As summarized by Michael Blake in anti-cosmopolitanism arguments:

> [t]he decisions about immigration are to be made with reference to the impact of such immigration upon the lives and projects of those already within the cultural group. If immigration would undermine cultural integrity and continuity, then such immigration may legitimately be precluded . . . outsiders . . . do not have an equivalent standing to challenge the actions and decision of the state in question. (2003: 23)

This is a fundamental difference from the cosmopolitan position that argues insiders' interests and outsiders' interests must both be weighed and taken into account from an impartial position.

The only other qualifying factor acknowledged by anti-cosmopolitans is the case of refugees and asylum seekers where there is a real likelihood of loss of life. Even these cases are qualified by the 'communitarian' criteria outlined here. If states have some discretion over 'who enters' and 'under what circumstance', does this mean they can be free to turn away those seeking refuge and asylum? Or do the claims of refugees and asylum seekers trump the exclusive claims of communities, even democratic ones? This is the topic of the next section.

Refugees and asylum seekers: the right to have rights

The omission of the question of membership and entry from international ethics and political theory speaks directly to both the situation of refugees and asylum seekers. Writing in the aftermath of the Second World War, Hannah Arendt (1951/1967) was one of the first to think seriously about the ethical problems associated with refugees. For Arendt, refugees are caught between states and are therefore technically no one's responsibility. She argued that refugees were arguably amongst the worst off in the world because they no longer had a state to protect or recognize their rights. In her memorable phrase, they had lost the 'right to have rights' when they left their home states. Arendt, of course, was not endorsing this situation; rather, she was pointing to the moral challenge to recognize the humanity of people who were no longer citizens anywhere (Arendt 1951/1967). She was articulating an idea of the need to recognize cosmopolitan duties to people who were without protection.

In recent years, the Italian philosopher Giorgio Agamben and the French philosopher Jacques Derrida (Derrida 2001) have both reflected upon the plight of the refugee. For Agamben, and those who interpret him (see Edkins 2003), the situation of the modern refugee who may have to spend years in refugee camps where there may be only minimal security is also a situation where they are not capable of making a future for themselves. They are reduced to the status of 'bare life', understood as merely physical sustenance. As refugees they are situated in a limbo where they have no agency and no capacity to determine their own future.

Arendt recognized that refugees present special claims that might override any justifications that states have to exclude other migrants because refugees have a claim based on need, rather than simply interest or desire. Thus, moral issues surrounding refugee claims don't extend from the claim to a right of free movement, but rather from a claim to end suffering. They invoke positive duties to aid (stop suffering) rather than negative duties (preventing movement). As we saw for Kant, there was a cosmopolitan duty to allow entry to those who may be harmed, hurt or killed by their exclusion. The types of harms refugees may suffer are multiform; they include loss of life, torture, physical suffering and religious persecution. For Arendt, they also suffered the harm of being 'stateless' which included the loss of their capacity to be members in a civil society, or *polis* – that is, their capacity for freedom and self-determination. Ultimately, refugees raise the claim that the moral duty to relieve suffering outweighs the claims of communal rights of self-determination.

Currently, the right of refuge is enshrined in international law in the international refugee convention (UNCRSR 1951) which stipulates that states have obligations to accept the claims of those (he or she) who:

> owing to well-founded fear of being persecuted for reasons of race, religion, nationality, membership of a particular social group or political opinion, is outside the country of his nationality and is unable, or owing to such fear, is unwilling to avail himself of the protection of that country; or who, not having a nationality and being outside the country of his former

habitual residence as a result of such events, is unable or, owing to such fear, is unwilling to return to it.

This means that states must offer hospitality to refugees or those fleeing persecutions and cannot return them to the state of origin. It is worth noting that the Convention does not include those fleeing war. However, many refugees from war can claim a risk of persecution if, for instance, one side wins. States are obliged by the principle of *non-refoulement* to provide asylum at least until it is safe for the refugees to return to their country of origin. This means refugees cannot be deported or returned home if they are likely to face persecution and so forth upon their return. States are not obliged to offer permanent residency or resettlement, but must allow refugees the opportunity to work and move freely within their borders until such time as their permanent status has been decided. In Kantian terms, they are to be treated as friends not enemies, but they are also to be distinguished from migrants and permanent residents or citizens.

Refugees and asylum seekers are often considered identical but there is an important distinction between them. Refugees often make claims upon more than one state, that is, they may arrive in one state but seek relocation or resettlement in a third state.[4] Asylum seekers prompt a different response. Their claims are more immediate because they claim asylum not from a third-party state, but directly by arriving at the borders of the state. They are on the doorstep, so to speak. In these cases, the claim is made directly to the receiving state for help, thus 'what gives asylum seekers a vital moral claim, however is the fact that their arrival involves the state directly and immediately in their fate' (Carens 2003: 101). This immediate claim is hard to refuse by any ethical standard. There is a direct claim to alleviate suffering 'if asylum seekers are denied entry and sent back, the state is directly involved in what happens to them, . . . (therefore) the moral responsibility for what happens to them is greater' (Carens 2003: 101). It is implied that by refusing such a claim states are denying the rights of others and contributing to the infliction of harm.

In practice, however, asylum seekers are often treated worse than other immigrants and forced into camps, or granted only limited and temporary rights in their new communities. This practice is becoming increasingly widespread as many states adopt tougher practices that implicitly reject any right of asylum (see Hayter 2000), For instance, between 2001 and 2008, the Australian government practised a policy of deterrence towards asylum seekers who sought to enter Australia by sea. This has involved a complicated arrangement called the 'pacific solution' in which asylum seekers are housed and their claims processed in third-party states after they have reached Australia's shores or territorial waters.[5] Arguably, the Australian government's response to asylum seekers, informed by the idea the 'we control who comes here', is in fact a rejection of any right of asylum because it implies that nobody has the right to turn up unannounced at the door. In Australia, the Howard government encouraged a view that asylum seekers are queue jumpers or people pushing their way to the front of the line, using unfair means to cheat the system. Why should people with the capacity to charter a boat and travel from Afghanistan to Australia not simply wait their turn? Though, of course, the Australian government does admit asylum seekers, it is often only after incarceration for up to several years and it has gone to extraordinary lengths to deter the relatively few asylum seekers who do arrive in this country (for detailed discussion, see Gelber and McDonald 2006).

While asylum seekers make a more direct claim to specific states, it is by no means clear that their claims outweigh those of refugees in third-party states. Carens has argued that there is a significant moral distinction between the two cases on the grounds that many refugees are relatively safe, i.e., in camps, whereas 'refusal of entry to a refugee seeking asylum leads directly to his or her suffering' (Carens 2003: 102)

While it is true that refugees in camps are making a more indirect claim for resettlement, usually via a third party like the UNHCR, it is actually more likely that their suffering is even greater than many who are counted as asylum seekers because life in a refugee camp is anything but 'safe'. This argument is supported, for instance, by evidence concerning the incidence of rape against women in refugee camps where, in some cases at least, most women are likely to be raped (see Pittaway and Pittaway 2004).

In short, to allow people to languish for years in refugees camps may in many instances involve imposing or being complicit in a continuing harm to both their physical person and their agency. These harmful conditions of refugee camps support the argument that states should be obliged to accept refugees or partake in a scheme to ensure that some state accepts them, so that they may have their rights recognized and not be harmed. But also it reinforces the argument that refugees and asylum seekers have a greater claim than do ordinary immigrants, and that refugees have an at least equal claim to asylum seekers. They therefore should be given priority both in terms of processing and in numbers accepted.

While many states seek to display their humanitarian credentials by accepting refugees, most liberal democratic states still accept more migrants than they do refugees. Duties to refugees and asylum seekers are given lower priority than state interests such as labour to fuel a growing economy. The discussion in the following section evaluates this practice from both cosmopolitan and anti-cosmopolitan perspectives.

Cosmopolitanism and refugees

Kantian hospitality provides the basic starting point for cosmopolitan positions on refugees and asylum seekers. Hospitality towards strangers in need is one of the basic cosmopolitan clauses of the 'pacific federation'. Kantian cosmopolitanism therefore favours an open-door policy with regard to refugees and asylum seekers. These people have lost the recognition of their moral status as ends in themselves, insofar as they are seen as throwing themselves on the mercy of others and insofar as they have lost their own political communities. In order for them to be recognized as ends in themselves, they need at least to have their human rights recognized by belonging to a republican state.

For egalitarian liberals, such as Carens and Goodin, it follows that if there is a right of free movement then, strictly speaking, there would be no refugees or asylum seeking as such. There would be no obstacles to people fleeing persecution and no need for a right of refuge or asylum. However, when they step from the realm of ideal theory to non-ideal theory (see Rawls 1972) – that is, when they recognize the reality of a world of states with boundaries – they argue that it is almost self-evident that refugees and asylum seekers have a greater and more immediate claim than others, based on their need to avoid suffering (see Carens 2003). Thus, Carens argues, if we accept a provisional right of state exclusion then that right is still overwhelmed or modified by the needs of refugees and asylum seekers.

The right to refuge and asylum is a basic human right to be free from persecution and suffering. For cosmopolitans, there is a corresponding duty for states to accept refugees and asylum seekers who appeal to them. Thus, individual rights trump communal rights when that individual faces suffering or punishment if not accepted into a new community. A liberal/egalitarian cosmopolitan perspective emphasizes that the consequences for outsiders and for insiders must be taken into account (and weighed against each other). This means that, in terms of individual refugee admissions, states clearly have a duty to individuals who are going to be significantly worse off, either by remaining in refugee camps or returning to their home country.

In the context of state policy, it means that refugee admission policy should be driven by the needs of the refugee before the needs of the state receiving the refugees.

For utilitarian cosmopolitans, the greatest good of the greatest number calculation suggests that it is only in states where the risk of suffering or persecution is equally high that a corresponding right to restrict entry exists. In this sense, utilitarians would argue that the overall utility would not be helped by fleeing genocide only to find a famine. Utilitarians would calculate that from a global position, overall utility would be achieved by allowing for movement of refugees and that, generally, in the case where it is rich states who are being appealed to, that the utility (welfare) of their residents should not outweigh that of the refugees. On the whole, the utility calculus is in favour of the right of refugees because 'the sacrifices (losses of well-being) made by those who must provide asylum will normally be considerably outweighed by the gains in well-being of those who thus find refuge from repression' (Penz 2000: 49).

However, as Penz (2000: 49) further explains, the obligation to provide asylum is not unlimited and 'the limit is reached when the effort to provide asylum costs more, in terms of human lives, than the lives saved by the provision of asylum'. Given that most of the world's refugees and aslyum seekers are housed by developing countries, then there might well be a case for restricting numbers because the costs to poor countries are high. Thus, the countries neighbouring Iraq, Afghanistan, Sudan or the Democratic Republic of Congo have to absorb millions of refugees while still struggling to feed their own populations. Instead, in most of these cases, the rights of asylum are respected while the ultimate destination of refugees is assessed, one major exception being the Democratic Republic of Congo. In many more affluent countries, as noted, the right of asylum is increasingly restricted even though the numbers are vastly lower.[6] The impact of absorbing refugees therefore actually falls disproportionally upon the poorer countries. However, it is also easy to believe that with equitable dispersal among the world's wealthier countries the impact of 33 million people would be relatively imperceptible (see Carens 2000).

Overall Penz draws the following conclusions from the utilitarian premise:

(1) Asylum is important to the global public interest and is to be instituted in a strong form, not merely as a right not to be returned to the country of origin, but also as a right of entry to other countries in the first place. (2) Refugees – those entitled to asylum – should be defined in much broader terms than those who have been persecuted and should include those

victimized by violence, famine, and disasters. (3) Asylum is to be provided with adequate assistance, but also at least cost. The balance is to be struck globally rather than in relation to local conditions, given the cosmopolitan frame at work. (4) The least-cost approach can mean that asylum is provided largely in neighbouring countries. (5) The least-cost approach may mean no more than temporary asylum in many cases. (6) The least-cost approach also requires that measures to prevent or minimize displacement, including humanitarian or preventive intervention, need to be considered first and that can also minimize the need for asylum . . . (7) *The dangers and deprivations of refugees are so important that their protection comes before practically all other concerns.* (8) Progressive levies to distribute the burden of providing asylum on the basis of international ability to pay are essential. (2000: 51–2; italics added)

In other words, Penz argues that the utilitarian approach would suggest a radical restyling of the current priorities of states and the international community, so that the overall amount of suffering could be reduced globally. I doubt many cosmopolitans would reject this formulation even if they disagree with the means by which it is achieved (utility) because of the emphasis on placing the suffering of refugees first (point no 7). In other words, because it recognizes that refugee suffering is amongst the worst forms of suffering in the current world and that the suffering of few, if any, citizens of the developed countries is comparable.

Matthew Gibney (2004) has argued that the both utilitarian and liberal egalitarian solutions are unrealistic and that the cosmopolitan principle of humanitarianism (mutual aid; see chapter 5) provides the best starting point. Humanitarianism requires that all states and especially liberal democratic states have a duty to accept refugees but not 'up to the edge of a morally undesirable state of affairs' (i.e., marginal utility) implied in utilitarianism (Gibney 2004: 234). In addition, Gibney argues that humanitarianism is capable of incorporating the anti-cosmopolitan concern with swamping. Humanitarianism is, in Kantian terms, an imperfect obligation of hospitality because 'as the cost of assisting outsiders comes increasingly to impinge upon these commitments a state's duty to help outsiders correspondingly decreases' (Gibney 2004: 234). Gibney claims that properly defined humanitarian duties provide a significant requirement to *balance* the absolute needs of refugees with their own ability to absorb them. Humanitarianism requires states to 'accept as many refugees as they can without undermining the civil, political and importantly the social rights associated with the liberal democratic state' (Gibney 2004: 230).

Thus, there is 'a prima facie case for liberal democracies giving refugees at least as high priority in entrance decisions as regular and family migrants' (Gibney 2004: 243). The problem with this formulation is that humanitarianism begins to sounds less like obligation and more like charity because, in another place, Gibney claims that 'states have an obligation to assist refugees (only) when the costs of doing so are low' (2004: 231). There is a significant degree of latitude between accepting as many as possible and accepting only those who impose low costs. If this is the case, then Gibney's humanitarianism skates very close to putting the interests of domestic constituency above the suffering for refugees and represents no major modification to current practices, and it is therefore only a marginally cosmopolitan solution.

For cosmopolitans, the clear ethical choice in refugee and asylum policy is to work through a balance of political and ethical considerations. But, in achieving such a balance, the overall guiding value should not be advancing the interests or the well-being of insiders; rather, it should be that of achieving overall well-being and relief from suffering for refugees. Refugees and asylum seekers should have equal if not first priority over other potential entrants in admissions because they present a special case. Their claims should be given equal weight with insiders.

One conclusion shared by cosmopolitans (and some anti-cosmopolitans) is that an ethically adequate solution to the problems posed by refugees requires an international system for assessing and distributing the responsibility for refugees. In the words of Penz, 'once one acknowledges that state have a duty to accept asylum seekers, the issue of justly distributing the asylum burden between states emerges' (2000: 56). If it is accepted that there is right of refuge and *non-refoulement*, it is not clear whose obligation it is and how that obligation may be dispersed given that no single country could really accept them all. This in turn suggests that refugees are not only a problem for 'us', in relation to 'them', but a problem of what we all owe to each other, that is, of justice. That is, even when any given state has accepted as many as is reasonable, it still has not discharged all its responsibilities; instead, it has continuing cosmopolitan duties to assist in finding global solutions to the needs of refugees.

These types of considerations are in keeping with cosmopolitans' transformative agenda, which requires a longer-term project of 'reshaping the political environment . . . in ways more conducive to the protection of refugees' (Gibney 2004: 257). Cosmopolitan egalitarians, such as Carens and Beitz, seek to establish a global egalitarian distribution regime (see chapter 7). For them, the question of a state's responsibility towards refugees cannot be understood without an

account of global poverty and affluence. Thus, policies for distributing the refugee burden must be conceptualized within the framework
of global distributive justice. Ultimately, this includes the duty to
reform the international order in line with principles of justice in
order to eliminate the factors such as poverty which generate refugee
flows (see Jordan and Duvell 2003). For this reason, refugee problems not only generate obligations in relation to admissions policies,
but include responsibilities, especially for rich states, to end refugee
suffering by aid, or policies targeting refugee-generating states.

Anti-cosmopolitanism, refugees and asylum seekers

The anti-cosmopolitan position is premised on the state's ultimate
right of exclusion and tends to give preference to asylum seekers
over refugees. Thus, anti-cosmopolitans tend to accept a duty of
hospitality or mutual aid in relation to certain outsiders under certain
circumstances, but this duty is heavily qualified by the community's
right of exclusion.

The logic of the anti-cosmopolitan position is best demonstrated
by Michael Walzer. Walzer claims that states do not have a perfect
obligation to refugees to end their suffering. They have at best an
imperfect duty of mutual aid. Walzer argues that states should
only take refugees who have some connection or adherence to the
dominant culture of the receiving states:

> So long as the number of victims is small, the mutual aid principle will gen-
> erate similar practical results (to justice), and when the number increases,
> and we are forced to choose among the victims, we shall look rightfully,
> for some more direct connections with our own way of life. If on the other
> hand, there is no connection at all, antipathy, rather than affinity, there
> can't be a requirement of any sort to take people in. (1983: 21)

Refugees' claims must be assessed according to suitability to the
host community. States have the right to reject refugees because communities 'depend with regard to a population on sense of relatedness
and mutuality. Refugees must appeal to that sense. One wishes them
success, but in particular cases, with references to a particular state
they may well have no right to be successful' (Walzer 1981: 21).
According to this logic, Christian states could rightfully discriminate
against Muslims on religious grounds, and vice versa, regardless of
the needs of those people. Of course, Walzer is not saying that states

can't take in refugees on any other grounds, rather that they are not *obliged* to take in refugees.

Human rights claims, or merely the duty of avoidance of suffering, do not matter in this context. While it might be cruel and indifferent not to help those in dire need, it would not be ethically 'wrong' in any basic sense. Thus, good samaritanism or mutual aid is ultimately trumped by communal autonomy. Communal autonomy overrides individuals' rights to avoid suffering. In a sense, Walzer's argument equates refugees with migrants because he does not acknowledge that by refusing entry to refugees a state may be exposing them to harm or depriving them of life. He implicitly accepts Carens's observation that refugees are 'safe'.

For Walzer, the only case that might override communal priority is the asylum seeker. The asylum seeker arrives on the shore of another country and has a claim of immediacy that is not mediated by third parties, such as UN agencies or other countries. The asylum seeker has a right to entry that might override the community that extends from a sort of communal right, i.e., the right to make a life, or the right to belong to a community. The asylum seeker has nowhere else to go, no other state that will take him or her, no capacity to make a life anywhere, and no community to be a member of. In the words of Walzer, 'Though he is a stranger and newly come, the rule against his expulsion applies to him as if he had already made a life where he is; for there is no other place where he can make a life' (1981: 22). What Walzer is claiming is that everyone has a right to be a member of a community and to make a life for himself or herself.

Walzer claims that asylum seekers, those refugees who are not situated in other states but who have arrived 'on our shores' or 'at our door', with a claim to be let in, are a special case. For them, it seems the situation of their need is so great that to turn them away is to deny them the opportunity to live or to make a life for themselves because they have nowhere else to go. Asylum seekers have no state, therefore we ought to provide them with a state and the opportunity to make a life. In this way, Walzer's view echoes Arendt's point about the right to have rights, only Walzer gives priority to asylum seekers over refugees. But, in so doing, he is claiming that in this instance communal autonomy comes second to an individual right to rights, or to a home, to belong somewhere.

In addition to this basic quasi-universal claim, liberal states also have special duties. Liberal states should, according to Walzer (1981: 23), grant asylum 'for two reasons: because its denial would require us to use force against helpless and desperate people, and because the numbers likely to be involved except in unusual cases, are small and the people easily absorbed'. However, even this is a pragmatic acknowledgement and is conditioned by the swamping concern because 'if we offered refuge to everybody in the world who could plausibly say that he needed it, we might be overwhelmed' (Walzer 1981: 23).

It is doubtful that Walzer's distinction between asylum seekers and refugees generates the special claims of asylum seekers that he defends.[7] As noted above, the lives of refugees in many parts of the world are more desperate in the majority of cases than those of asylum seekers. Nor, on the other hand, is it clear why, according to Walzer's logic, asylum seekers' potential incompatibility to the community should be overridden by the immediacy of their claim or their physical proximity when, in the case of refugees whose need may be just as great, it is not.

David Miller would seem to concur with Walzer that the immediacy of the asylum seeker's claim is what makes it a specific responsibility of the receiving state. However, he accepts that the refugees are owed the same standing as asylum seekers. Miller nonetheless goes further than Walzer because he is willing to apply the criterion of need, and not just communal compatibility to refugees. According to Miller:

> states have an obligation to admit refugees, indeed refugees defined more broadly than is often the case to include people who are being deprived of rights to subsistence, basic healthcare . . . [because] refugees are owed more than the immediate protection of their basic rights – they are owed something like the chance to make a proper life for themselves. (2005: 203)

However, for Miller, this recognition generates no corresponding obligation on any *particular* state, instead 'the responsibility for ensuring this is diffused among states in such a way that we cannot say that any particular state has an obligation to admit refugees. Each state is at some point entitled to say that it has done enough to cope with the refugee crisis' (2005: 204; see also Meilaender 2001). Miller claims that, in the absence of a universal system of allocation, then 'there can be no guarantee that every bona fide refugee will find a state willing to take him or her in' (2005: 204). In sum, both Miller and Walzer reiterate the anti-cosmopolitan argument that places the needs of the national community ahead of the rights of the foreign individual and this can, for Walzer at least, qualify even the limited cosmopolitan responsibilities of mutual aid.

But Walzer, Miller and others accept that the anti-cosmopolitan position is consistent with obligations to refugees extending from the natural duty to do no harm. Thus, according to Walzer, the US and Australia in the years after the fall of Saigon had a special responsibility to accept refugees from Vietnam. Having played a major role in the social upheaval that was the Vietnam War, the US and Australia can be said to have a causal responsibility generating a positive duty to accept refugees from Vietnam (Walzer 1981). Likewise, today, they and other members of the 'coalition of the willing' have a special responsibility to accept Iraqi and Afghan refugees fleeing the wars in those countries de-stabilized by their interventions. Thus, Walzer indicates that anti-cosmopolitanism acknowledges that a responsibility for the harm caused by one community to another leads to ethical duties to outsiders.

Ethics of membership

The final ethical problem confronting states in response to the movement of people (and especially in the case of refugees and asylum seekers) is whether or not, once permitted entry, they should be granted full membership or citizenship. Most states make a distinction between citizens and mere residents. In many countries, this is expressed in a variety of ways, such as short-term work visas for temporary residents, longer-term work visas for 'guest workers', temporary protection visas (TPV) for refugees, or rights of permanent residency. In many cases, the new migrants are not allowed voting rights but are still taxed. In some cases, their movement may be restricted, and sometimes their children are also denied permanent residency or citizenship even if born in that country. All of these types of measures place the new immigrant or arrival in a different category from the citizen.

In addition, many states place refugees and asylum seekers in camps or detention centres while their asylum claims are processed. These practices place asylum seekers in limbo indefinitely, and can legitimately be seen to be inhumane or unethical because while in asylum they are unable to continue to live as full human beings. In Walzer's terms, they are denied the right to 'make a life' or, in Arendt's terms, 'the right to have rights'. In some states, such as Australia, temporary protection visas were given to asylum seekers on the grounds that the conditions in their home country may change and then they can return. However, this may take many years. This policy comes close to denial of the right of *non-refoulement* (the right to not be returned to one's point of origin if the cause of departure has not changed), as it is up to the receiving state to determine when conditions are safe. For instance, the Australian government has repatriated asylum seekers when they are still likely to suffer persecution on ethnic grounds, or torture, and indeed there is evidence that at least nine deportees have died since their return (ARRA 2007).

Anti-cosmopolitans and cosmopolitans share common ground in rejecting these practices. It is clear that an individual's freedom is inconsistent with prolonged detention and exclusion from the political community. Therefore, in general, the logic of cosmopolitan thought, with its emphasis on rights, freedom and autonomy, is in favour of associating residence with membership. In other words, once you are in you are presumed to be entitled to full participatory membership.

While bordering on the inhumane, current practices of states in this regard do not depart too much from the obligations Kant thought accompanied the cosmopolitan right of hospitality. Individuals can be refused entry if it is not going to lead to their deaths but they cannot be excluded if it is likely to lead to their destruction. The costs of these practices in the contemporary world help us to see the limitations of Kant's interpretation of the duty of hospitality identified by Benhabib (above). Hospitality, as Kant understood it, is not enough to ensure an individual's treatment as an end in itself; membership is also required. Benhabib argues that hospitality is not, as Kant argued, a 'sovereign' prerogative but a basic human right: 'Permanent alienage is not only incompatible with a liberal democratic understanding of human community it is also a violation of the fundamental human rights' (2004: 3). Hospitality includes not only a right of transit, but a right of permanent residency and citizenship. For Benhabib, this is achieved by extending the discourse ethics interpretation of the categorical imperative (see chapter 1) because 'I cannot justify to you with good grounds why you should remain a permanent stranger upon the land. This would amount to a denial of your communicative freedom' (2004: 140). Once people have been allowed into a political community they ought to be, or have the option of being made, full members or citizens of the community so that they can participate in political life:

In the meantime, the practical outcome of democratic cosmopolitan standpoint in relation to questions of entry and membership requires:

> Recognizing the moral claims of refugees and asylees to first admittance, a regime of porous borders for immigrants, an injunction against denationalization and the loss of citizenship rights, and the vindication of the right of every human "to have rights" that is to be a legal person entitled to certain inalienable rights, regardless of the status of their political membership. (2004: 3)

Incorporating this recognition, Benhabib argues, provides the most important cosmopolitan corrective to state policies regarding entry and membership.

The logic of anti-cosmopolitanism on this issue is mixed because, on the one hand, it follows that communities should decide for themselves what criteria should be used for membership, i.e., citizenship rights. It could mean that residents have to pass citizenship tests that indicate a commitment to and familiarity with their new country. There is also no intrinsic reason why communities should not keep immigrants in a state of second-class citizenship, if that is what their traditional values suggest. Despite this logic, few anti-cosmopolitans take this line and instead they emphasize that because membership in some community is a universal need then no one should be denied that need. Thus, for Walzer, if you are to be allowed in then there is no reason not to be granted full membership rights, as long as it is clear you intend to stay and partake of the community. Full citizenship should be granted so the person can make a life. Walzer argues that within liberal democracies this is especially the case because in the basic premises of liberal democratic thought if individuals live, work, buy property, pay taxes and participate in the life of the community, then they ought to be able to partake in the political process that determines and influences that life. Miller agrees that 'what is unacceptable is the emergence of a permanent class of non-citizens, whether these are guest workers, illegal immigrants or asylum seekers waiting to have their applications adjudicated' (2005: 205). In this sense, individuals cannot remain mere subjects but must become citizens.

In sum, cosmopolitan and anti-cosmopolitan authors agree that once entry is granted it is not justifiable for states to continue to enforce moral distinctions between insiders and outsiders (though it is unclear whether such a position is actually consistent with the premises of anti-cosmopolitanism understood as communitarianism). What this conclusion points to, in fact, is a recognition of the universalism, and indeed liberalism, contained within many anti-cosmopolitan positions.

Conclusions

The debate between those who advocate open borders and those who defend states' rights threatens to repeat the mistake of pitting the principles of local self-determination, and communal autonomy and cultural difference, against cosmopolitanism. Instead, what the discussion in this chapter has shown is that group self-determination should be understood as necessarily couched in and mediated through a cosmopolitan framework and balanced by the needs of individuals. There are good reasons for thinking that neither the 'open borders' policy nor the states' rights policy are entirely adequate or realistic options. As Mathew Gibney (2004: 230) argues, 'While accepting the full logic of impartialism might lead to policies which would undermine the conditions necessary for communal self determination and the provision of public goods, adhering to partialism risks sacralizing entrance policies that attach little weight to the claims of refugees.' Open borders accounts of migration pay too little attention to the meaning of community and the value of self-determination. The claim that national communities are equivalent to distinctions of races is somewhat misleading. States and other political communities are not simply a given, except by nationalist ideologues, but rather are 'shaped' by their members and so embody, or attempt to embody, certain values and norms. While there is no reason for always believing the claims of communities about how they do this, there is also no doubting the value that most people see in communal self-determination.

In this context domination by 'outsiders' is a legitimate fear for many, especially post-colonial communities. On the other hand, the implications of an unqualified right of self-determination of entry and membership is that the right to maintain an identity is used to justify the exclusion of those in dire need or at risk of 'destruction'. The advantage of the cosmopolitan argument is that it denies states the right to use cultural preservation as a trump card over the well-being and sometimes the right to life of other human beings. As we have seen, the anti-cosmopolitan position gives insufficient weight to the suffering of outsiders and the harm done to them by continued exclusion.

The arguments presented above are best (but not perfectly) reconciled from a Kantian perspective. The argument for open borders, based as it is on a fundamentalist rights account, while universalist, is not Kantian. The main problem is that it emphasizes freedom as an individual and absolute right and not as a contextual capacity. If we recall, the test of the CI was whether a principle could be universalized, not whether it was inherently owed to all. The CI emphasizes the compatibility of any individual's right of freedom with all others' capacity to exercise freedom. Thus, any freedom of movement would always be limited by the freedom of others. There are no absolute freedoms in this sense. It is quite conceivable that the CI does not justify freedom of movement as an absolute, or perfect, duty; rather that it is an imperfect duty, or a secondary right, as suggested by Miller. Therefore, an individual's absolute right of freedom would be curtailed by the rights of others, including the rights of political self-determination. In other words, because autonomy is exercised in relation to others, one's freedom is always limited by what is acceptable to others. Therefore, any right to freedom of movement is going to be conditioned by its impact upon the conditions of others' freedoms. Democratic citizenship is one condition for individual freedom. Therefore it becomes possible to restrict membership or entry according to whether it will undermine democratic freedom, i.e., the condition of individual freedom. That is, there is good reason to think that the universal freedom of movement for all would undermine the conditions of freedom itself. In this sense, universal free movement is not universalizable. Hence hospitality is an imperfect duty.

This does not mean that states are always justified in excluding outsiders, or that there are no rights of free movement. Any individual's right of free movement can be legitimately compared with the individual's rights to participate in a community of self-legislating agents. States have a duty to maintain the conditions of their democratic practices and their own democratic identities. States which are not democratic but are merely national, republican or otherwise, have less rights of exclusion, that is, if they do not enable their citizens to treat each other as ends, they cannot exclude outsiders on the grounds of preserving autonomy. Nationalism and communal identities are relevant only insofar as they provide the conditions for individual agency. When they function to deny individual rights and cause suffering, then they are unjustifiable exclusions. Ultimately, the question of entry and membership comes down to whether identity matters over survival. If exclusion results in people's significant persecution or a more serious harm, such as exposure to genocide or death, the principle of hospitality or individual rights should override the principle of identity or group rights.

The second conclusion to be drawn from this position is that those escaping persecution and unfreedom have the greatest right of entry, because they are unable to exercise their autonomy. Kant's argument for an imperfect duty of mutual aid was justified on the grounds that suffering prevented effective agency. Therefore, there was a duty to aid others to achieve the conditions of agency. Thus, the weight of argument is in favour of first priority to asylum seekers and refugees over 'economic migrants' because in principle their agency, i.e., their status as ends in themselves, is at stake.

The other way of framing the same argument is to say that to deny asylum seekers and refugees the right of entry is to clearly harm them or to contribute to a continuing harm. However, it is not clear that denial of entry is *in itself* a harm in the same sense as others such as poverty, torture and statelessness. Because suffering or unjustifiable harms are the worst things we can do, and because they present the bedrock of human agency – i.e., when suffering is so great that humans cannot exercise agency – then relieving suffering is the first priority of cosmopolitanism. The next chapter examines this aspect of cosmopolitan thought in the context of the practice of humanitarianism, or mutual aid.

5

Humanitarianism and Mutual Aid

Kindness, . . . need(s) to be supplemented by the clarity about what the moral point of helpfulness is that can be derived from attention to the duty of mutual aid. Our goodheartedness is to be tempered by the moral need for self-development and struggle in others. So we should not meddle and we should be wary of impulses to paternalism not because they may bring more harm than good (as they may) but because they go against the grain of the respectful help we are morally required to give.

Barbara Herman 1984: 601

Introduction

This chapter discusses the ethical issues associated with the principle and practice of humanitarianism, as well as the philosophical and moral background to the concept. Humanitarianism is one of the first and most successful cosmopolitan principles to be applied and institutionalized in the international order. Discussing these here includes examining the nature and meaning of humanitarianism, its connection to cosmopolitanism, the ethical dilemmas faced by contemporary humanitarian actors and the limits of humanitarianism as an approach to international ethics. Also discussed are the relationship between humanitarian theory and practice, the idea of rights and the emerging doctrine of the humanitarian imperative, and claims that some of the dilemmas faced by aid agencies and other actors stem from its conceptualization as a principle of both charity and justice.

In contemporary parlance, humanitarianism has come to have several different meanings. It refers to everything from the provision of emergency relief for the effects of natural disasters and wars, through long-term development aid to military assistance and armed intervention. Insofar as humanitarianism has a presence in the international realm, Ramsbottom and Woodhouse argue that it has three manifestations:

(i) the international humanitarian law of armed conflict,
(ii) the cluster of enterprises referred to as 'international humanitarian assistance', and
(iii) what some call 'international human rights law'. (1996: 10)

This chapter focuses on international humanitarian assistance.

In recent times, humanitarianism has come under fire both literally and metaphorically. This is especially so in the case of humanitarian aid in emergency situations where the possibility is real that such aid may contribute to conflict rather than help end suffering. Humanitarianism refers to positive duties to assist or aid rather than negative duties to avoid or cease harming. At its simplest, it means 'The impartial independent and neutral provision of relief to those in immediate danger of harm' (Barnett 2005: 724). Humanitarianism brings the tension between deontological and consequentialist criteria to the foreground. The realities of humanitarian assistance confront practitioners with the classic ethical problem of how to remain true to basic principles while assessing the unintended consequences of actions. For these reasons, the ethics of humanitarianism have become a significant area of controversy in the field of international ethics and in the practice of international relations, with a split emerging between 'classical' and 'new' humanitarianism.

Humanitarianism relies upon a universalist principle that all human beings deserve aid in times of need and that a duty exists to give such aid in order to alleviate or prevent unnecessary suffering. According to former ICRC director Cornelio Sommaruga (1999: 27), 'The universality and independence of humanitarian work, transcends national and political considerations to focus on the human conditions [and] reflects the universality of suffering.' Thus, humanitarianism invokes the cosmopolitan goal of ending suffering, together with the idea that when people suffer from extreme poverty, starvation, illness or other avoidable harms, then their belonging to any particular subset of the human family should not provide an obstacle or encumbrance to their receiving assistance to escape that condition and end their suffering.

At the core of this argument is the cosmopolitan claim that there is

such a thing as a common humanity, that humans share morally significant attributes as a species that are due recognition as such. This means
that no human ought to be excluded from moral consideration when it
comes to the meeting of their needs. In employing the notion of 'humanity' as its moral bedrock, humanitarianism clearly can be designated
as a basic, if not the basic cosmopolitan principle. Humanitarianism
represents a cosmopolitan value because it puts individuals of humanity at the core of moral concern. Humanitarianism has been guided by
an interpretation of the core cosmopolitan principles of impartiality,
individualism and universality, as well as neutrality and consent.

The principles of humanitarianism have also found support in anti-
cosmopolitan traditions in terms of the doctrine of mutual aid, or good
samaritanism, the duty to assist those in need without causing harm to
oneself. As we saw in chapter 3, Walzer, Miller and Rawls all endorse
mutual aid in cases of great need. This suggests that anti-cosmopolitans
in general endorse the practice and philosophy of humanitarianism, at
least in its less ambitious form. Given this agreement between cosmopolitanism and anti-cosmopolitanism, the more significant question,
and point of difference between them, concerns how far the duty of aid
goes. In other words, how much should one be prepared to give, or sacrifice, in order to come to another's aid? However, in keeping with the
moral priority given to fellow nationals, anti-cosmopolitans have little
to say about how humanitarianism, or mutual aid, is delivered. Simply
agreeing that aid is owed to those in need is not the end of the ethical
issue. Once aid is provided, those providing it are faced with a range of
political and ethical challenges that require further deliberation upon
the meaning and purpose of aid and of how it can be delivered.

This chapter discusses the relationship between grounds of humanitarian doctrine and the practice of humanitarian emergency aid. The
first part of this chapter examines some of the most important ethical
problems facing those who seek to apply humanitarian principles in
the field. The second part examines the concept of humanitarianism.
It also examines the expression of this doctrine in the core doctrines
of the International Committee of the Red Cross (ICRC) and other
NGOs, and concludes with some discussions about the place of the
principle of humanitarianism in the field of international ethics.

Humanitarianism and the Core Principles of the ICRC

This section discusses the core principles of the ICRC and the problems associated with them. Much of the debate surrounding 'new

humanitarianism' has focused upon the meaning and possibilities of humanitarian practice as set down in the principles of the ICRC. These principles include *universality, neutrality, impartiality* and *consent*. Most humanitarian agencies and actors are committed to these principles or something similar and use them as a guide to practice. These four basic principles have an important role in guiding the ICRC's actions and operations. Significantly, they provide the key to access to areas of conflict and allow the ICRC to operate in areas that might otherwise be inaccessible, such as war zones.

The first thing to note about these principles is that they directly parallel the core principles of liberal cosmopolitanism as outlined in chapter 2. This is no mere coincidence because humanitarianism is one interpretation of the meaning of cosmopolitanism. The humanitarian duty is to relieve suffering without discrimination and according to need alone because one's standing as a human being, as a member of humanity, is the only relevant criteria other than need. Humanitarianism represents a core cosmopolitan value because it puts individual humanity at the core of moral concern. Humanitarianism relies upon a cosmopolitan principle that all human beings deserve aid in times of need and that a duty exists to give such aid. These criteria delineate the just scope of relief efforts, or, in Kantian terms, beneficence.

Universality

The principle of humanity claims a universal scope, that is, it applies to all humans. All people are to be regarded as human and therefore deserving of aid in times of emergency. One practical conclusion of this principle is that the victims of war on all sides are deserving of relief. It also claims universality in the sense that it has transcultural legitimacy. No claim to cultural difference can override the principles of suffering and most cultures claim to recognize some form of principle of humanity that includes a commitment to alleviate unnecessary suffering. In support of this claim, the ICRC points to the near-universal commitment by all states to the Geneva Conventions which embody this principle. This commitment means that at least in principle all states acknowledge that, in regard to an entitlement to relief from suffering during times of war, all humans are equal and that an international agency, the ICRC, has legitimate authority to dispense humanitarian relief. In recent times, many states and some NGOs have not demonstrated this commitment in practice, refusing or neglecting, for instance, to give aid to the Serbian victims of the NATO bombing campaign in 1999 (see Fox 2001).

Neutrality

Neutrality, for the ICRC, means that their activities are non-political, that is they do not take sides or speak out in relation to the merits or otherwise of conflict, or the activities of parties. Neutrality means that humanitarian actors are not involved in either realpolitik or party political activity. In other words, they are not a party to the conflict. This idea of neutrality is better expressed as non-partisan, rather than non-political, because it refers to the idea of not taking sides. It is hard to overestimate the importance of neutrality to human relief assistance agencies. In order to get access to volatile environments, aid agencies need to be seen to be non-participants in the conflict. This allows the combatants to be reassured that they are not giving comfort or aid to their enemies by allowing the humanitarians into the scene of conflict. In this sense neutrality is akin to disinterest in the outcomes and causes of the conflict.

Neutrality has been brought into question in the context of humanitarianism on at least two fronts. The first is the charge that neutrality can mean indifference or inaction in the face of political causes of violence and conflict. Neutrality has required the ICRC to be silent about the causes of suffering in order to attend to some of the victims. For the critics, neutrality has come to mean to be indifferent, unprincipled and vacillating (Slim 1997: 347). The implication is that humanitarians need to take sides in some way and to recognize the politics of the contexts in which they operate, and to be able to judge them. These criticisms have come from NGOs with expressly human rights or social justice missions. For these groups, neutrality prevents them playing an advocacy role on behalf of the victims. For the critics, neutrality must sometimes be sacrificed in order to 'bear witness' to suffering and to identify perpetrators. At its most extreme, this may mean that an agency has to withdraw from a conflict situation, as MSF has done on occasion, or to risk not being allowed in.

The most obvious case of the detrimental nature of neutrality here is the behaviour of the ICRC during the Nazi Holocaust. In this situation, the principles of neutrality which gave the ICRC access to prisoners of war and displaced peoples required them turning a blind eye to the deliberate state policies targeting Jews and other minorities for genocide and forced slavery (Favez 1999). Because neutrality means not taking sides in political matters, the ICRC took the position that comment on the Holocaust would be a political intervention or criticism of state action.

In order to gain access to victims or those in need, the ICRC relies on the argument that it is non-political and does not take sides. It is neutral in relation to the terms and issues of the conflict. However, when it is the population itself that is being targeted, or when aid flows to an enemy people or it is interpreted as aid to the enemy, then neutrality is harder to maintain. To provide humanitarian aid to a town that might be under siege from enemy forces could be seen to be aiding and prolonging the siege, and thereby the associated suffering. This type of aid could also be viewed as feeding people only to release them later to be slaughtered by the enemy. This is the argument in relation to the so-called UN safe havens in Yugoslavia. The UN was seen to be complicit by neglect in the massacre of the male Muslim population of the town of Srebrenica. Furthermore, especially under these circumstances, allowing access to the ICRC can be manipulated by the perpetrators of violence to show their supposed humanitarian credentials, while still engaging in harmful actions, as Nazi Germany did when it allowed the ICRC to inspect Theresienstadt concentration camp. The ethical decision confronting aid agencies, therefore, is whether they are contributing to the problem by maintaining neutrality or whether they should risk not being able to deliver relief or assistance if they abandon neutrality.

Perhaps the frontrunner in engaging and challenging the ICRC on these issues, as well as its practice of neutrality, has been MSF (Médecins Sans Frontières), which was set up precisely to correct certain aspects of the ICRC practices. While often presented as a complete rejection of the ICRC principles, MSF is better understood as a modification and correction of these examples. MSF rejects the ideal of total neutrality in favour of the doctrine of 'care and bear witness', which can include lobbying, advocacy and speaking out. The key point here is that neutrality must be understood not as indifference or a lack of principle, but as a principle itself with a moral purpose, to ensure delivery of emergency aid based on needs alone.

It is worth noting that humanitarian neutrality is different from the political neutrality of, say, Switzerland. Political neutrality, for Switzerland, allows all sides to use Switzerland for their own purposes, and allows Switzerland to deal with everyone in ways which benefit Switzerland itself. Slim (1997: 347) argues that humanitarian neutrality involves abstention, prevention and impartiality. In other words, neutrality entails no involvement in the political or military conflict, treating all parties on equal terms so that 'neither party is able to use the organization to its advantage'. Neutrality in the humanitarian sense constrains the type of dealings an NGO may have with parties at war.

Maintaining this type of neutrality entailed in humanitarianism is inherently difficult in complex emergencies, and it requires hard choices in terms of deciding how and whether one's aid is helping or hurting one side or another, or reaching the intended recipients. Maintaining neutrality is not a simple technical task which can be decided in advance. But the difficulties of making these decisions do not automatically undermine the principle. It simply means that the principle is, like all moral and ethical rules, decided in the interpretation and action itself, that is, in its application. More recently, the idea of integrated or coherent humanitarianism has effectively jettisoned the principle of neutrality and gone beyond bearing witness to actively taking sides. Neutrality, it is alleged, has stood in the way of more fundamental transformations which require addressing political issues such as human rights and the rule of law and democracy.

Impartiality

The third principle of the ICRC is impartiality: the victims of all sides of conflict are entitled to humanitarianism assistance. Sometimes this is confused with neutrality, but impartiality refers to a practice of non-discrimination between innocents and perpetrators, or between aggressors and defenders. It concerns who will receive the aid. This is the basic principle used to argue for IHL, which seeks to protect all those affected by conflict on all sides, so long as they are no longer in the field of warfare. Once individuals are non-combatants they deserve humanitarian assistance just like everyone else. As Ramsbotham and Woodhouse (1996: 16) put it, impartiality means that the ICRC 'endeavours to relieve the suffering of individuals being guided solely by their need and to give priority to the most urgent cases'. Impartiality means that individuals, regardless of origins, are entitled to equal treatment of having their needs met, in terms of their welfare and the alleviation of suffering. Hugo Slim points out that many who reject neutrality favour the idea of impartiality. MSF, for instance, has emphasized impartiality because it allows them to be judgemental. In other words, 'public criticism will be made against people or groups on the basis of what they do, but not on the basis of who they are'

(Slim 1997: 349). This sense of impartiality sits more easily with the liberal cosmopolitan sense of a position that is capable of judging and assessing from outside.

Impartiality, however, has come under criticism as well. Most clearly impartiality has been seen to be problematic in the case of the refugee camps set up to cater for those fleeing the Rwandan genocide of 1994. In this context, impartiality meant that, in many cases, UN and other relief agencies provided aid to the perpetrators of the genocide and allowed them to continue their practices inside the refugee camps themselves (see Fox 2001). This was because the refugees consisted of both Tutsi and those Hutus fleeing the advancing Tutsi army which was seeking to stop the holocaust. The practice of impartiality meant that anyone who was a refugee was accepted into the camps and because of the overwhelming numbers it was impossible to discriminate between Hutus and Tutsis, yet alone between victims and perpetrators. The Rwandan episode provoked a crisis of conscience for many humanitarians and resulted in a joint new code of conduct for the International Red Cross and Red Crescent Movement, and NGOs in Disaster Relief Programmes.

In other not dissimilar circumstances, MSF has been willing to withdraw from situations where there is no 'humanitarian space', where it is not actually possible to deliver aid without political interference. Humanitarian space 'entails the ability to independently assess the needs of the population; retain unhindered access to the population conduct, monitor, and evaluate the distribution of aid commodities; and obtain security guarantees for local and expatriate aid personnel' (Tanguy and Terry 1999: 33). For MSF, there was no such humanitarian space in the refugee camps along the Thai–Cambodian border where they were required to cooperate with the Khmer Rouge. MSF made the difficult decision to withdraw from these camps. Since then, MSF has also withdrawn from Iraq and Afghanistan, citing lack of security for their workers.

The Rwanda example raises the question of whether it is permissible to deliver aid to perpetrators of violence who are now refugees. Martone (2002) is clear that the Geneva Conventions provide the basis for the answer, as they stipulate that food is a basic right. But this is a different issue from the consequentialist one of deciding whether aid is actually 'funding' human rights violators. Impartiality means that aid can be given to perpetrators if they are suffering and not engaging in violent acts, but if they continue to perpetrate violence against others there are indeed grounds for withholding aid. Making these decisions requires complex calculations of likely costs and benefits.

Consent

The ideas of neutrality and impartiality are also expressed in the doctrine of consent, as the ICRC's fourth principle. The ICRC must seek the consent of the warring parties in order to deliver relief. Clearly, this is a pragmatic decision designed to make their work and access easier, but it is also a means by which warring parties are held to account because the responsibility is on warring parties to recognize humanitarian principles and international conventions (ICRC). However, the critics also argue that seeking consent may limit access, and therefore it might not be possible for assistance to be provided. Alternatively, it is possible that the price involved in seeking consent, silence, or perhaps agreeing to deals with warlords and so on, may be too high and undermine the original aim by contributing to an ongoing war effort.

While many such as Doctors Without Borders (MSF) have challenged the ICRC as a model of humanitarian practice, they remain largely committed to the same type of enterprise. Most humanitarian NGOs take the core principles of the ICRC as their own but interpret them differently. For example, the Sphere Project and the Humanitarian Charter are attempts by a number of agencies to move beyond disagreement and establish and broaden the meaning of core humanitarian principles in more detailed fashion. They do not represent an attempt to abandon the core goals of humanitarianism as set out by the ICRC, but rather to reinterpret and elaborate on them under new conditions.

However, in the contemporary era, the four principles of neutrality, universality, impartiality and consent provide the focus for a set of debates about the ethics of humanitarianism and the delivery of assistance in practice. It is neutrality which has proven to be most challenged by the context of complex emergencies.

Humanitarianism in theory and practice

Since the end of the Cold War, the number and the scope of calls for humanitarian assistance have expanded dramatically. During the Cold War, as many observers noted, humanitarianism was largely limited to the work of the Red Cross and to contexts of natural disasters. Since at least the 1990s, however, the number of occasions in which humanitarian assistance and relief has been required or called for, and the number of agencies involved in such work, have grown.

Most significantly, this has revealed a far greater complexity of issues in applying humanitarian principles than previously acknowledged. Instead of simply attending to battlefield situations or displaced civilians, the ICRC and other agencies have found themselves attending 'complex emergencies'.

Complex emergencies are either international or intrastate conflict situations, or a combination of both, which might have a variety of parties in conflict, from states, to militias and international agencies such as peacekeeping forces. Such complex emergencies 'are characterised by a combustible mixture of state failure, refugee flight, militias, warrior refugees, and populations at risk from violence, disease and hunger' (Barnett 2005: 726). Somalia in the 1990s, Sudan/Darfur, the Central African Republic and the Democratic Republic of Congo today all exhibit these characteristics.

In such situations the distinction between combatants and non-combatants, central to traditional humanitarian practice, becomes harder to maintain or identify. In addition, it is often civilians, rather than enemy military forces, who are the targets of the conflict. This lack of distinction between combatants and non-combatants is most obvious in cases of ethnic 'cleansing' and genocide, but also in the case of state breakdown such as in Somalia, where the violence occurs between rival militia or warlords. In these cases, control of resources, territory and populations is contested by governments, militias, criminal gangs or warlords. The civilian populations are often identified by the combatants as legitimate targets of violence or extortion.

Hugo Slim has captured the nature of the difficulties of humanitarian practice as trying to 'represent the values of humanity and peace within societies which are currently dominated by the values of inhumanity and violence' (1997: 343). Creating even further problems for humanitarians attempting to supply assistance to civilians is the fact that not only do many actors remain ignorant or disrespectful of IHL, but they also target and manipulate relief agencies and their resources to help further their own war efforts. Aid workers themselves are increasingly likely to be abducted, raped or murdered, as is the case in contemporary Afghanistan.

Under these conditions, the complexities of the situations give rise to the possibility that the materials and food supplied by aid agencies can themselves provide unintentional material support for the conflict. Thus, many humanitarians find themselves asking whether they are in fact contributing to solving the problem or making it worse. If, for instance, the food that is being supplied to a population is also being used to support soldiers, either voluntarily or involuntarily, then it becomes a factor in consideration of the conflicting parties.

Humanitarian actors then have to address whether their assistance, while saving the lives of some, may help perpetuate a cycle of violence. Mary Anderson (1999) has argued that aid affects conflict through both resource transfers and through implicit ethical messages. In particular, she identifies five 'predictable' impacts of aid resources upon conflict and seven implicit ethical messages that aid workers have to confront if they wish to 'do no harm' (Anderson 1999: 39).

Resource transfers occur in a number of ways, such as when they are stolen by warriors and used to support armies and buy weapons. In addition aid affects and distorts local markets when it substitutes for local resources, and the distributional impacts of aid affect inter-group relationships when they benefit one group over another. Also, aid can free local resources to support conflict and can legitimize certain people but not others. The implicit ethical messages in aid delivery include endorsing a connection between arms (authority) and power by dealing with or using local militias and so forth. Anderson also argues that inter-agency competitions support the idea it is unnecessary to cooperate with people. More importantly, when aid workers enjoy privileges denied locals, from food to public transport and security, they are seen to act with impunity, thereby valuing aid workers' lives differently (above) from the lives of local staff (Anderson 1999: 59). In short, the delivery of aid in complex emergencies is not only logistically but also ethically complex as aid workers and agencies negotiate the task of helping those at risk of serious harm.

The arrival of complex emergencies in the post-Cold War period has prompted a great deal of debate and soul-searching amongst humanitarian agencies regarding their purposes and their methods. The most important question to have emerged from this process is whether humanitarianism, as classically understood by organizations like the ICRC, is viable or whether the relief of suffering requires aid agencies to engage in more comprehensive societal solutions to conflict. The classic interpretation of the role of humanitarian agencies, as noted above, is to deliver aid to the suffering according to impartial, non-partisan and needs-based criteria. The principle aim is to provide relief to the suffering regardless of cause, based on need, and without taking sides in any conflict. However, complex emergencies have raised the possibility that providing relief leads only to the phenomenon of 'well-fed dead'. By providing only immediate relief, humanitarians ignore the likelihood that later stages of the conflict will threaten the lives of victims, resulting in, as one recipient stated, 'you save my life today, but for what tomorrow?' (Anderson 1998). Such claims led to the emergence of what has been called the 'new' humanitarianism.

New humanitarianism is '"principled", "human rights based", politically sensitive and geared to strengthening those forces that bring peace
and stability to the developing world' (Fox 2001: 275). In this view,
humanitarianism becomes an active participant in capacity-building,
peace-building, conflict resolution and finding long-term solutions to
the causes of suffering. Thus, for instance, agencies like Oxfam incorporate both development and emergency relief into their projects. In
some forms, new humanitarianism goes beyond emergency relief and
begins to look more like development assistance or post-conflict reconstruction and development, 'democracy promotion and even building
responsible states' (Barnett 2005 723). At the core of new humanitarianism is the incorporation of a commitment to human rights as a
fundamental legitimizing value and as a practical goal of aid delivery.
The aid agencies' purpose is not only to relieve suffering but also to
protect the human rights of the victims of complex emergencies.

The claim is that humanitarianism cannot remain, and indeed never
was, 'non-political', but must instead become part of the solution if it
is to avoid being part of the problem. This development should not be
too much of a surprise. It is a logical step from addressing the suffering of individuals in emergency situations to asking how that situation
arose and how it could be prevented in the future. For any committed
humanitarian, it is predictable that they will ask themselves if the aid
they provide is going to provide simply a band-aid solution to more
fundamental problems. According to Michael Barnett, the overall
effect of these reflections has been the politicization and institution-
alization of humanitarianism in general and the emergence of two
different types of humanitarian agencies, the Dunantist, committed
to the classic approach of impartiality, neutrality and independence, such as ICRC and MSF, and the Wilsonian (Save the Children,
Oxfam, World Vision), committed to the transformation of 'political,
economic and cultural structures' (Barnett 2005: 728). This move
has culminated in the shift to what has been called an 'integrated' or
'coherence' approach to emergency aid.

The integrated approach aims to develop and pursue 'comprehensive durable and just resolution of conflict' (de Torrente 2004: 3).
Since 1992, the UN has operated the Office of Humanitarian Affairs
(OCHA 2008) which 'facilitates the work of operational agencies
that deliver humanitarian assistance to populations and communities
in need. (and) . . . has overall responsibility for ensuring coherence
of relief efforts in the field' (OCHA 2008). The OCHA brief is to
coordinate both UN and non-UN agencies and to effect a 'coherent
interagency response to humanitarian emergencies'. Integration arguably reached its apex in the US and NATO invasions of Afghanistan

in 2001 and Iraq in 2003. In both these cases, humanitarian NGOs were integrated into the planning of the military action, in order to anticipate and address the likely humanitarian consequences of the military operation.

However, integration is not without its critics and, rather than solving the problems raised in the 1990s, has generated another set of ethical questions for the humanitarian conscience to address. The core issue concerns the costs and benefits of the politicization 'of Humanitarianism, that is, the subjecting of humanitarian assistance to' the 'international community's political ambition' (de Torrente 2004: 3). What this means is that instead of being autonomous actors oriented to relief, humanitarian agencies have become part of a larger goal that includes political aims. This in turn has required them on occasion to deny relief or make it conditional upon acceptance or compatibility with the political aims of states (see Fox 2001; Stockton 2002). Thus, instead of being aid to the needy, such relief becomes a reward for compliance or an incentive to change behaviour or, worse, denied as a sanction. The problems with the integration approach were dramatically illustrated in both Iraq and especially in Afghanistan, where humanitarian efforts were seen by the military as essentially a 'force multiplier . . . an important part of our combat team' (Colin Powell, in Barnett 2005). This resulted in, amongst other things, associating the distribution of aid with collaboration or informing against the Taliban. One pamphlet dropped along with aid said: 'Pass on any information in relation to Taliban, al Qaeda, and Gulbaddin to the coalition forces in order to have a continuation of the provision of humanitarian aid' (in de Torrente 2004: 6 n.7). For classical humanitarians, this sort of linkage privileges the political goals over the needs of individuals, with the consequences being the loss of lives that could otherwise have been saved. More starkly, the victims of conflict become sacrifices to longer-term goals.

The integration of relief work with human rights discourse has also led to a situation where the actions of humanitarians may involve supporting, or participating in, armed intervention, what one author calls military humanitarianism (Chandler 2001), associated with humanitarian intervention. Arguably, Somalia in 1992, when the US led a UN force to allow the distribution of famine relief, is the first instance of this type of action. The Kosovo intervention by NATO in 1999/2000 was undertaken primarily for humanitarian reasons, though in this case it was to prevent a crime against humanity, but also contributed to a large humanitarian emergency through the displacement of Kosovo Albanians. The underlying argument is that in certain instances a humanitarian imperative requires a military action. In this case, there is moral responsibility to prevent or end human suffering by the use of military force.

This idea that states have humanitarian duties has now taken root in the doctrine of the Responsibility to Protect (ICISS 2001). This doctrine argues that states and the international community have a responsibility to protect vulnerable populations from avoidable suffering in the form of crimes against humanity and genocide. This responsibility includes, but is not limited to, a responsibility to engage in military action. The obvious moral difficulty arises because the use of military force necessarily causes avoidable suffering not only to the 'guilty' but also, highly likely, to the innocent or non-combatant civilians. Thus, the irony of military intervention for humanitarian purposes is that humanitarian NGOs could find themselves tending to the victims of military action for humanitarian purposes, as well as to the victims of violence to which that action was directed. In this sense, military intervention is likely to cause human suffering as well as alleviate it.

Many people, for instance, argue that the NATO intervention in Kosovo caused the humanitarian crisis that followed with the deportation of Kosovo Albanians. If this is the case, then there is a good argument that the military intervention should not have taken place because it created another, arguably greater, humanitarian emergency. But this is only the case if the intervention did indeed cause the deportation of the Kosovo Albanians and if the resulting emergency was significantly worse than what might have happened otherwise.[1] The dilemmas of humanitarian intervention take the dilemmas of humanitarianism to the logical extreme. Is it possible to cause harm, including death, or at least accept harm as an unintended consequence, in order to relieve suffering? The crisis of traditional humanitarianism and the costs of the new humanitarianism have left many looking for a new guiding principle or 'moral banner' (Fox 2001). The remainder of this chapter explores these issues and dilemmas, and suggests that a Kantian reading of the doctrine of mutual aid can help provide not only a moral 'banner' but a more satisfactory moral foundation for the humanitarian project, which helps to overcome some of the limitations of both classical human rights and new humanitarianism.

Defining and justifying humanitarianism

It is actually rather difficult to find a single definition of humanitarianism. The concept is usually equated with an equally poorly defined notion of humanity and/or the activities of humanitarians, or of humanitarian organizations such as the ICRC. For one-time director of the ICRC Jean Pictet (1979), humanitarianism descends from the basic idea of humanity or humankind: 'Humanitarianism is a doctrine which aims at the happiness of the human species, or, if one prefers, it is the attitude of humanity towards mankind, on a basis of universality.' Humanitarianism is also related to the ethical/political project of humanism, 'the belief that the sole moral obligation of humankind is the improvement of human welfare' (qtd in Gall and O Hagan 2003: 4). For early humanitarians, humanism was connected to the belief in human perfectibility. Humanism was the product of Enlightenment rationality and humanitarianism was an expression of the belief that not only could suffering be ameliorated, but it could be eradicated. More specifically, humanitarianism, as a humanistic practice, seeks to address the needs of all humans who are suffering from avoidable failures to have their basic needs met. Humanitarianism at its simplest refers to the most basic of human moral values: the commitment to respond to the suffering of others.

While humanism has undoubtedly played the foremost part in the emergence of a secular humanitarian doctrine in the nineteenth and twentieth centuries, the role of religious and theological justifications for universal sympathy should not be neglected. Christian doctrines of compassion and Quaker sensibility regarding war and suffering were evident in early humanitarian movements such as the anti-slavery movement. Charity and mutual aid also have their equivalents in Islam (hence the Red Crescent Society) and other religions. Thus, like cosmopolitanism in general, humanitarianism has both religious and secular roots. Most importantly, humanitarianism is cosmopolitan in scope and intent while not necessarily liberal in justification, beginning as it does with the universal capacity of suffering.

Of course, the ICRC and similar organizations do not set out to end all human suffering. Their goal is not the total transformation of the human condition. Instead, they take humanitarianism to mean the more limited task of attending to immediate avoidable suffering. In the words of the ICRC, the humanitarian goal is to 'prevent and alleviate human suffering wherever it may be found. Its purpose is to protect life and health and to ensure respect for the human being' (in Ramsbotham and Woodhouse 1996: 16). The classic doctrine of humanitarianism in practice has been one of assistance, usually emergency assistance. For the Red Cross, this means 'protecting human beings in the event of conflict and of relieving their suffering' (Pictet 1979: online). This refers to the attempts to address the needs of those who find themselves in the situations where they are likely to suffer from displacement, dispossession, famine, poverty and so on. Classical humanitarianism aims to provide temporary relief of human suffering while motivated in part by a transformative agenda of ending unnecessary suffering per se. Humanitarianism has largely been devoted to alleviating suffering caused by either natural disasters or warfare. In the words of Ramsbottom and Woodhouse (1996: 12), humanitarianism is 'concerned with the immediate relief or assistance and is concerned with immediate needs of victims of natural or political disasters, not necessarily in war zones and not necessarily connected with explicit violations of human rights'. The basic moral assumption is that no human should suffer needlessly from avoidable causes when there is a capacity for others to assist, ameliorate or end that suffering.

However, the alleviation of suffering can be both an immediate goal of relief or assistance, or it can be a more ambitious commitment to end unnecessary suffering per se. Pictet's definition of humanitarianism reveals the dual and sometimes contradictory characterization of humanitarianism as a principle of both charity (philanthropy) and justice. Pictet claimed:

> Modern humanitarianism is an advanced and rational form of charity and justice. It is not only directed to fighting against the suffering of a given moment and of helping particular individuals, for it also has more positive aims, designed to attain the greatest possible measure of happiness for the greatest number of people. In addition, humanitarianism does not only act to cure but also to prevent suffering, to fight against evils, even over a long term of time. (1979: online)

The dual motivation of charity and duty (justice) identified by Pictet generates a tension within humanitarianism. This tension clearly lies at the heart of the split between the Dunantist and the Wilsonian approaches. The tension is precisely over whether and to what extent the relief of suffering requires not just temporary relief but transformation of the circumstances of suffering.

Charity and justice are both present in the ICRC's aims of tending to the victims of war, reforming the practices of war and of eradicating war altogether. At one level, the idea that the victims of war should be cared for, regardless of their role in the conflict, is, in historical terms, a revolutionary doctrine indicating an expansive sense of morality not often witnessed in human civilization. This transformative ambition of humanitarianism is evident in the evolution of international humanitarian law (IHL), the body of international law that stipulates the rules of warfare and especially the treatment of prisoners and non-combatants, and the restrictions upon states' practice in warfare. According to the ICRC (2007: online), international humanitarian law seeks 'to limit the effects of armed conflict, protects persons who are not or are no longer participating in the hostilities . . . [and] restricts the means and methods of warfare'. In these cases, humanitarianism clearly attempts to transform state practice in order to reduce human suffering and to aid those who have been harmed by a state's violent action.

The debate about the relationship between humanitarianism and human rights expresses the tension between the humanitarian impulses of charity and the idea of justice. The doctrine of human rights represents a more fully fledged transformative political agenda than is encapsulated by the idea of humanitarianism assistance. Because humanitarianism in areas of natural disasters is largely apolitical in origin it is relatively uncontroversial. However, where the duty of humanitarian assistance extends into alleviating the effects of warfare more significant ethical questions arise. In particular, the humanitarian claim is that the ethical duty to provide aid overrides any political allegiances, secular loyalties or military aims. This claim, while stemming from a notion of humanism, is more commonly expressed today in the language of human rights but is also embodied in international humanitarian law.

Humanitarianism as charity

The dilemmas arising in the delivery of humanitarian aid, and the trade-offs that have to be made, point to the tension between relief of suffering to victims (charity) and the achievement of justice and social transformation that the principle embodies. Many of the problems faced by practitioners in the field should be understood as stemming from this foundational ambiguity.

For this reason, addressing these tensions requires some reflection on this relationship and the meaning of these terms. Jean Pictet distinguished charity from mere alms-giving and instead related it to Christian love, which is for Pictet a form of altruism prompted by pity:

> Charity is an effort demanded of us, either inwardly or from the outside, which becomes a second nature, to relieve and put an end to the sufferings of others . . . Charity is above all an expression of Christian morality and is synonymous with love for one's neighbour . . . we are speaking of altruistic and disinterested love, which can be required of us, which calls for a certain

degree of self-control, a love which is extended even to our enemies . . . Pity is one of the driving forces of charity . . . that stirring of the soul which makes one responsive to the distress of others. (Pictet, ICRC online)

Charity as selfless altruism and solidarity with others' suffering provides an important motivating factor for many people. It is clear that much good work has been done by those who, motivated by love, are willing to help others in desperate situations by engaging in acts of charity.

As charity, humanitarianism is understood as primarily an expression of virtue, of what it is good to do and of an individual conscience. It can be seen as philanthropy, which essentially is recognition by the well off that it is a good thing to help those who are worse off. It is clear that charity has informed the evolution of IHL and the ICRC as much as any sense of moral duty. The idea of charity partly explains why the ICRC and other organizations can claim a non-political status. By being depicted as charitable acts, humanitarians can claim that providing assistance to the victims 'does not constitute interference in the conflict itself' (Gall and O'Hagan 2003: 12).

It is also clear that charity is not necessarily socially transformative. Furthermore, for a universalist and cosmopolitan doctrine, the idea of charity has some negative consequences, the most important of which is the implication and acceptance of a certain degree of inequality between giver and recipient. This logic is present and is arguably a source of the implicit ethical messages of impunity and inequality identified by Anderson (1999). When recipients are seen as victims, then it is easier to allocate special privileges to those providing aid. After all, the aid givers are doing good work and helping others when they don't have to, therefore they surely deserve some sort of reward or compensation. In addition, the aid givers understand themselves as possessing legitimate authority over resources and can 'use them for personal purposes and pleasure' (Anderson 1999: 57). It is 'their' aid to give, after all. The message is even stronger in the case of the different policies adopted for expatriate and local staff, which include differential salaries, use of vehicles, radios and so on, and, most seriously, when it comes to evacuation of international staff. In many cases local staff have often been left behind or given lower priority in evacuation than material goods. As Anderson (1999: 58) rightly notes, the 'implicit ethical message is one of inequality'.

Because charity is ultimately seen as a gift of the giver to the receiver, it inevitably raises the possibility of inequality between the two parties. By virtue of being a gift to one who is in need, aid is likely to create a sense of superiority on the part of the giver, who is in the position to give, and inferiority on the part of the recipient because it obligates them to receive it. The recipient is obligated to the giver who has power over them, including the power to withdraw aid if they are not sufficiently grateful. Charity raises the question of why the gift was necessary in the first place. Perhaps the recipients are *by nature* incapable of helping themselves and therefore the superior giver should be beneficent towards them. In the case of charity between Europeans and non-Europeans, Hugo Slim argues that, historically speaking, 'The fact that the gift was necessary seemed to justify the "fact" that these people were not fully human "like us"' (2002: 11) (because they were apparently clearly incapable of providing for themselves). In other words, charity was necessary because of inherent inequality, not of situations, but of individual capabilities and capacities. Those who receive charity should be grateful and humble in their receipt of it, and they should not complain or ask for more or different forms of charity. According to Slim, contemporary and past international NGOs and UN humanitarian organizations have compounded this inequality by couching 'the moral case in favour of those suffering war and disaster . . . in terms of such people's extraordinary and immediate "needs", their pitiful state and their inherent miserable righteousness as "victims"' (2002: 6). In other words, if you are on the receiving end of charity, your life must be so reduced in quality that you have become nothing but a victim (hence the common sense of a loss of dignity felt by those who see themselves as 'reduced to charity'). Charity as a concept invokes the common phrase that 'beggars can't be choosers'. Charity reinforces the idea that the recipients are inherently powerless to help themselves, to meet their own needs or change their circumstances. In this way, charity 'undermines the idea that people are the subjects of their own survival and of equal worth to their benefactors' (Slim 2002: 6). In this, there is little difference between the charity extended to the poor and providing for or 'protecting' suffering animals.

At its worst, charity takes no regard for the interests of the recipient, and is ultimately focused on the giver. In the situation of complex emergencies, ignoring this can become of life-threatening significance and contribute to a lack of effectiveness. While a sense of *moral* duty is not necessarily a guarantee of success, it can provoke reflection that is missing from a charitable focus on the giver. If we look, for instance, at the practice of food aid in times of famine, such aid is often inappropriate to the recipient. For instance, wheat may be an inappropriate food to deliver to a community used to a rice-based diet. Understanding aid as charity, i.e., something it is good to do but that is not morally required of us, arguably informs much official development aid which is often tailored to the needs of the donor state. For instance, official US policy on USAID food aid, until the 1990s, listed 'the development of export markets, the containment of communism and the reward to loyal allies as objectives of food aid, in addition to humanitarian concerns' (Neumayer 2005: 395; see also Clapp 2005). This sort of misdirection of effort is arguably more likely when the source of motivation is the giver's own need to do good (charity) rather than actual needs of the recipients.

The most important implication of this aspect of charitable work is that the attention to immediate relief deflects attention from deeper political and social questions of causality and responsibility. Charity is piecemeal in its approach and does not lend itself to addressing solutions. As Slim (2002: 5) argues, 'a system of "good works" can serve as a smooth gloss over more structural violations and injustices'. For this reason, charity is an unreliable and ultimately inadequate guide for action. These limitations suggest one reason why many are beginning to use the language of universal human rights or the humanitarian imperative in association with humanitarian work and goals. These are discussed in the next section.

Humanitarianism as rights work

The problems identified with classic humanitarianism's commitment to neutrality can in part be derived from its heritage as a form of non-political charity. The new humanitarianism therefore rejects this notion of charity in favour of the notion of human rights. As many authors have noted, the language of international ethics is focused on human rights, with more and more actors appealing to an international consciousness of rights and employing the idea of a right as a means of achieving their ends. For its advocates, the advantage of a human rights approach is that it provides a clear moral foundation and a set of values to guide humanitarian work, while also grounding it in international law. Thus, humanitarians can claim that their humanitarian goals are upheld and defended by international law, and that states and other actors have responsibilities to recognize and uphold that law. The advantage of this is that it makes clear to both the providers and the recipients of humanitarian assistance exactly where the justification for their work lies and what its purposes are. In the words of Hugo Slim:

> An ideology of charity and philanthropy alone could simply demand pity, compassion and care. But the moment one uses rights-talk, one becomes

explicitly in a demand for responsible politics, law and justice. Where this demand is rejected in war becomes the point at which the struggle for humanitarian action to protect these rights is begun. (2002: 7)

The language of rights also refers to the relationship between people and their state, and is therefore overtly political. Because basic human rights are the standard below which no one ought to be allowed to slip, all political systems and parties to a conflict retain an obligation to prevent anyone falling below that minimum standard. By using the language of rights, humanitarians are explicitly entering into a political discourse. Humanitarianism in defence of rights therefore represents a political intervention because it is a claim to restrict and curtail state activity.

At the same time, the appeal to the language of rights directs humanitarianism away from charity and towards the transformative language of justice. The idea of human rights is socially transformative because it is part of a political project to transform the world into one in which such rights are realized. The ultimate advantage of rights language over that of charity is that it changes the way in which recipients are perceived, and indeed of the nature of the 'gift' received: 'rights dignify rather than victimize or patronize people, they make people more powerful as rightful claimants rather than unfortunate beggars. Rights reveal all people as moral political and legal equals' (Slim 2002: 16). In this context, humanitarianism is invoked as a means of restoring or meeting human rights obligations. NGOs now view themselves as providing humanitarian protection, or protection both of individuals and of their rights. As rights bearers, individuals claim protection of those rights, and not just 'relief'. This has been signalled by a shift from the language of assistance to that of humanitarian protection. As Slim notes, 'What was "relief" [the great philanthropic term of the Victorian poor laws and the defining term of Britain's ancient charity laws] became "assistance" in the 1990s and is now merging with practical legal notions of rights in war and asylum to shape a new over-arching term "humanitarian protection"' (2002: 14).

Many NGOs have had troubles with the idea of humanitarianism being connected too tightly to human rights because humanitarianism is traditionally seen as 'above the contests for power and interest' (Gall and O'Hagan 2003: 3). The shift to a vocabulary of rights in the delivery of humanitarian aid presents the risk of politicizing what has previously been understood as non-political. The danger in this is that it may prevent humanitarians from doing their work, by preventing access to conflict zones. However, the defenders of a rights-based approach point out that not taking sides in conflicts is not the same as

being non-political. Humanitarianism has always been deeply political. Organizations like the ICRC have always, since their founding,
necessarily been involved in the inherently political task of trying to
secure humanitarian space for their own work and getting states to
respect the lives of non-combatants. The ICRC began not merely by
providing aid to the suffering, but also by lobbying states to develop
a set of humanitarian rules to allow assistance to the victims of war.
Those rules have been codified and are now embodied in international humanitarian law. As Slim (2002: 2) argues, humanitarianism
is 'a project that is actively engaged with challenging those in power
to limit violence and protect civilians'. In addition, because humanitarianism invokes a universal community of humankind, humanity
itself, it also directly challenges the state's claim to exclusive national
sovereignty over its people and their loyalties.

The more important limitations of the rights-based approach
have emerged in recent crises in Iraq, the great lakes region of Africa
and Afghanistan. While human rights as a doctrine is (as noted in
chapter 1) grounded in a number of ethical traditions, in the context
of post-Cold War humanitarianism, it has become linked to consequentialist values. Thus, as Fox claims, 'One look at the way the
rights-based approach is being used in humanitarian conflict shows
that the human rights approach means the elevation of political rights
over basic needs' (Fox 2001: 283). For instance, in Afghanistan,
'Several aid agencies suspended humanitarian aid programmes . . .
when the Taliban issued their edicts restricting women's rights. Here
these agencies were clearly putting the basic needs of the Afghan
people second to human rights concerns' (Fox 2001: 283). Most
controversially, this has meant that the saving of lives 'now' has been
sacrificed to the possible long-term saving of more lives later, through
finding viable political solutions. The most stark demonstration of
this occurred in the refugees' camps in Zaire (now the Democratic
Republic of Congo) in 1994–7. After the successful aid efforts to
support those fleeing the Rwandan genocide, the refugee camps were
flooded with fleeing Hutus fearful of retaliation by the new government. The camps then became the scene of continued violence and
harassment by the 'genocidaires'. Eventually, the Rwandan army
invaded, the camps were closed, an action endorsed by many NGOs,
and hundreds of thousands were expelled. Many of these were forced
back to Rwanda; many, however, were not and were left to their
fates in Zaire and neighbouring countries. In short, the humanitarian
effort was shut down in order to facilitate a political solution (which,
however, did not arrive) (see Stockton 2002; Fox 2001).

These sorts of failings ultimately involve the sacrifice of the basic humanitarian call to end suffering to the political goals of the powerful. While of course seeking political solutions is necessary to the longer-term goals of ending suffering and achieving peace, such aims cannot be a substitute or excuse for inaction now. Thus, rather than providing the answer to the humanitarian crises of the early 1990s, politicization of emergency aid has created far more serious problems for humanitarians. As we have seen, this has resulted in the split between traditional Dunantist and transformative Wilsonian NGOs. Thus, as many note, there still remains a need to provide a more coherent moral foundation for humanitarian activity to enable the criteria for providing and delivering aid. The next section identifies Kantian ethics as providing just such a morally coherent grounding for a humanitarianism that can inform practice as well as policy.

Mutual aid: a humanitarian imperative?

Paralleling the use of the discourse of rights has been the development of the notion of a humanitarian imperative. The *Sphere Handbook* (1996: 16) identifies the humanitarian imperative as 'the belief that all possible steps should be taken to prevent or alleviate human suffering arising out of conflict or calamity, and that civilians so affected have a right to protection and assistance'. The idea that humanitarians are fulfilling an imperative is one that emphasizes the moral *obligation* to assist. Where rights-based discourse specifies only negative duties, to not violate rights, the imperative discourse refers to positive duties. Imperatives are categorical, which means that they are unconditional and apply regardless of outcomes or consequences.

The language of imperatives is distinct from consequentialist ethical frameworks which would make aid conditional upon, or connected to, some prior political goal or outcome such as democratization or transparency, or even peace. Instead, the humanitarian imperative is directed to all affected by a conflict or crisis situation, as ends in themselves. In this, it offers an advance upon Pictet's understanding of humanitarianism as charity, while retaining the universality of a conception of humanism associated with some form of justice, that is, of what is owed to everybody. Insofar as they use the language of imperatives, humanitarians are making a claim that can be said to go beyond human rights because the humanitarian imperative specifies a universal duty to assist those in need. The notion of an imperative remains under theorized, but points us to an alternative to both charity and rights discourses.

What lies at the core of classic humanitarianism is the argument that there is some sort of duty to render assistance to those who are unable to assist themselves and that this is a duty based primarily on need and on a sense of common humanity. The common term for this is 'good samaritanism', but the philosophical term is 'mutual aid' or sometimes 'beneficence' (though some make a distinction between the two). This is simply the moral duty to help others in need so long as helping does not harm oneself.

Mutual aid is distinct from charity or supererogation (what it is good to do but not a duty to do). Mutual aid is generally understood as owed to all humans. Mutual aid is required in circumstances where an actor has the capacity to aid another who is suffering or in need, usually in dire need. So we think of mutual aid as being owed in times of famine by those with plenty to those with little or nothing. To withhold aid in this situation is to do wrong in a moral or ethical sense. The doctrine of mutual aid suggests that all persons owe this duty to all others, when they are in need. There is, however, no duty to help others who do not need it. Mutual aid is distinct from duties of justice as understood by Rawlsians because it does not refer to a basic ordering principle of society, but rather to what is owed by individual actors to each other. Mutual aid is defended by many pluralist and communitarian anti-cosmopolitans.

The language of imperatives links directly to the Kantian tradition of cosmopolitanism. As noted in chapter 3, mutual aid is a cosmopolitan principle derived from Kant's CI. Kant argued that the principle of mutual aid, promise-keeping, a prohibition against suicide, and duty to cultivate one's talents were universal duties (Guyer 2007). Each of these was derived from the CI and was concerned with the other's status as ends and therefore was a moral principle. Helping others in times of need, when they cannot help themselves, is not merely good but is morally required. This is because, according to Barbara Herman, 'In the Kantian account of beneficence, the point of the help we may be required to give, in both emergency and normal cases, is not to alleviate suffering per se, but to alleviate suffering because of what suffering signifies for beings like us' (Herman 2001: 244). What suffering signifies for beings like us is a particular form of harm, that is, the loss of agency, the loss of the capacity to make a life for oneself. When one is suffering from severe deprivation one is suffering from the lack of this capacity, as well as from the more mundane physical pains and sorrows. Thus, the duty to provide aid is a moral duty to support:

> the other's active and successful pursuit of his self-defined goals. I promote another's well-being or happiness by supporting the conditions for his

pursuit of ends. That is, what I have a duty to do is to contribute to the meeting of his true needs when that is not within his power. (Herman 1984: 601)

Thus, mutual aid for Kant was premised on a recognition not of suffering per se but, rather, on what was owed to reasonable beings, i.e., ends in themselves. It is worth elaborating on this point here in order to see its significance for humanitarianism. While rights discourse is directed to one's status as an end, it does not provide an adequate specification of why I should aid you in achieving your rights (see O'Neill 1986). The Kantian account attempts to provide a reason beyond mere empathy for a binding duty of care:

> As a person's true needs are those which must be met if he is to function (or continue to function) as a rational, end-setting agent, respecting the humanity of others involves acknowledging the duty of mutual aid: one must be prepared to support the conditions of the rationality of others (their capacity to set and act from ends) when they are unable to do so without help. (Herman 1984: 597)

We can contrast this duty with both the idea of charity and rights discourse. In Kantian terms, if you are on the receiving end of charity you are seen as without agency, the capacity to determine your own life, and you are not being treated as an end.

For Kant, mutual aid is a positive duty to aid that is not dependent upon any causal relationship. In Kant's terms, mutual aid is nonetheless an imperfect duty. Perfect duties are those that it is always wrong to ignore. Imperfect duties are those we can be excused from under certain circumstances. Mutual aid is an imperfect duty because we cannot be expected to give aid to the point where we suffer. Herman argues that for Kant mutual aid means: 'If giving aid undermines the life activity of the giver, the point of mutual aid is not achieved. (It is a duty of mutual aid, not sacrifice.) The requirements of beneficence do not interfere with what is necessary for one to continue to live a human life.' (1984: 598). A perfect duty of aid would require us to give until we can give no more.

Mutual aid is a moral duty, but understanding it requires processes of moral judgement. In other words, because it is an imperfect duty it is not always clear exactly what and how much I can be expected to do or give in the way of aid. The Kantian focus of the duty of mutual aid points directly to the relations between means and ends, or the manner of aid delivery. In particular, the duty of beneficence in seeking to meet another's needs as ends in themselves means that:

> The *how* of needs response, that is, the manner in which one meets anoth-
> er's needs, is no less than crucial to the dignity of the agent. If needs are met
> in a way that demeans the one in need, . . . her dignity and worth will in no
> sense be protected, let alone further fostered. Agents can be harmed by the
> incivility and humiliation of insulting care. (Miller 2002: 158)

To address this, humanitarianism must keep in mind the meaning of the categorical imperative. Our duty of mutual aid requires us to help others to help themselves and not just to keep them alive. This type of Kantian practice has resonance with Mary Anderson's (1999) concern to 'do no harm'. Her work indicates that in order to be effective, to achieve good consequences, recipients of aid must be acknowledged as equals and not just 'victims'. Thus, rather than being members of the 'deserving poor' who are unable to help them-selves, most recipients of humanitarian aid are in fact people suffering from severe situations and breakdowns of societal mechanisms but who are otherwise endowed with the capacities and capabilities of other humans.

It is possible that one could derive a consequentialist view from the Kantian account, because it could be taken to mean that the creation of a viable political culture, or of human rights institutions, or the act of military intervention, are means for realizing the conditions where others are treated as ends in themselves. However, if this requires neglecting one's duty to aid individuals 'here now', i.e., during this emergency, then it misunderstands the meaning of mutual aid in this context. As an expression of the CI, mutual aid means that no one's needs can be sacrificed to another's in this way. To make emergency aid, for instance, conditional upon achieving political ends would reduce the recipients to means to an end, and this is incompatible with mutual aid and the CI.

It is possible that the reference to meeting another's real needs could be taken to reinforce a conception that the aid worker is in possession of superior knowledge and knows what the other needs better than they do themselves. However, the recognition of the other as an end in themselves mitigates against precisely this type of inter-pretation, because what defines a moral agent as an end is in part the capacity to know what their own needs are. As Sarah Miller notes:

> The duty of beneficence commands that I promote others' happiness in
> accordance with their self-determined, self-defined ends (hence avoiding
> paternalistic practices). As Kant notes, 'I cannot do good to anyone in
> accordance with my concepts of happiness . . . thinking to benefit him by
> forcing a gift upon him; rather, I can benefit him only in accordance with
> his concepts of happiness' (MS 6: 454, 203). (In S. Miller 2005: 154)

Thus, carrying out the duty of mutual aid requires, as Herman notes, 'the acquisition of dispositions of appropriate helpfulness (attitudes of humility and respect; wariness about paternalism and dependence, and so forth)' (2001: 245). The Kantian understanding of mutual aid can also help overcome the criticism made by Edkins and others (1996, 2003) that humanitarianism replicates the logic of 'bare life' where people become merely bodies to be fed and monitored, or governed. In so doing, humanitarianism dehumanizes individuals. At the core of Edkins's claim is the possibility that in responding to others' needs merely as sufferers, in addressing people who are receiving aid as merely bodies, their culture and identity, humanity and agency will be forgotten or overlooked.

Kantian beneficence therefore reminds humanitarian aid workers to be both careful and caring in how they carry out their responsibilities. Providing care also means that aid workers recognize the agency and capacities of those whose care they are charged with. (It is worth noting that humanitarianism is also well served by the 'ethics of care' (see Robinson 1999; Held 2006; S. Miller 2005).)

In sum, the duty of mutual aid understood in Kantian terms provides a moral foundation for humanitarian aid because it places the task of meeting the basic (or what Miller calls the 'constitutive') needs of individuals, who are unable to meet these themselves, at the centre of moral concern. It is precisely addressed to people in 'emergency' situations and, while demanding, is also limited in its scope. Mutual aid is distinct from justice in that it is an individual moral duty; therefore it is not addressed to the structure of political or social institutions that might realize the individual's rights. It is a less ambitious individual duty to help others in immediate need.

In the context of 'emergency aid, or complex emergencies, it does not generate an obligation to solve all the problems of development, peace-building or human rights (though it does involve a negative duty not to contribute to anything that might prevent the success of these things). However, it does require that in meeting the duty of mutual aid the recipients must be understood not merely as recipients or victims, but as people who must be assisted to re-establish their own agency. The people who receive emergency humanitarian aid are people suffering a temporary loss of agency.

The duty of mutual aid is consistent with the values of classical humanitarianism, but it provides them with a new footing that places the needs of recipients at the core. It guards against the dangers of political humanitarianism, because sacrificing aid to political goals is not acceptable. However it also avoids the paternalism of charity. Mutual aid cannot provide a practical solution to the problem of the

'well-fed dead'; nor does it provide the rules for assessing the consequences of humanitarian actions after the supply of emergency relief
has ended. Mutual aid is a reminder of the limited nature of this duty
and of the limits of beneficence. Thus, if aid keeps people alive but
becomes a substitute for their own self sufficiency, or if it keeps them
in relations of 'welfare' dependency, then it is not meeting its own
moral obligations. If aid keeps people alive and healthy when they
would otherwise die, the obligation is fulfilled.

In the case of the 'well-fed dead', there is a responsibility not to put
people in the way of harm but there is not a responsibility to end the
conflict or engage in peace-building. The responsibility for these is a
social responsibility and that is a question of justice. This account of
mutual aid suggests that NGOs engaged in the more ambitious 'new
humanitarianism' are stepping beyond the realm of beneficence and
are seeking to be agents of justice. Duties of justice are distinct from
duties of mutual aid. Where mutual aid finishes is where the duties
of justice begin. Duties of justice are primarily the duties of states or
societies as a whole. Thus, states have duties to their own subjects
and citizens to avoid, prevent and alleviate unnecessary and avoidable
suffering. States cannot prevent all suffering but they can attempt to
ameliorate it, and prevent it. This is the part of the scope of justice.
Humanitarianism, or mutual aid, is a responsibility that falls to these
agencies only when the state has failed in its duty to protect its citizens (see Wenar 2007).

Conclusion: humanitarianism and cosmopolitanism

Humanitarianism addresses the issue of basic needs and conditions
necessary to achieve a meaningful life. Humanitarianism invokes the
idea that humans have duties to alleviate suffering when it occurs. As
such, humanitarianism is the first principle of a cosmopolitan practice.
By drawing upon suffering as its frame of reference, humanitarianism
begins with the basic facts of human life. It confers a degree of recognition on the social and biological unity of human community. The
most important insight to have come out of the humanitarian debate
of the 1990s is precisely the need to supplement this concern with a
recognition of the agency of those receiving help or protection. The
limits of humanitarian practices indicate the necessity for recognizing
the moral importance of individual agency, which is at the core of
the Kantian cosmopolitan tradition. Once we recognize that humans
do suffer and that we may have an obligation to help, then we need

to recognize that in fulfilling our obligations we need to take their moral standing as autonomous individuals (ends in themselves) into account.

Anti-cosmopolitans have endorsed this type of general mutual aid principle as compatible with communitarian values. The principle of humanitarianism has the advantage that it does not require a shared thick conception of justice or the good life. The delivery of aid may be tainted by cultural conceptions, paternalism, prejudice or ignorance, but in principle the alleviation of suffering in emergency situations does not require any shared culture. At its core, humanitarianism calls on a general sense of a common humanity and solidarity with distant strangers, rather than a full-bodied notion of citizenship and shared political or cultural identity.

Humanitarianism does not require that we understand ourselves as belonging to a *homogenous* global community. It neither endorses a global Rawlsianism nor settles for a neglect of duties to outsiders. Most importantly, humanitarianism draws upon a recognition of and identification with the suffering of others, regardless of their identity or belongingness to a specific community, and demands action based on that recognition. It interprets the principle of equality in the context of empathy, compassion and understanding of another's needs. A minimal humanitarianism addresses the issue of basic needs and conditions necessary for a meaningful life. For these reasons, communitarians and pluralists can and do endorse the principle of mutual aid. However, anti-cosmopolitanism has provided little guidance as to how the principle of mutual aid should be interpreted and implemented. The discussion above has shown that the Kantian account of beneficence is able to provide some guidance. Thus, the duty of mutual aid cannot be understood without reference to cosmopolitanism and, therefore, even 'communitarian' ethics are incomplete without this.

The practices of emergency humanitarian aid, which are informed by a humanitarian ethics (but which are not the limit of such an ethic), are the most concrete and pervasive form of humanitarianism. Beyond this minimal conception of humanitarianism is a more fully developed cosmopolitan ethos which refers to a more comprehensive duty to alleviate suffering wherever it is found, and not just in extreme or emergency cases. A full-blown humanitarianism addresses the alleviation of poverty and hunger wherever it is found. However, because mutual aid is associated with a limited scope of practice and aid, it is insufficient from a cosmopolitan perspective because a more fully fledged attempt to end suffering requires a commitment to justice and to transforming social institutions. This commitment is the focus of chapter 7.

6

The Ethics of Harm: Violence and Just War

Introduction

Chapter 4 examined the ethics of membership and entry, and argued that international ethics begins at home. Chapter 5 addressed the ethics of humanitarianism understood as a duty of mutual aid. This chapter focuses the discussion on the negative duties to avoid or minimize harm in the context of violence between states. In particular, the chapter examines the central debates of the (European) Just War tradition (JWT). The JWT aims to regulate violence and to address the issue of when it is acceptable to harm others. The JWT is concerned with the nature of the harms that states are permitted to inflict upon outsiders. It provides a set of guidelines for determining and judging whether and when a state may have recourse to war and how it may fight that war, that is, the types of harms that are allowed and forbidden once an exemption has been granted. It aims to clarify the moral limits to states' recourse to war and the negative duties to limit harms that states can commit against other states' military forces and civilians.

The JWT is one of the first and most firmly established traditions of thought specifying the ethical obligations that states have to each other. The JWT traditionally consists of two parts: the *jus ad bellum* (or justice of war) and the *jus in bello* (the justice in war), and a third, *jus post bellum*, has recently been added. Where *jus ad bellum* refers to the occasion of going to war, *jus in bello* refers to the means – the weapons and tactics – employed by the military in warfare, and *jus post bellum* refers to the consequences of the war. The aim of this chapter is to give a clear picture of the nature of the JWT and under what circumstances it allows and curtails permissible harms, and what ethical quandaries these arguments generate. One of the major questions in contemporary Just War thinking is whether war can be waged, and harm committed, for 'humanitarian' or cosmopolitan reasons such as defending human rights. In other words, whether under some circumstances there is a positive duty to wage war. The chapter spells out the major issues associated with the use of violence and provides an assessment of cosmopolitan and anti-cosmopolitan contributions to Just War thinking, and the chapter concludes with reflections about the adequacy of Just War thinking and its relationship to cosmopolitanism.

Pluralist, communitarian and cosmopolitan aspects are present in the JWT. This tradition invokes cosmopolitan principles insofar as it says that even during war there are duties to limit the harm done to outsiders. However, the JWT also aims to balance these rights to outsiders with rights to communal autonomy in terms of a legitimate right to self-defence.

Broadly speaking, the *jus ad bellum* tradition is generally associated with pluralism. The rules it lays down refer to times when it is legitimate for states to wage war. In this view, what are acceptable or unacceptable causes for war are formulated in terms of rules about and for states, concerning what states owe each other. The justifications for war are given not to God or humanity, but to other states. Michael Walzer (1977) calls this the legalist tradition or the 'war convention', a matter of informal but effective agreement between states. The only acceptable justifications for war in terms of the *just ad bellum* are the defence of individual state sovereignty and, arguably, the defence of the principle of a society of states itself. We can compare this with the more cosmopolitan elements of *jus in bello*, which refer explicitly to civilians and to what is owed to them in terms of harm minimization in war. The ultimate referent is humanity, and the rules about proportionality, non-combatant immunity and discrimination all refer to the rights of individuals to be exempt from harm (see Walzer 1977). The *jus in bello* principles inform, and have been codified in, international humanitarian law, such as the Geneva Conventions (see chapter 5), as well as in a number of other treaties limiting the use and deployment of certain weapons, including chemical weapons, landmines and weapons of mass destruction (WMD).

The JWT also demonstrates how arguments concerning natural duties and cosmopolitan arguments regarding universal human rights are largely in agreement on the essential components of the JWT. It also demonstrates how the principal differences between natural duties and cosmopolitan arguments, outlined in chapter 4, re-emerge in the context of the principle of civilian immunity and the doctrine of 'supreme emergency'. For anti-cosmopolitans, the JWT reflects the limits on ethical responsibilities of states and, of course, for realists, even these ethical responsibilities are severely qualified by the prudential calculations of necessity.

However, for cosmopolitans, the use of violence for political ends is far more problematic because, as Kant observed, war is a violation of the categorical imperative. This raises the question of whether it can in fact be possible for cosmopolitans to agree with the 'sorry comforters' of the JWT. The discussion below will show that, for many cosmopolitans, it is certainly possible to endorse several, though not all, of the core JWT principles. The difference, however, is that cosmopolitans endorse these principles for cosmopolitan and not statist reasons. However, what distinguishes most cosmopolitans from other defenders of the JWT, including the pluralists and legalists, is the emphasis on the moral obligation to make war vanish from the practice of international politics. Pluralists and anti-cosmopolitans see no end to war itself, instead seeking to accommodate the necessary evil of war without surrendering entirely to its murderous logic. Whether the end of war is in fact possible, or desirable, is one of the most important issues raised by the JWT. This chapter argues that the JWT remains inadequate from a Kantian cosmopolitan perspective because it fails to address itself to the possibility of eradicating war.

What is Just War thinking?

The JWT is one amongst many approaches to thinking about the relationship between war and ethics (see Ceadel 1989). Just War thinking is common to many ethical codes and different cultures. Confucian and Islamic scholars both engaged with the questions surrounding the need to reconcile the necessity of violence with its clear breach of everyday morality. The Islamic JWT is arguably the most comprehensive rival to the European tradition. However, while it continues to provide moral guidance to Islam, it has not been incorporated into international law as the European JWT has.

For most of its history, the JWT was a matter either of theological reflection or customary international law. Since the late nineteenth century, customary international law about Just War, and in particular about justice in war, has been codified into formal agreements and treaties. These treaties have covered everything from the state's right to make war to the banning of particular weapons, such as anti-personnel landmines. The most famous of these agreements are the Geneva Conventions which govern the treatment of captured enemy soldiers and which outlaw torture and other forms of mistreatment.[1]

Many writers refer to a Just War Theory (see Elshtain 1992), thus implying that thinking about Just War forms a coherent body of thought that can be applied to specific cases in a relatively mechanistic way, a little like act or rule utilitarianism. The framework views Just War principles as relatively straightforward universal moral principles with relatively straightforward applications, involving 'a moral slide rule from which legitimate instances of the use of force can be read off whenever necessary' (Rengger 2002: 360).

Other scholars argue that this is a misreading of the nature of the doctrine and that Just War thinking should be understood as a tradition with many different contributors. A tradition in this sense is a certain set of questions which are common to many thinkers but generating no agreed-upon single answer (see Rengger 2002; Gunnell 1974). In other words, Just War thinking generates different answers to similar cases at different times. Thus, the 2003 US invasion and occupation of Iraq has been both condemned and supported by reference to the Just War doctrine. If we understand Just War as a tradition, then it becomes impossible to say which of these is the correct analysis. For this reason, therefore, debate about the JWT cannot be reduced to simply applying the 'theory' to specific cases. The JWT itself, and its core values themselves, must be treated as debatable, because it gives rise to as many ethical quandaries as it attempts to solve. While this makes some people very uneasy, it ought instead to remind us that making ethical judgements is ultimately a matter of interpretation of universal principles in particular contexts, and reflection on these contexts provokes change in the interpretation of universals. Some of these quandaries will be discussed below in more depth.

The European JWT claims a heritage at least as far back as St Augustine. It is usually argued that the JWT began as a response to Christianization of the Roman Empire. Augustine is usually cited as the first Christian to identify when it was permissible, or at least defensible, for Christians to engage in warlike activity in the service of the state. Until then, Christian Orthodoxy had been firmly pacifist. While initially concerned with duties of individual Christians, over time, Augustine's contributions evolved into a doctrine of state, providing an account of when it is acceptable for states to wage war.

According to Bellamy, it is possible to identify a number of distinct traditions of thinking about Just War: 'positive law, natural law and realism' (2006: 6). Positive law refers to the rules made by states (Walzer's legalist tradition) and corresponds to the pluralist under-standings of international morality. As noted in chapter 3, natural law is Christian tradition, and a universalist framework that is not necessarily cosmopolitan in the modern or liberal sense. The moral scope of Christian laws is not restricted to any individual community and enjoins us to recognize our duties to humanity, and therefore our responsibility for providing good reasons for violating the basic commandment 'thou shalt not kill'.

The legalist tradition understands Just War to refer to the rights and duties that states have, by virtue of their 'social contract' in inter-national society, while the Christian and natural law traditions refer to the 'higher' law ordained by God, or natural law, and by which individuals are judged. Realism, of course, refers to the discourse of necessity and the consequentialist concerns of statecraft (see chapter 1). Bellamy's categories overlap but do not correspond directly to either cosmopolitan or anti-cosmopolitan positions. While Bellamy's framework is useful, this chapter will instead employ and focus on the cosmopolitan and pluralist approaches to the JWT as they best reflect the themes of this book.

The Christian JWT often represents itself as a *via media* between the amoralist realism of Machiavelli and the utopianism of pacifism. From the position of the realist, the JWT provides unjustifiable limits upon statecraft. According to realists, international politics is the realm of necessity and in warfare any means must be used to achieve the ends of the state. Necessity overrides 'ethics' when it is a matter of state survival or when military forces are at risk. According to real-ists only the state can judge for itself when it is most prudent to wage war and what is necessary for victory. On the other hand, from the position of the pacifist, the core doctrine of the JWT only encourages war by providing the tools to justify and provide war with a veneer of legitimacy.

A division exists between those who understand the JWT to mean wars that are just and those who mean they are justifiable. For the first, they are a bit like crusades because they are fought for a just cause. For the second, Just War refers simply to the justification of war, that is, to the idea that wars, because they are so serious a breach of the normal moral code, require justification. Depending on where you sit in this debate, you can come up with very different interpre-tations of the core doctrines of the JWT. For example, Jean Bethke Elshtain (2003) has justified the American war against Iraq in 2003 as a just cause because it is concerned with fighting the evil of al-Qaeda. However, even in Elshtain's case, the JWT is not to be confused with Holy Wars or Crusading, which are wars designed to spread a particular faith or political system, whereas the US government claims to be spreading liberal democracy by invading Iraq.

Thus, according to Rengger (2002: 361), 'the just war tradition . . . has justice – or more accurately the opposition to injustice – as its central assumption, and assumes as a result there may be circumstances where war is preferable to peace, if peace would amount to a surrender to injustice'. For most writers, the aim of the JWT has not been to achieve 'positive' justice per se. Rather, Bellamy (2006) suggests, the emphasis is on the limitation of war. Just war writers 'share a concern that recourse to war ought to be limited and conduct of war made as humane (or as least brutal) as possible' (Bellamy 2006: 5). In recent times, this has meant restricting harms to necessitous acts, and to defining what that necessity ultimately is.

At the core of the European or Christian JWT is a set of propositions, which cover both *jus ad bellum* and *jus in bello*. The next section discusses each of these elements and some of the important qualifications and difficulties associated with each. Scholars disagree over the exact content and number of these propositions, but they are usually identified as including the following:

- *Jus ad bellum*: just cause; Right authority; Right intention; Last resort; Reasonable hope of success; Restoration of peace; and Proportionality of means and ends.
- *Jus in bello*: proportionality; Non combatant immunity; and The law of double effect.

Just ad bellum: just cause

The basic assertion of just cause is that if you intend harming someone or doing wrong to them, you had better do it for the right reason, that is, with good justification. The idea of just cause is something like an essentially contested concept.[2] It is agreed that one should have a just cause but not what constitutes such a cause. A just cause could be preserving order, regaining territory, or, in more recent times, protecting human rights.

According to Bellamy (2006: 122), just cause in the modern era usually consists of 'self-defense, defense of others, restoration of peace, defense of rights and the punishment of wrongdoers'. Martin Ceadal

(1989) has noted that, historically, Just War theorists did not make any real distinction between offensive and defensive action, which has meant that until the 1870s, at least, it became very easy for states to justify any warlike actions. In particular, Ceadal (1989: 11) argues that this lack of distinction gave rise to the possibility of '"simultaneous ostensible justification", a situation in which both sides in a war could make an equally good case for having a "just cause"'. If we think of a contemporary controversial example, it might be possible to say that in 1990 Iraq had a just cause for invading Kuwait because Iraq claimed that it was redressing a past injustice (by retaking historical territory) and defending itself against an aggressive action by a neighbour (Kuwaiti oil-pricing policy). (Of course, seeing things this way requires that one takes Saddam Hussein's claims at face value or accept him as a legitimate leader, neither of which the international community was particularly inclined to do.) On the other hand, the US, Kuwait and the international community as represented by the UN claimed just cause in reference to the preservation of Kuwaiti sovereignty and rejection of the principle of violence as a means of sorting out historical disputes.

This situation has changed somewhat with the legalization of the JWT, especially since the signing of the UN Charter, which effectively ended the right of states to aggressive war. The UN Charter makes it clear that 'aggressive warfare is an illegal means for settling . . . grievances' (Ceadal 1989: 13). The UN Charter of 1945 also nominates the UN itself as the only agency that can legitimate war and assess just cause (Ceadal 1989: 13). Until this time states had claimed recourse to war, including aggressive war, as a right of statehood that accompanied sovereignty and indeed was something of a duty for the great powers. This consideration of war as a right is indicative of the difference between the legalist war convention, an agreement amongst states, and the Christian theological and natural law parts of the tradition.

For the legalists, war between states was a part of the constitution of international society, whereas, for theologians, war could only be a last resort and was never a right. Clearly, for the legalist tradition, a just cause is whatever the states party to international law agree to. The natural law tradition with regard to the JWT attempts to provide a firm benchmark that has a more transcendental moral standing because self-defence is a basic moral claim. States who violate this right are committing a moral, and not just legal, wrong.

From a legalist position, just cause ought strictly to refer only to the right of self-defence or of redressing a wrong, such as invasion of territory, because 'any use of forces or imminent threat of force by one state against the political sovereignty or territorial integrity of another constitutes aggression and is a criminal act' (Walzer 1977: 62). Therefore, without a doubt, the most widely accepted cause is self-defence because, as Walzer (1977: 62) says, 'nothing but aggression can justify war'. This reflects the basic commitment of pluralist international society to the values of state sovereignty (Walzer 1977). Invading another state is a violation of sovereignty and of the international social contract. In terms of this sort of violation, two kinds of responses are legitimate or just and include 'a war of self-defence by the victim and a war of law enforcement by the victim and any other members of international society' (Walzer 1977: 62). One recent challenge to traditional just cause thinking has been the Bush administration's claim to an expanded right of self-defence which allows for preventive warfare. Preventive war is the 'initiation of military action in anticipation of harmful actions that are neither presently occurring nor imminent' (Buchanan and Keohane 2004: 1). Preventive war is distinguished from pre-emptive war because in the latter the threat is imminent or about to commence. The Bush administration claimed that its attack on Iraq in 2003 was a preventive war against a possible, but not imminent, use of weapons of mass destruction against it.

The self-defence account of just cause is clearly supported by the pluralist communitarian perspective for two reasons. First, states' borders represent the boundaries of political communities whose members have made a common life for themselves, and thus defending those boundaries is defending the rights of those individuals to that common life. Second, that common life requires an international society of states in order to be recognized. The defence of that society of states as a principle, therefore, lies in the defence of any individual state's independence 'for it is only by virtue of those rights that there is a society at all' (Walzer 1977: 59). For Rawls, a law of peoples would not support the sovereign's right to wage aggressive war. Instead, the only justifiable just cause of war for decent peoples is self-defence (1999: 92). Nevertheless, Rawls endorses the idea of defending human rights as a just cause for war in certain exceptional 'grave' circumstances. At the same time, Rawls opens the doors to aggressive wars because liberal societies cannot tolerate 'outlaw states'. The difference between Rawls and Walzer on this point is that for Walzer the international society is a regime of tolerance and the only grave circumstance that can override a right to be tolerated is the case of genocide, where the communal life that tolerance allows has in fact broken down. However, for Rawls, the liberal states have no duty to recognize the independence of outlaw states and he implies at least a duty to act against them. Thus, for Rawls, a just cause might extend beyond defending basic human rights through to restoring or aiding the restoration of a 'decent' society.

It remains an open question as to who defines what a just cause is. From the critics' point of view, this is an inevitable consequence of the legalist focus on positive international practice. Cosmopolitans offer an account of just cause that begins not with the morality of states but with the idea of a common, universal good and the moral equality of individuals. According to Dower (1998: 18), cosmopolitanism stands outside the war convention because it offers an 'independent moral yardstick' that goes beyond what is stipulated by natural law. While cosmopolitanism has a long-standing opposition to war of all sorts, cosmopolitans are not always pacifists (though most pacifists are cosmopolitans).

Moellendorf (2002) and Caney (2005) have both ventured accounts of just cause from a cosmopolitan perspective. According to Moellendorf, the problem with the traditional account of just cause is that it gives a right of war to illegitimate states. States are human institutions which can be 'wicked, corrupt, repressive and inhumane. And where they are, there can be no ground on which to say that they have a moral right to defend themselves' (Caney 2005: 203). For the cosmopolitan, 'the right to wage war in self-defence is a right possessed only by a legitimate state' (Luban, in Caney 2005: 203). To outlaw any war of aggression and allow any war of self-defence means that states could continue to do what they please domestically, whether it be just or not. In other words, the universal right of self-defence protects unjust states from external intervention. An example might be the case of Zimbabwe, where the Mugabe government is clearly causing great suffering, but the international community is unwilling to violate Zimbabwe's rights of sovereign self-defence in order to create a more just political order.

This raises the question of what counts as legitimacy from a cosmopolitan position. For Moellendorf, it is the Rawlsian criteria of whether a state possesses a just basic structure which guarantees justice to its members (see chapters 1 and 7). Thus, Moellendorf argues that the war against Iraq in defence of Kuwait was an unjust cause because the Kuwaiti regime was unjust in its basic structure, for example, by denying the vote to women.

Caney argues that Moellendorf's account of just cause is too restrictive because it does not allow for a war between two unjust states that might result in a more just state of affairs, or at least a less unjust one. Caney points out that the situation in Kuwait deteriorated after Iraq's invasion. Therefore, it was possible that the intervention or defence of Kuwait was justifiable because it led to or prevented the continuation of a situation that was worse than the one existing prior to the invasion by Iraq. In other words, 'it would be perverse to claim that a regime has no just cause simply because it has a poor human rights record if not waging war would result in an even worse human rights record' (Caney 2005: 204). Thus, from Caney's position, cosmopolitanism has three things to say about just cause:

a that self-defence is not necessarily a priori a just cause;
b that cosmopolitan principles apply to the legitimacy of states; and
c that preventing a more unjust condition from emerging can provide grounds for a responsibility to act.

Nigel Dower (1998: 118) has noted that a cosmopolitan 'commitment to moral political or religious ideal' can in principle lend itself to crusades, stemming from the need to convert or promote this ideal amongst others. Thus, the danger in the cosmopolitan account of just cause is that it may actually extend the use of war beyond defence to the promotion of substantive justice, either in terms of the promotion of human rights or of a Rawlsian basic structure. Therefore, it at least raises the prospect that cosmopolitanism might support, in principle, the idea of a war to rid a country of dictatorship, such as the 2003 war against Iraq. Indeed, some liberals did support this war largely for such reasons.

In recent times, the biggest shift in just cause thinking has occurred in relation to the issue of humanitarian intervention. Humanitarian intervention is armed intervention to stop or prevent serious human rights abuses and atrocities like genocide. Humanitarian intervention represents a change in the legalist interpretation of Just War, which has focused primarily on the issue of defence against aggressive war. The idea of humanitarian intervention threatens to overturn the prohibition against aggression and replace it with a limited right of intervention (aggression). Indeed, with the emergence of the doctrine of the responsibility to protect, it seems that just cause now includes not just a right but a duty to intervene to protect civilians from major human rights abuses such as genocide. Thus, it appears there is a conflict between an emerging norm of humanitarian intervention, emphasizing human rights and a duty to protect, which sometimes might justify aggressive war, and the norm of non-aggression. (This issue is discussed in more detail below.)

Regardless of the particulars of any case for just cause, it is a necessary, but not sufficient, reason to justify war, 'because it does not require that there be good reason to believe that action will remedy the injustice, that such action is necessary to remedy the injustice, and that greater harms will not also be done in the course of attempting to remedy the injustice' (Moellendorf 2002: 119). Thus, the cosmopolitan claim is that upholding human rights is prima facie a just cause, but not necessarily a sufficient cause for humanitarian intervention. For cosmopolitans and anti-cosmopolitans, a sufficient case requires the other elements of JWT. Examination of these other requirements will allow a more accurate assessment of whether cosmopolitanism contains sufficient restraints on any states' ability to use war.

'Right' intentions

A more controversial, and 'slippery', concept is that of right intention, which stems from the idea that the cause may be justified but it is not just unless undertaken in good faith or with good intention. Thus 'the emphasis in the just war tradition on right intention makes it unethical to have ulterior motives behind the decision to resort to force' (Fixdal and Smith 1998: 300). Right intent means that even though outcomes might be good, say, the deposing of Pol Pot's regime and the ending of the genocide in Cambodia by the Vietnamese, the action must also be done for the right reasons. By this clause, the intentions of the Vietnamese, if they established a client state with a friendly government, detract from the achievement and undermine any claim that the Vietnamese action could count as a Just War.

Arguably, this clause of right intention only makes sense if you believe in an everlasting soul and/or judgement in another life, or reincarnation, where one's intentions are taken into account by God. This reflects the origins of the JWT in Christian thought. Christianity recognized that war was bad and that its consequences were always bad, but, as Augustine acknowledged, war was sometimes necessary; therefore it should be fought only for good reasons. According to Fixdal and Smith (1998: 300), 'At stake is the health of the soul and prospects for eternal life . . . nothing is hidden from the deity. Therefore you must not only act well but mean well.' In this case, it would matter what one's intent was because the fate of one's immortal soul depended on it. In other words, if you are going to do bad things, and cause bad consequences, then you ought to at least do them for the right reasons.

Historically, the clause regarding intention appears to have been directed against individual state leaders or sovereigns who might be tempted to undertake a Just War for reasons of personal aggrandizement or gain, or out of hatred for enemies or neighbours. That is, they may be able to mount a case for a just cause but their intention might be something else, such as personal or political advantage or, for instance, securing domestic political support. Right intent is not included in all Just War accounts and could arguably be included under the heading of just cause, but that would assume a congruence between cause and intent that philosophers would find troubling.

However, two important cosmopolitan theorists reject the relevance of right intent as a cosmopolitan principle justifying violence. Both Moellendorf and Caney argue that good intent is not necessary from a cosmopolitan viewpoint. Moellendorf and Caney clearly depart here from the Kantian tradition of cosmopolitanism. For Immanuel Kant, intention was everything. One should always act because one has been convinced of the rightness of the action, and not because one may gain from that action, or simply because that is what custom or law dictates. In the arguments of both Moellendorf and Caney, the influence of Rawls overwhelms Kant, because they agree that it matters not what the intentions of states' leaders are so long as 'justice' (i.e., the basic structure) is improved upon. This reflects the liberal cosmopolitan emphasis on substantive justice. For these cosmopolitans, Just War can only be acknowledged in the context of an account of justice understood as basic structure.

However, having a good intention must surely be an important criterion when setting out to break the fundamental commandments 'do not kill' and 'do no harm'. If we are going to allow killing, then surely it must be not only for just a cause but also with the right intention. Thus, Bellamy (2006: 122), in opposition to Moellendorf and Caney, argues that 'eschewing right intention begs the question of how to justify killing in war at all'. For Bellamy, killing for the common good and not individual self-aggrandizement, whim, greed, hatred, or advantage, is the only justification that is valid. Bellamy's refutation of the liberal cosmopolitans' rejection of right intent points to his understanding of the role of Just War thinking as a restraint on state action rather than a source of encouragement or permissiveness to make war. Bellamy's case is buttressed by reflection on the relationship between intent and outcome. As we know, the path to hell is paved with good intentions, but does that mean intentions are irrelevant to outcomes? If one's intentions are good, then does this outweigh any bad consequences of one's actions, and if so at what point?

How can we think adequately about the role that intent should play? What is clear is that the outcome of the war makes it easier to question the intent and motives of those who began it. Evidence suggests that the Bush administration was intent on removing Saddam

Hussein from office for its own reasons. The main reason for thinking this is not that no weapons of mass destruction were found, but that little or no thought was given to the responsibilities of the US after removing Saddam Hussein. Had they been more concerned with the welfare of the Iraqi people, the US would have been more likely to have given greater thought to the consequences of their actions and the post-war arrangements. Had the US been genuine in its intention of liberating the Iraqis from their dictator, rather than, say, getting rid of a menace for the US, or settling a grudge left over from a previous war, then it is more likely that serious thought would have been given to the post-war situation and how to preserve order within Iraq. Instead, because the underlying intention was arguably different from the stated intention, post-war requirements were not considered until the last minute.

The contrasting case would be the Kosovo bombing campaign of 1999. In this case, NATO had to be seen to be fighting not only a Just War but to be fighting it in a just manner as well, especially because the war was undertaken in the name of human rights. Thus, if the intention was to save Albanians from genocide and in doing so to protect human rights, then the means for doing so must also be consistent with human rights as much as possible. Due to the nature of intent, a further commitment was required to help reconstruct these societies, to prevent another war, and to be humanitarian in the way the wars were fought.

Intention ultimately refers to what the agent is intending to achieve, which implies or raises the question of how they are to do it, and not just why (cause) they are doing it. Thus, intentions are important in that they relate to the consequences of an action, because they can determine the nature of the action itself.[3] However, like just cause, good or right intention is not sufficient to establish a case for a Just War. The JWT also requires that further criteria be met with regard to how the war is to be fought.

Proportionality

Proportionality refers to the principle that 'the harm judged likely to result from the war is not disproportionate to the likely good to be achieved' (Ceadal 1989: 11). States should be limited to wars where winning them is not outweighed by harms incurred. The proportionality criterion is a response to the problems that arise when basic harm conventions are suspended as in war. If we are going to commit a basic harm by engaging in war, we must restrict further harms as much as possible. States should also offer some reasons for thinking that going to war will outweigh the costs of not going to war. If the initial harm has been slight, or perhaps significantly long ago, then other means ought to be found for redress. If the harm has been major, such as to territorial integrity, then war is more likely to be justifiable.

Proportionality is designed to restrain states and to keep their aims within reason. But it can also, of course, lead to an escalation if the stakes are high enough – i.e., if universal perpetual peace is the result, then what is considered proportionate might be quite high. This clause can be supported by the just cause argument that the ultimate goal of a Just War is to re-establish peace. This is a particularly strong part of the legalist tradition which emphasizes maintaining order (and therefore peace) between states. In Hedley Bull's formulation, war is justified in order to maintain the egalitarian principles of sovereignty against the hierarchical one of empire or suzereignty (Bull 1983). Additionally, the peace established after the war must be preferable to the peace that would have prevailed if the war had not been fought. How big could a war become before it was disproportionate? Was the Second World War justifiable because of the peace which has lasted in Europe as a result? And was it therefore better to have had that war than not? Thus, if a war could be fought that would establish, say, a realm of peace between Europe's states that would last for 100 years, then it might be justifiable in terms of the proportionality clause. However, this type of calculation would also lead to the making of utilitarian calculations as to the cost of wars and of peace.

Ultimately, however, proportionality raises the question of proportionate for whom? From a cosmopolitan perspective, it must take into account the effects on everybody involved, not just the initiators of war but also those who are being warred against. Bellamy (2006) points out that proportionality has a cosmopolitan scope because it takes not only the costs to those who initiate war but also the costs to all parties involved or affected by the actions of war as its scope – that is, costs to all affected by the actions. The proportionality principle refers beyond the realm of state to something like a universal interest, or universal cosmopolitan concern for the overall effects of war.

Last resort

At its minimum, the last-resort measure means that states should not only resort to war as a last measure to solve their problems, but they should delay the recourse to war as long as is possible. War should not simply be the main means for achieving foreign policy goals or, in Clausewitz's terms, the extension of foreign policy by other means. Last resort does not mean the 'exhaustion of every means short of force' (Bellamy 2006: 123). Such a goal is too demanding for most states, as war can always be put off in favour of negotiation. Rather, force must be the most *feasible* means of resolving conflict. According to Bellamy (2006: 123) 'actors must carefully evaluate all the different strategies that might bring about the desired ends, selecting force if it appears to be the only feasible strategy for securing those ends'. All reasonable peaceful means of conflict resolution must have been attempted or at least considered before recourse to war.

The criteria of last resort are particularly topical in the context of the war on terror and the recourse to the so-called preventive war against Iraq. Last resort has traditionally been understood to be reconcilable with a doctrine of pre-emption, that it is acceptable to launch an attack on another state in order to pre-empt a certain and imminent attack. The Israeli attack on their Arab neighbours during the six-day war is an example of pre-emption. Under these conditions, the Israeli attack was seen a defensible action because the Arab attack was certain to occur within a very short period, a matter of days or hours. Preventive attack, on the other hand, is intended to prevent another state from being able to attack at some uncertain and unspecified time in the future. Pre-emption occurs at the moment before a war would otherwise start. Prevention is an attempt to prevent the emergence of a possible but not certain threat which may or may not lead to war. The danger of this approach is that it opens the door to war as the first option for diffusing conflict, and as such is a potential reversal of the last-resort clause. In this sense, prevention may achieve a good result by preventing a larger war but it cannot be considered a last resort.

Legitimate authority

The origins of the rule that war can only be undertaken by a legitimate authority lie in the emergence of Westphalian states from the wreckage of the Middle Ages when private armies, mercenaries, criminals and pirates all competed and engaged in warfare. The chief result was to de-legitimize other forms of violence and to legitimate state, or sovereign, violence. For pluralists and anti-cosmopolitans, it is self-evident that the state, or the political community, should have the right to defend itself or have just cause in self-defence, because the state is a legitimate form of political community. However, for cosmopolitans, this is not self-evident. A state's legitimate authority, and therefore its legitimacy to make war, is always conditional upon other factors. As Caney (2005: 205) notes, 'we should not simply assume without supporting argument, that there should be a world of states and hence that the authority to engage in warfare should rest with states'. The rule of legitimate authority forces us to ask who is a legitimate authority in the contemporary world? While possessing sovereignty, many states today have questionable legitimacy (see Buchanan 2000).

In contemporary debates the presence of many non-state actors, including private security forces such as Blackwater, and the use of non-conventional violence (terrorism) also challenge the criteria of the sovereign state as the only legitimate authority. Some non-state actors, such as revolutionary forces, might be considered to have more legitimacy than certain state actors. While many may object to the methods of these groups, which may fall outside the rules of *jus in bello,* they nonetheless claim legitimacy, even if that claim is not shared by everybody else. Thus, there is no prima facie reason why non-state actors cannot be considered legitimate actors and therefore bound by the rules of Just War. Because, in principle, many of these non-state actors claim to act in the common good or on behalf of a certain people, they can be distinguished from those who practise private violence and organized crime.[4] It is possible, therefore, that legitimate authority can be given to political actors, rather than private actors, who act in the name of the common good. There is also good reason for claiming that today states have to act in a way that is legitimate in the eyes of international society as a whole, in the form of permission or under a license from the UN Security Council. This is especially so in the case of humanitarian intervention.

Reasonable chance of success

The possibility of war being fought for just cause has to be weighed with the likelihood of success. Thus, a noble, but doomed, cause, should not be undertaken. It would be wrong to engage in a noble crusade if it is unlikely to work, in part because the result would be disproportionate or would be outweighed by the harms committed. Thus, the consequences of action ought to be realistically assessed. There is no point committing one's troops to a lost cause as it will only end in unnecessary suffering on all sides. We might think perhaps of a hypothetical war of liberation against the Chinese occupation of Tibet. By most accounts, this occupation is unjust and therefore a case could be made that war to liberate the Tibetans was justified. However, the costs and the likelihood of long-term success of that war would outweigh the cause itself. For this reason, while the cause might be just the consequences would not be just. This is a reference possibly to cosmopolitan elements as it suggests a concern to limit unnecessary suffering to all those involved. Both cosmopolitan and anti-cosmopolitan thought generally agrees that this reasonable chance of success clause is justifiable and essential to any reasonable ethics of force.

Jus in bello

Where *jus ad bellum* refers to the occasion of going to war, *jus in bello* refers to the means for fighting a war, to the weapons and tactics employed in warfare. Some writers have traditionally argued that *jus ad bellum* and *jus in bello* are logically separate. In other words, any war fought for an unjust cause cannot be considered just by any measure, no matter how well it is fought, and a war fought unjustly, but for just cause, is still an unjust war – the ends do not justify the means. For instance, NATO action against Yugoslavia over Kosovo fits this latter model because the use of certain munitions types, cluster bombs, and the targeting of civilian infrastructure cannot be considered just means for fighting a war.

The *jus in bello* principle forms the majority of international law of armed conflict, perhaps reflecting some recognition that states may be more willing to exercise restraint in how they fight the wars they do engage in. That is to say, states are not really willing to renounce war but it is more believable that they may renounce certain weapons and tactics. However, there is still plenty of evidence of states doing neither, or in some cases doing a bit of both. The US defence forces have extensive briefings and codes for their forces as well as a great number of legal resources, including the JAG (Judge Advocate General) arm. At the same time, the US continues to use methods and tactics that are outlawed by international law and that are highly controversial. Examples of these methods are cluster bombs and phosphorus bombs, and targeting practices that are less selective than target practices of other states.

Perhaps even more than *jus ad bellum*, *jus in bello* rules invoke the idea of cosmopolitan duties. By making a clear distinction between who is a legitimate target and by urging restraint, *jus in bello* rules invoke the idea that war is not to be waged against a people as such. In the twentieth century, these *jus in bello* rules have become highly codified in international humanitarian law, representing for many the pinnacle of cosmopolitan values in the international order. However, differences remain between cosmopolitans and pluralists, especially about how to ground these rules and, ultimately, how extensive or restrictive these rules are. The crucial consequence of this difference emerges in the discussion about the extent of civilian immunity, or the discrimination principle that exempts civilians from being targeted. The two core demands of *jus in bello* are the proportionality principle and the principle of discrimination or non-combatant immunity.

Proportionality

Proportionality means that the methods used in the war must be proportional to the ends and limited to achieving the just goal of the war. The best example of this type of question is the case of the dropping of the atomic bombs on Hiroshima and Nagasaki, which brought the Second World War to an end. The dropping of these bombs was an unprecedented action as they were used against non-military targets, destroying whole cities. Could such methods of violence be justified? The US position held that this would drastically shorten the war and therefore reduce the overall number of deaths, especially of US and allied forces. Therefore, according to the US, this action was proportionate to the larger goal of ending the war. In other words, the proportions of the war had become so great that it was necessary to take this step. The more common understanding of proportionality relates to the methods of fighting between combatants, ruling out massacre of the enemy's troops.

Proportionality involves a minimal cosmopolitan sense of humanity through:

> a basic respect for life urged on all those who engage in war. It demands economy in the use of force; that commanders should not waste the lives of their own soldiers in the pursuit of unattainable or relatively unimportant military objectives, and that they should not inflict undue and unnecessary suffering on an adversary. (Coates 1997: 227)

It should not be underestimated how 'revolutionary' this proportionality clause is. It demands that even in the midst of the breakdown of morality that is war it is still incumbent upon warriors to minimize the harm they cause to their *adversaries*. However, proportionality is not enough as it is a very elastic and subjective term that gives great scope to individual judgement as to what is or is not proportionate. Therefore, there is general agreement that proportionality is incomplete as a *jus in bello* principle without the more explicit principle of discrimination or civilian immunity.

Discrimination and civilian immunity

This principle states that the weapons and tactics used in war must discriminate between combatants and non-combatants and that the civilian population of the enemy is never a permissible target. This rule provides a fundamental and cosmopolitan restriction on the prerogative of military commanders and politicians, because it focuses on the civilian status of human beings and demands that military commanders and politicians respect those who are not part of the war in any immediate sense. Non-combatant immunity is central to Just War thinking because were a war to ignore this principle it would become total war and lose any grounds for wider justification. As Coates (1997: 263) claims, 'How can a theory that claims to regard wars as an instrument of justice countenance the injustice involved in the systematic suppression of the rights of non-combatants?' Just War tradition must place the well-being of individuals and non-combatants at its centre or else it succumbs to *raisons d'état*. Any coherent account of Just War must accept that humanity is the ultimate moral referent and therefore necessarily place the well-being of human beings not engaged in the war (civilians) at the centre of its concern.

In order to understand the justification of non-combatant immunity, it is necessary to understand the logic of warfare itself. Warfare should be understood as an exception to the normal rules of life, whereby everybody is immune from violence. In warfare, soldiers or those engaged in aggressively hostile activity lose that immunity. Likewise, the Geneva Conventions spell out obligations to respect enemy forces outside the field of combat. The argument is that once the soldiers have been removed from the field of battle they are no longer legitimate targets; they revert to their normal status. In this way, civilian immunity should be understood as the norm from which targeting combatants is the deviation. This fits in with the natural law understanding of the JWT because it is referring not to any right of war or right to kill civilians, but at best is a temporary lifting of the 'do no harm' principle that governs all humans.

The most obvious examples of lack of discrimination in the area of tactics are the carpet bombings of German cities and the fire bombing and atomic bombings of Japanese cities by the US during the Second World War. In pursuance of their war against Hitler, the British undertook massive bombing of Germany, destroying many cities and killing hundreds of thousands of civilians. The most famous of these was the bombing of the German city of Dresden. Dresden was especially controversial because it had no military significance at all. In the firestorm that was created by the allies, at least 100,000 people died. Likewise, the Americans, during the closing stages of the war against Japan, repeatedly bombed Tokyo and other major Japanese cities in raids that targeted cities rather than military sites. The main argument used to defend these clear breaches of the discrimination principle was that it was necessary to break the will of the people to continue fighting. By breaking the will of the people to fight, the war would be drawn to an earlier close. It was also argued these actions were necessary, and justifiable, because the war was not restricted to military forces alone but to entire societies, and therefore everyone was a potential target. In hindsight, both these practices clearly broke the immunity principle (indeed, they were also criticized at the time, especially by the Church) and are morally inadequate.

Arguments against civilian immunity usually employ a consequentialist logic – the cost of protecting civilian immunity is higher than the cost of not protecting it. So, for instance, one argument for the atomic bombings of Japan in the Second World War was that it would save lives in the long run, in particular the lives of US soldiers, by bringing the war to a speedy end and avoiding a bloody and prolonged full-scale invasion of Japan. Avoiding one form of suffering outweighs the other.

The other consequentialist argument is the more 'realist' one that in war necessity triumphs over morality. That is, military necessity can justify violating the discrimination principle. This idea stems from a belief that winning is the ultimate goal of war and if a particular military action brings about that goal more quickly, or is necessary for victory, then the non-combatant immunity is outweighed by the military action that will lead to the winning of the war.

Military necessity can be interpreted in two ways, as either the necessity of winning, or the necessity of survival or not being destroyed. The logic of this argument is that it is better to win badly than to lose and suffer the consequences. This is aggravated by a belief that a given war, or even a given battle, is one for survival and not just victory because a given battle could perhaps be a turning point in a war and hasten the overall end. Of course, the danger of taking this line is that survival can be used to justify anything, and if the outcomes override the means then we end up with the argument that the ends justify the means. In the case of war, this could result in defending any tactic that helped achieve victory. Thus, it could be argued that the tactical use of nuclear weapons is justifiable if they bring about a greater or quicker victory, as in the Second World War.

The danger of the rhetoric of necessity is that it becomes a licence to do anything. In the contemporary context this is emphasized by the discourse of the war on terrorism, which implies that the stakes in this war are so high that it is necessary to suspend certain aspects of the Just War rules such as the ban on torture. In this type of war it is claimed we must be prepared to use anything to defend ourselves. The JWT, as Coates (1997) points out, is built upon the opposite aim – to restrain as much as possible the activities of those who go to war. The purpose of the Just War approach is to address precisely the extreme situation of warfare and spell out rules for engagement that are morally just, and to bring war within the boundaries of justice insofar as that is feasible. Coates (1997: 237) makes the point that while it is often hard to draw a line, 'a line needs to be drawn some-where if liberty is to be preserved'. The *jus in bello* rules are defined *in extremis* and are precisely intended to overcome the argument that necessity allows for everything or anything. In terms of this logic, necessity itself does not permit the breaking of the discrimination rule and to do so would risk undermining the entire Just War project.

The fundamental issue raised by the argument of necessity is whether it is ever reasonable to target non-combatants and break the immunity clause. There are two possible arguments that qualify the non-combatant immunity principle. These are the argument of double effect, which allows for unintended civilian deaths, and supreme emergency, which allows suspending non-combatant immunity under extreme conditions.

Double effect

The law of double effect states that while it is not permissible to harm non-combatants, if such harm occurs as an unintended con-sequence soldiers can escape censure. The double-effect principle refers to the difference between whether the death of innocents, or non-combatants, is intended or unintended, or foreseeable but unintentional. However, the issue is more complex than simply intentionality suggests. The real issue is whether deaths can be unintended but probable, likely or foreseen. If deaths are foreseen that adds a further complexity to making judgements because it means one has knowledge that a death will occur from one's actions even if that death is an unintended by-product. So, for instance, a passerby close to a military site is killed when the site is bombed. This is fairly clear-cut. However, the principle of double effect seems more compromised where, say, as in the December 2008 Israeli attacks on Hamas in the Gaza strip, the military targets are situated amongst a civilian population. In choosing its targets in Gaza, because of the density of the population and the Hamas tactic of firing rockets into Israel from this location, Israeli planners would know that the likelihood of civilian casualties is high. In this context civilian deaths are unintended but highly foreseeable.

Is this a legitimate consideration in terms of the double effect or should avoiding the likely death of civilians override the military goals? The dilemma facing Just War theorists is whether we are then responsible for those deaths in the same way as we would be for intended deaths, or not?

For the critics of Just War, the double-effect principle does not place enough emphasis on anticipated deaths. Rather, it focuses simply on the difference between intended and non-intended targets, and actually gives planners license to commit murder, that is, to factor-in civilian deaths even when they are not intended. The critics say that if we draw the line only at intended deaths, military planners can still get away with anticipating as many civilian deaths as they wish. In this manner, the double effect undermines the rules of discrimination and renders them insufficient if not altogether pointless (e.g., Sjoberg 2006).

Michael Walzer (1977) suggests that double effect needs to be replaced by the notion of something like due care that takes foreseeability into account. Walzer (1977: 156) argues that simply not intending civilian deaths is not enough and 'what we look for in such case is some sign of a positive commitment to save civilian lives'. The principle that should be followed is 'when it is our action that puts innocent people at risk, even if the action is justified, we are bound to do what we can to reduce those risks, even if this involves risks to our own soldiers' (Walzer 2004: 17). Thus, in many cases, Walzer argues for serious consideration to be given to choices, say, between commando raids and aerial bombardment.

The principle of civilian immunity clearly states that individuals' moral standing trumps military goals and states' interests when it comes to fighting wars. The discrimination principle is the most clearly cosmopolitan element of the JWT because it invokes the individual human as the relevant moral focus. This point is acknowledged even from the communitarian and pluralist position. Walzer (1977: 158), for instance, claims that the argument for due care extends from an account of human rights which 'stands independently of political allegiance . . . it establishes obligations that are owed, so to speak to humanity itself and particular human beings and not merely to one's fellow citizens'.

Supreme emergency

A supreme emergency is a situation where not merely victory but survival of a state or community is on the line. For Walzer (1977: 254), a supreme emergency exists when there is 'a threat of enslavement or extermination directed against a single nation'. Such a fear occurs 'when we face moral as well as physical extinction, the end of a way of life as well as of a set of particular lives, the disappearance of people like us' (Walzer 2004: 43). Under this situation, war becomes an all-or-nothing situation. Supreme emergency rules suggest that it is necessary to do whatever it takes to win or survive. The clear inference, though Walzer does not use the term, is to say that in cases of attempted genocide, understood as the complete physical or cultural destruction of a people or group, then civilian immunity might be legitimately compromised. Walzer makes it clear that it is only when extinction is imminent that a supreme emergency might be said to exist, that is, when all other options have failed or no other option is available. He claims 'there is fear beyond the ordinary fearfulness . . . of war, and a danger to which that fear corresponds, and that this fear and danger may well require exactly those measures that the war convention bars' (1977: 251). Walzer argued that Britain faced this challenge in the early days of the Second World War when it looked as if Hitler would conquer Britain. Walzer implies that had Nazi Germany conquered Britain, then Britain would simply have ceased to exist or would have been forced into slavery, like the Eastern European states (see Bellamy 2006, and Coady 2004, for critical examination of this claim).[5] Nonetheless, the supreme emergency exception suggests that community rights are more important than cosmopolitan human rights.

There are at least two questions raised by the use of necessity in this context. The first is to ask whether necessity does in fact override other concerns and, if so, how or when? The second concerns the assessment of what constitutes a necessity and the point at which an action becomes necessitous. It is not clear why supreme emergency itself constitutes a reason to override the normal rules of discrimination. Why, for instance, should the survival of the community, or the communal identity, be more important or necessitous than the survival of the individuals who comprise it?

This defence of violating non-combatant immunity is clearly derived from Walzer's communitarian pluralism. Walzer's doctrine says that under some circumstances the community matters more than the (foreign) individual because 'the survival of and freedom of political communities whose members share a way of life, developed by their ancestors, to be passed on to their children, are the highest values of international society' (Walzer 1977: 254). At this junction, the contradiction and the tension at the heart of the anti-cosmopolitan position is revealed. Walzer appeals to both cosmopolitan principles, such as human rights and natural duties, which are owed to all, *and* to the highest values of international society such as communal autonomy. According to Walzer, human rights mean we cannot take innocent lives because 'it is the acknowledgment of rights that puts a stop to such calculations and forces us to realize that the destruction of the innocent, whatever its purposes, is a kind of blasphemy against our deepest moral commitments' (1977: 262). Nevertheless, communal autonomy allows us to do just that. The issue of non-combatant immunity dramatizes and crystallizes the point at which a position has to be taken in favour of the priority of the individual or the community. Walzer's defence of the supreme emergency clause, and its endorsement by others including Rawls, marks another point at which anti-cosmopolitanism sides with community over humanity.

For a number of reasons, the anti-cosmopolitan argument does not stand up. First, states are not individuals and not every person in a state is likely to suffer or be threatened by the loss of the political community in the same way. Walzer does not answer the question as to why any particular community's (cultural) existence is more important than the lives of innocent civilians. In other words, given a choice between cultural extinction and killing other civilians, why is any particular community's existence more important? Why is it not better to refrain from committing an evil than to commit one – even if that means a greater evil is committed against oneself or one's community? Walzer does not give satisfactory answers to these questions.

The most obvious limitation to relaxing the discrimination clause is that it increases the chances for abuse. It opens another avenue for state leaders to suspend the discrimination rules and leaves unanswered the question of who decides, and how, when a supreme emergency exists. As Bellamy points out, 'Any political leader, as realists would argue, can construct a plausible case that what he or she is facing is a supreme emergency. Read this way, the "exception" could be cast so broadly that the rule of non-combatant immunity would cease to offer much protection' (2004: 836). The purpose of the discrimination rule is precisely to make a distinction between Just War and massacre or murder. Relaxing the discrimination clause is to collapse that distinction.

It could be argued, then, that only a fully cosmopolitan account of Just War holds out the possibility of providing more adequate guidelines. Or, stating this another way, it is only by extending the basic cosmopolitanism of Walzer's reading of Just War, and of the JWT itself, that the JWT can resolve some of its inadequacies.

Terrorism

The attacks on the US on September 11, 2001, by terrorists of al-Qaeda have in a number of ways brought the issue of the Just War alive. The response to these attacks prompts reflection upon whether terrorism can ever be justified and whether the response to terrorism ought to be bound by the laws of the JWT. The crux of the matter is the argument concerning whether terrorists are engaging in just cause.

Beginning with the technical requirements of Just War and putting aside the issue of state terrorism, terrorists do not meet the criteria of just authority because they are non-state actors. However, it is often the case that terrorists do achieve international recognition as legitimate actors even if they do not control a state. In many cases, terrorists are also aspiring to control a state and therefore should be understood as seeking all the rights and responsibilities of statehood. This would distinguish them from criminal organizations and private violence. Such was the situation experienced by the founders of Israel who employed terrorism to gain momentum for their struggle to gain independence from Britain. To condemn political violence purely on the grounds that it is not committed by a state is to effectively de-legitimize all armed resistance and struggle, including against illegitimate states. Therefore, the right authority clause, because it focuses on states only, cannot adequately deal with the problems of terrorism without unconditionally approving the status quo.

The argument that those who use violence for political ends, such as national liberation, use it to justify armed struggle relies most heavily on the case for a just cause. This usually takes the form that great injustices have been, or are being, perpetrated against or experienced by a certain group or people and therefore a violent struggle is required. Such arguments rely upon some form of equivalency between the state's right of self-defence and the situation of the aggrieved group.

The critical issue here arises when the armed struggle moves from targeting military or government actors to indiscriminate targeting of civilians. Terrorism against military targets, such as has been used by guerrilla fighters for at least a century, appears to be covered by most of the JWT. However, terrorism directed against civilians is covered by the law of discrimination and can never be justified in the JWT. Therefore, there is no prima facie reason why the rule of non-combatant immunity should not apply to non-state actors. If these actors wish to claim, as for instance the IRA did, that they are engaged in military conflict, then it follows that they ought also to be restrained by the rules of the JWT. If they are not constrained by the JWT, they run the risk of wishing to claim legitimacy as equivalent to states but without taking on the obligations that such legitimacy entails. The only argument they can therefore deploy with any consistency is a consequentialist and realist one that the end justifies the means, that the common good overrides the rights of individuals. If this is the case, then terrorists are clearly stepping outside the confine of the JWT.

Jus post bellum

The criteria with which to assess the cessation of hostilities and the movement from war to peace have been recognized as equally significant as moral considerations of war. *Jus post bellum* seeks to regulate the ending of wars, and to ease the transition from war back to peace, ensuring 'the just goal of a Just War, once won, is a more secure and more just state of affairs than existed prior to the war' (Walzer, in Orend 2000: 122). In recent years, a third component of the JWT that has been developed by Just War theorists as well as by critics (Bellamy 2006; Orend 1999, 2000, 2002; Walzer 2000, 2002; Williams and Caldwell 2006), has evolved to address the termination and aftermath of war. Standard conceptions of a Just War may have held, as Walzer (2002: 18) explains, that a war of aggression is justly terminated when aggression is rolled back and old territories are re-established. Recent conflicts, however, demonstrate the need for more comprehensive termination and restoration, and which are guided by principles of justice (Orend 2000).

Jus post bellum is clearly cosmopolitan as it is concerned with not just the return to status quo as it existed before the war, but also with the achievement of a measure of justice. This is especially so in the case of humanitarian intervention. In these cases, if the war is to be just, it must not end with the restoration of the status quo ante because 'the war is from the beginning an effort to change the regime that is responsible for the inhumanity' (Walzer 2002: 19). Walzer cites the case of Rwanda to demonstrate that if this intervention had occurred as it should have, part of its aim would have included replacement of the Hutu regime responsible for the genocide (2002: 19–20). Additionally, guidelines are required to prevent states, which take on the responsibility of a replacement of an unjust regime, from failing to submit themselves to a set of moral principles or require-ments (2002: 18–20). Such a case is illustrated by Vietnam's expelling of the Khmer Rouge from Cambodia, followed by its establishment of a satellite regime (the PRK) in 1979. There needs, in short, to be an ethical 'exit strategy' from war (Orend 2005).

Humanitarian intervention

In recent years, the issue of humanitarian intervention has raised many of the issues traditionally covered by the JWT. Much of the discussion of humanitarian intervention has not expressly acknowl-edged this (see Fixdal and Smith 1998), focusing instead on either the legal justifications, or on the prudential and pragmatic arguments. In particular, the debate about humanitarian intervention has focused on the legal issue of whether the state or the international community has the right to violate state sovereignty.

Humanitarian intervention challenges traditional JWT criteria in a number of ways. First, humanitarian intervention raises the pros-pect of a shift from negative to positive cosmopolitan duties and a consequent expansion of the category of Just War. As noted above, it challenges the prohibition against aggressive war by, in its most recent formulation, proposing a duty to intervene to prevent crimes against humanity. The development of the doctrine of a responsibility to protect suggests an emerging consensus that genocide and crimes against humanity are sufficient cause to overturn a state's right of non-intervention. Second, humanitarian intervention also raises the possibility of the emergence of a new source of legitimate authority, in the form of the UN or the international community more generally.

Third, humanitarian intervention raises questions about *jus in bello* because it draws attention to the increased duty of states to fight justly. If the war is being fought for humanitarian reasons, then it must be more responsible in its methods. The NATO campaign in Kosovo provides a good example because of the use of certain targeting practices by the US and of certain sorts of munitions, such as cluster bombs and depleted uranium warheads. Both of these weapons represent threats to non-combatants, including after the cessation of hostilities. Their use in so-called humanitarian interventions threatens to undermine the legitimacy of the war because of the harm they can do to non-combatants.

Despite these challenges, there is no reason why any case for humanitarian intervention should not also meet the other criteria of Just War – proportionality, last resort and reasonable chance of success. This has been recognized by the ICISS criteria for military action (see ICISS; also Bellamy 2008).

That said, a number of other issues are raised by humanitarian intervention that don't necessarily fit within the confines of the JWT. For defenders of humanitarian intervention on human rights grounds, the biggest issue is whether it is possible to justify denying some people their human rights in order to save others. On one hand, this is simply a case of proportionality. On the other hand, it could be seen as a case of basic principles in conflict. Humanitarian intervention presents a case where the values of harm avoidance and of humanitarianism may come into conflict. To uphold humanitarian values some people may have to be harmed, including in all likelihood some innocent people. This is a crucial test case for cosmopolitan values and for cosmopolitan states, and it speaks to the very meaning of how cosmopolitanism is to be realized in a world of states. The case of Kosovo provides one of the most interesting examples because the NATO allies had to make a judgement on what the anticipated reaction of the Serb leadership would be. Many argued that the expulsion of Kosovo Albanians from their homes was directly the result of the NATO intervention, or was at least hastened or made worse by that intervention. This suggests that the harm of intervening was greater and that things would have been better had NATO not intervened (see Bellamy 2006 for an alternative reading).

Humanitarian intervention has received qualified support from both cosmopolitan and anti-cosmopolitan writers. To be sure, some such as Jackson reaffirm the pluralist account, and the privileging of order over justice. For Jackson (2000: 291), 'the stability of international society . . . is more important, indeed far more important, than minority rights and humanitarian protections'. However, others usually associated with pluralist concerns, such as Walzer and Rawls, argue that under certain conditions humanitarianism provides a just cause for war. For Walzer, humanitarian intervention is justified in order to protect the victims of severe human right violations, or more commonly severe persecution, and genocide in particular. For Walzer (2004: 81), this is consistent with his pluralism because 'the victims of tyranny, ideological zeal, ethnic hatred . . . are not determining anything for themselves'. That is, these individuals are being denied the capacity for self-determination and to make a common life for themselves. Therefore, it is in fact required or obligatory for outsiders to intervene in this context, and 'whenever the filthy work can be stopped it should be stopped' (Walzer 2004: 81). This does not necessarily involve a rejection of non-intervention as the basic norm, but only a slight qualification of it. Intervention is not justified to uphold, for instance, the right of freedom of speech, or religion, or even individual liberty. According to Walzer, it is only the collective right of self-determination or, more specifically, the communal right to existence, which provides the grounds for denying the sovereignty of a larger collective. It is surely this qualification that separates Walzer from the other plural-ists such as Jackson because it distinguishes him as a communitarian rather than a statist. For Jackson, it is not communal autonomy that is primary but rather the institutional structure of the modern state and the society of states, which provides the only viable form of world order and therefore the possibility of any international ethics at all.

In contrast to the qualified support of pluralists, cosmopolitan writers have a different set of ethical issues to address. Cosmopolitans reject the pluralist claim that order is sufficient justification for not intervening, For example, Caney (2005: 240) argues that 'Appeals to international order are . . . incomplete and need to be supplemented by an argument showing that the international system is fair and morally legitimate.'

Simon Caney argues that cosmopolitan approaches to humanitarian intervention have two forms, the standard and the liberal egalitarian arguments. The standard argument involves four assumptions:

1: all persons have fundamental interests
2: political institutions do not have value except insofar as they respect these interests

3: external agents have duties to protect people's fundamental interests
4: External intervention is occasionally required as an effective means for protecting these interests. (2005: 233)

The liberal egalitarian model claims that 'persons have political human rights . . . and economic human rights . . . political institutions . . . have worth only so of far as they protect these values . . . given that all persons have duties to respect and protect these human rights it follows that intervention is justified when it could successfully protect these rights' (Caney 2005: 235). In keeping with this logic, Moellendorf claims that 'just cause for the use of military force exists if and only if the intervention is directed toward advancing justice in the basic structure of the state or the international effects of it domestic policy' (2002: 159). Thus, cosmopolitan law overrides the state's automatic right of self-defence (norm of non-intervention). This does not in itself justify any particular intervention; instead, it removes the automatic presumption of sovereign inviolability from intervention.

Ultimately, if the intervention is going to cause more harm than it prevents, then it is not justifiable. For cosmopolitans, humanitarian intervention therefore also needs to meet the other criteria of Just War, especially proportionality, last resort, right authority and reasonable chance of success. Caney makes his cosmopolitan case for humanitarian intervention in such terms of just cause, proportionality, least awful measure, reasonable chance of meeting success and legitimate authority. He reformulates each of these with cosmopolitan components (see below). According to Caney (2005: 251), there are five conditions that must be met for an act of humanitarian intervention to be considered legitimate:

1 When it is against a regime that is violating human rights (both economic and social).
2 Proportionality; the costs cannot be 'disproportionate in comparison to internal wrongs' which the intervention is addressing.
3 Humanitarian intervention resorted to only when least awful options have been considered. For instance, it could be argued that economic sanctions, or doing nothing, could both result in more awful results than humanitarian intervention. In other words, the different costs of different harms have to be measured, including the harm of doing nothing.
4 Humanitarian intervention must have a reasonable chance of meeting its objective, that is, of preventing the violation of human rights or preventing a worse violation of human rights than might otherwise occur.

5 Right authority. Ideally, this means an 'impartial transnational political authority'. (Caney disagrees with Moellendorf on this clause, and argues that in the absence of such a legitimatizing authority the intervenors require 'as wide and ecumenical a coalition of support as possible'.)

Caney's revision of the Just War clauses in relation to humanitarian intervention serves two functions. First, it serves to deflect or diffuse the possibility of a cosmopolitan crusade to enforce a human rights regime universally. It also, by placing rights as the basic criteria, employs wider criteria than Moellendorf's argument. By making conformity with a Rawlsian basic structure as the criteria, Moellendorf's argument opens the door to an interventionary, crusading foreign policy that is incompatible with cosmopolitan values identified by Kant, for example. In contrast, Caney's reinterpretation of the Just War clauses provides evidence of the underlying flexibility and adaptability of Just War thinking, and in particular of its uses as a brake on war. Caney's approach to humanitarian intervention is much closer to the spirit of Just War thinking because it recognizes that while justice might require the use of force on occasion, this should be the exception rather than the rule. Overall, however, liberal cosmopolitans see the JWT as a means for achieving justice or, at the very least, they see achieving justice as the ultimate, and only, justification for warfare.

Kantian cosmopolitans such as David Held, Jürgen Habermas and Andrew Linklater all argue that the Just War provisions seeking to limit recourse to war are incomplete until they are legitimized in a cosmopolitan institutional and legal framework. Under such a framework, the use of violence becomes an instrument of law and not foreign policy. As such, it is also constrained by that law and is made more accountable. Within this framework, doubts about intentions and causes are minimized by the specification and legalization of the legitimate use of force according to cosmopolitan rules. In this form, violations of human rights, including the targeting of civilians by terrorists and states, are to be treated as criminal offences subject to the law.

The thrust of the argument here is to focus on the procedural and democratic legitimacy of international institutions which authorize the use of force. In the meantime, this means that humanitarian and other interventions must approximate legitimacy not just in terms of their possible consequences, say, the removal of a dictator, but in terms of degree to which they can command an authoritative international consensus and not just a 'coalition of the willing' (see Habermas 1999: 2003).

Finally, humanitarian intervention raises the question of whether a greater harm or injustice may be committed by not acting. Is doing nothing or failing to act the same as committing harm? If by not doing something, a bad result occurs, such as a death, are we responsible in the same way as if we ourselves directly cause the death? Certainly, the history of international inaction suggests that most states have few qualms about doing nothing, thus endorsing inaction as a morally acceptable practice. However, on the other hand, it is clear that most traditions of ethical thought argue that the principle of mutual aid, or beneficence, means that if we can act without causing serious harm to ourselves then we would be wrong not to act to help another. This suggests that mutual aid provides an answer to the question of the moral justification of humanitarian intervention in general.

While the JWT provides useful guidelines for assessing the recourse to humanitarian intervention, it does not actually provide an adequate justification. Such a moral justification, as Terry Nardin (2002b) notes, must come from outside the JWT. This raises the possibility that, in keeping with the discussion of humanitarianism in the previous chapter, humanitarian intervention should be understood as a form of mutual aid. This chapter has demonstrated that mutual aid has played little role in the discussion about Just War or humanitarian intervention. However, as in the discussion of humanitarianism more generally, mutual aid is a useful term in helping to overcome the limitations of rights thinking and of justice-based arguments. The advantage of using mutual aid in the context of the JWT is that it permits action in the aid of others, outsiders, while limiting the nature of that assistance, preventing it from turning into imperialism or an over-permissive criteria of justification. Thus, humanitarian intervention should be understood as acts of assistance rather than of 'justice' in the strict sense. The purpose of military action against another country is to stop violence or prevent it being used against 'innocents' (Nardin 2002b), and not to impose a just basic structure.

The Kantian principle of mutual aid could be interpreted as supporting a practice of humanitarian intervention. To do so, however, it would have to be able to reconcile the duty of aid with the necessity of killing and, therefore, of using others as means to an end. As Nardin explains, this is possible because mutual aid (or what he calls common morality) allows us 'to defend the rights of others when those rights are threatened' (Nardin 2002b: 65). Defending these rights on occasion requires the use of violence because mutual aid is a duty 'to employ force against the violent if their victims cannot otherwise be protected' (Donagan, in Nardin 2002b: 66). In other words, humanitarian intervention is primarily an action of self-defence undertaken by others on the victim's behalf. Such a Kantian view dictates that any interventions be limited to the minimum force and engagement necessary to cease attacks or persecution. It is not clear, however, if that duty then also extends to a duty of reconstruction or a *just post bellum*. This suggests that projects such as spreading liberal democracy, or a 'just basic structure', fall outside the purview of humanitarian intervention or indeed the JWT in general.

The limitations of JWT

For as long as there has been a JWT there have been critics of the tradition. The most long-standing critical frameworks are pacificism and realism. Pacifists reject entirely the possibility of an ethical use of violence. On the other hand, realists reject the possibility of restraining violence of ethical reasons. However, between these two positions there have been others, including the Kantian cosmopolitans who reject the solution to the ethics of violence offered by the JWT. This section briefly discusses some of the criticism of the JWT itself and in particular its claim to represent an acceptable compromise between the violence of war and ethics.

The first major objection to the JWT is that it fails in its aim of providing a brake on states' actions and in limiting the instances and the manner of the use of force. Instead, it is argued that the effect of the JWT is to legitimate war and in particular the ethics of military necessity. Thus, as Anthony Burke (2004: 330) argues, 'moral discourses are part of the warrior's political armoury; they are party of war's machinery, not a rod in its wheels'. Burke suggests that 'Just War theory invokes concepts like "proportionality" and the "double effect" to remove thousands of people from the space of moral concern' (2004: 352). Therefore, the JWT is 'not completely adequate to the problem and phenomenon of war' (332).

In the absence of standards that ultimately aim to avoid the use of force, the JWT seems to continue to encourage the legitimation and entrenchment of the use of war by states. The basic argument here is that by trying to make tame and civilize war, we also contribute to its permanence. In other words, international 'legal efforts to regulate war have often come to sanction the behaviour they were ostensibly designed to prevent' (Jochnick and Normand 1994: 51, 58). This sets up a tension or a feedback loop where war is further defended on the grounds that it can be made just or fought humanely. Jochnick and Normand claim that 'the laws of war have been formulated deliberately to privilege military necessity at the cost of Humanitarian values. As a result the rules of war have facilitated rather than restrained wartime violence' (1994: 50).

The liberal cosmopolitanism of Moellendorf et al. is not exempt from the charge that 'the rule of law helps protect the entire structure of war-making from more fundamental challenges' (Jochnick and Normand 1994: 58). Liberal cosmopolitanism gives licence for liberal interventionism, because there is a prima facie case for war whenever there exists a society with an unjust basic structure. Likewise, Buchanan and Keohane (2004) offer an institutional cosmopolitan proposal for a regime, which makes preventive intervention in cases of massive violations of basic human rights conditional on a higher degree of cosmopolitan accountability. The aim of this model is to provide cosmopolitan elements which update Just War thinking but which also improve upon it by granting human rights priority over sovereignty. However, the rider that comes with Buchanan's and Keohane's argument is that liberal states will have special privileges as a result of their higher degree of internal legitimacy. The problem here is that not only does this invoke a hierarchical conception of international order (Reus Smit 2005) but also that it continues the same trajectory of the JWT by further institutionalizing the right of war. Buchanan and Keohane share a relatively sanguine view of the role and legitimacy of force in international life. So long as decisions to use force are reached through a specified procedure, and its use is limited by ethical constraints, the use of force is both normatively right and practically effective (Buchanan and Keohane 2004: 82).

These criticisms reveal the differences between Kantian and liberal (Rawlsian) cosmopolitanism. The Kantian claim is that, by legitimating war and its associated roles, the JWT serves to perpetuate war not limit it. Specifically, the JWT does not envisage a means to work for perpetual peace or to make war obsolete. In so doing, the JWT continues to provide a justification for warfare itself and not just individual wars.

Returning to Kant's perpetual peace, we recall that he argued that war presented a basic violation of the categorical imperative because it reduces people to the means of others' ends and prevents the exercise of universal freedom. In this light, the cosmopolitan aim is to make warfare impossible. Putting it differently, the aim of cosmopolitan theory is perpetual peace, which is not just a break in the cycle of violence but an end of it. The liberal cosmopolitan theorists who grapple with the problem of Just War have in many cases forgotten or denied this purpose. The goal ought not to be that of making violence and war more acceptable, but to see it ended. If war was seen as basically unjust and a problem to be eradicated, then it would generate different outcomes. The Kantian solution was to create peace through the example of the pacific federation, not through force or conversion (Kant 1795/1983).

Anthony Burke argues that the JWT needs to be replaced by the ideal of 'ethical peace', which works not to limit strategic violence but eradicate it (2004: 349). Ethical peace is more in keeping with Kant's moral vision because it 'imagines a universal moral community in which no ethical obligation can be traded away in times of emergency, and no humans can be put in mortal danger so that others may be safe' (Burke 2004: 333). The central clauses of the JWT would need to be rethought so as to facilitate this vision and not the vision of 'just' war. The value of ethical peace is not restricted to *jus ad bellum* but includes the *jus in bello* principles. In this context, the bar for acceptable violence needs to be raised so that the law of double effect no longer applies and proportionality is rejected, meaning that all 'avoidable death and suffering are condemned and prosecuted' (Burke 2004: 344). An account of ethical peace would be informed by a more robust cosmopolitan harm principle which would 'declare the illegality of *avoidable* harm' (Burke 2004: 551). For instance, in the case of the January 2009 Israeli attacks on the Gaza strip (and the Hamas attacks on Israel), ethical peace would have made such an action impossible without a clear case that it was necessitous, and not just prudent or expedient. This argument is also consistent with the feminist ethics of care which would seek to raise the bar so that any actor seeking to use war for political purposes would be accountable for *all* the harm they cause (Sjoberg 2006).

Following the line of argument suggested at the conclusion of the last section, a Kantian approach to the JWT would posit only a right of self-defence as just cause. Self-defence allows states and communities to defend their autonomy against violence but also to come to the aid of the 'innocent' victims of aggression abroad. Thus, humanitarian intervention should be understood as a defensive rather than an aggressive just cause if undertaken in this limited way. Such a formulation prevents the abuse of the JWT by those wishing to justify wars of conquest or liberal reform, while still allowing a cosmopolitan response to needs of foreign victims.

Conclusion

This chapter has discussed the content and purpose of the JWT from both cosmopolitan and pluralist positions. It has demonstrated the contradiction that lies at the heart of the pluralist account of Just War and international ethical life and demonstrated that this contradiction can only be resolved by employing a cosmopolitan framework. At the same time, while states may use the JWT to justify a variety of actions, Bellamy is most likely correct that the JWT as it is most commonly interpreted provides little ammunition for states to wage aggressive wars. In this way, the JWT is compatible with cosmopolitanism. However, this chapter has also demonstrated that liberal cosmopolitanism as offered by Moellendorf and Caney remains insufficient from a Kantian perspective because it opens the way for wars of liberation and this implies at least a continued legitimacy for interstate war as long as cosmopolitan goals are upheld.

At the same time, critiques of the JWT demonstrate that higher thresholds should be set to further constrain the use of force and seek to find a way out of the cycle of legitimating and entrenching war. Thus, the JWT provides many useful ways of thinking about the ethics of war but it does not exhaust them. To be truly consistent with a cosmopolitan ethics, and indeed with the pluralist concern with cultural autonomy, all communities must be able to be secured from the threat of arbitrary violence from outsiders and domestic sources. The rights of communities and individuals can only be guaranteed when war itself has become illegitimate.

7

Impermissible Harms: Global Poverty and Global Justice

For the first time in human history it is quite feasible, economically to wipe out hunger and preventable diseases worldwide without real inconvenience to anyone.

Pogge 2002: 14

Is hunger a misfortune which calls for beneficence and help? . . . or is ending hunger a matter of justice?

O'Neill 1986: 3

Introduction

The early years of the twenty-first century have been unusual from the international perspective because they have witnessed, for possibly the first time in human history, a near global awareness that the vast differences in life chances, quality of life and standards of living between the rich and the poor *globally* is a matter of political and ethical significance for everybody. In 2000, members of the UN signed up to the UN Millennium Goals. The UN millennium goals were a response to the idea that global poverty was a serious challenge for the international system and that something could be done about it collectively. This campaign has been accompanied by a high-profile public campaign called Make Poverty History, intended to keep the eyes of the world focused on the task.

This chapter addresses the ethical issues arising from the existence of severe widespread poverty, or destitution (understood as the point at which life is unsustainable), on a global scale (see Nandy 2002 on the distinction between poverty and destitution). The focus of this chapter is in understanding exactly what type of moral problem global poverty presents and for whom, and on assessing the different responses to it. Recognizing the existence of global poverty provokes the question of whose (moral) responsibility is it? That is: 'who has what obligations to end the everyday suffering of millions of people'? Another way of thinking about this is to ask: is poverty in fact a global problem, for everyone, or is it primarily a problem for the people of poor countries? The issue of severe global poverty or destitution provides perhaps the most important moral challenge to the view that compatriots should always or automatically take priority over outsiders and humanity. If we indeed argue that severe poverty, or destitution, is primarily a local problem then we are effectively abandoning the poor to their fate. Given the numbers of people today classified as destitute this is, to say the least, morally troubling.

Without a doubt, most academic attempts to address the problem of global poverty rely upon or are derived from some or other account of distributive justice: the distribution of rights, duties and material resources. The issue of global justice has perhaps more than any other helped to define liberal cosmopolitanism over and against anti-cosmopolitanism. As David Miller (2002: 976) notes, cosmopolitans and anti-cosmopolitans differ thus: 'cosmopolitans advocate global principles of distributive justice, anti-cosmopolitans hold that distributive principles only apply within nations and other smaller communities'. This would suggest that anti-cosmopolitans are indeed willing to abandon the poor to their fate. However, while such a conclusion might seem to follow logically from the 'communitarian' rejection of universalism, it would not accurately portray the position of many anti-cosmopolitans. The chief difference between cosmopolitans and anti-cosmopolitans in the case of global poverty concerns whether global poverty is subject to justice, or whether it is covered by natural duties or humanitarianism. In other words, the argument is over whether global poverty is the subject of mutual aid, beneficence or justice?

Deciding on this matter requires answering a number of questions. What are the circumstances of justice and do they apply in the case of global poverty? If they do not exist, then what if any obligations or duties do the rich have to the poor? In addition, because poverty is a moral question it also requires an analysis of the nature of moral obligation and its relationship to questions of causation and capacity. In other words, what role does cause play in assessing responsibility?

This chapter begins with a discussion of world poverty and some historical background. It then discusses the liberal cosmopolitan claim that Rawlsian principles of distributive justice are global and the anti-cosmopolitan critique of this claim. For anti-cosmopolitans, global *inequality* is not in itself a morally troubling issue because different societies value the distribution of resources differently. Global *poverty*, however, remains a serious moral problem and anti-cosmopolitans argue that a policy of basic rights and natural duties, mutual aid and the commitment to do no harm, can address it adequately. The next sections demonstrate that a far-reaching account of global justice can be derived from natural duties and basic rights. In particular, it will be demonstrated that the strongest arguments for responsibilities to address global poverty extend from cosmopolitan readings of the principles of mutual aid and the duty to do no harm, and these are reconcilable with the values of communal autonomy and cultural diversity.

Historical background

The emergence of a truly global international system in the twentieth century brought with it a consciousness for many, for the first time, that there might be good reason for considering ourselves to have binding moral obligations to people in all parts of the world. As we have seen, this was not a new thought. The Stoics, the Christians and Kant all worked on the argument that the human species was indivisible. However, these voices were less appealing when there was little or no sense that the world was actually interconnected. What happened in faraway places was the concern of those directly and perceptibly affected by them. Arguably, this was because prior to nineteenth-century imperialism, and twentieth-century globalization, the impact of many human decisions was felt by relatively few. A decision made in an imperial capital could affect the lives of millions of subjects, but a decision made in an Indian or Polynesian village, for instance, was not seen to have any appreciable impact on the imperial core.

In the twentieth century, and especially the late twentieth century, the emergence of a global trading system and the global rules under the GATT, along with decolonization, brought about an awareness that economically and politically there was a degree of global interdependence and unity. Decisions made in any part of the world could have an impact and, more importantly still, be seen to have an impact upon people in almost any other part of the world. So what happened in an Indian village (or in a million Indian villages) was seen to be of some importance to people beyond that village.

The emergence of a global trading regime after the Second World War, along with the difficulties that many newly independent countries faced in competing in this regime, raised the issue of global justice in two ways. First, there might be an obligation on behalf of the former colonial powers to make some redress for the costs borne by their former subjects. Continued poverty and economic underdevelopment in the third world were seen to be a result of imperialism and therefore there was a degree of historical restitution, or retributive justice, with a responsibility to compensate on the part of imperialists.

At the same time, in the economically developed parts of the world the post-Second World War period saw the triumph of the welfare state. The welfare state encapsulated the rejection of the nineteenth-century idea that 'the poor are always with us' and the complacency that such a belief engenders. Instead, the post-war period was characterized by the idea that solutions could be found to both domestic and international problems, which previously had been thought irresolvable. Poverty in many first-world countries was drastically reduced in the economic boom following the Second World War and by the adoption of welfare practices targeting the poor in these states.

In this context, many people began to argue that the obligation to end poverty was not one that ended at the national border but extended across the globe. This development was spurred on by the recognition of increasing levels of economic interdependence between states. Indeed, the contemporary debate about global justice can be characterized as a debate that focuses on the nature of the moral obligations arising from economic interdependence. In turn, the different arguments regarding global justice extend from different accounts of the nature of this economic interdependence.

The extent of hunger inequality and poverty

In order to understand why many think that global poverty is a moral issue for everyone, it is best to begin with what is currently known about the extent and nature of poverty, understood on a global scale. According to Thomas Pogge, citing the World Development Report, '[A]bout one-quarter of all human beings alive today, 1.5 billion, subsist below the international poverty line' (2001: 7). The poverty line is defined as the level of 'income or expenditure below which a minimum nutritionally adequate diet plus essential non-food requirements are not affordable' (UNDP 1996: 222, cited in Pogge 2001b). According to Pogge, this means that 790 million persons are malnourished, 'while one billion are without adequate shelter and two billion without electricity' (2001b: 8). The extent of global poverty and hunger and the unequal distribution of the world's wealth means that starvation and preventable diseases cause about one third of all human deaths, which was about 18 million in 1988. Pogge points out that this contrasts with the estimated number of deaths due to war at 588,000 and 'other homicides and violence' at 736,000 (2001b: 9).[1]

These figures point to the extent of severe poverty around the globe, understood as the capacity to maintain basic health and bodily integrity. Severe poverty of this type and extent, on this scale, should in itself be a cause for concern because of the sheer amount of human suffering it involves. This is further increased if we also examine the distribution of wealth globally. Poverty, or destitution, is cause for concern because of the human suffering involved, but it may be that there is not enough wealth to go around to end it. If this were the case, then it might be possible to say that indeed the 'poor are always with us' and that there is little that can be done until such time as population and resources are in balance.

While that may have been the case at a certain time in the past, an analysis of contemporary distribution of wealth suggests it is no longer so. Looking at the same statistics in another way, the global distribution of wealth is hugely unequal and the gap between the richest and poorest people in the world is not closing but is becoming greater. According to Pogge, 'The income gap between the fifth of the world's people living in the richest countries and the fifth in the poorest was 74 to 1 in 1997, up from 60 to 1 in 1990 and 30 to 1 in 1960' (2001b: 13). This amounts to a situation in which 'the collective income of the bottom quintile is about US$100 billion annually, or one-third of one percent of the annual global product, the high income economies have 14.9 percent of world population and 78.4 percent of the global product' (2004: 18). In other words, 'one percent of our collective income is equivalent to 235 percent of theirs' (Pogge 2004: 34–5).[2]

The conclusion to be drawn from these figures is that the problem of poverty is not getting better despite the global economic boom period of the last twenty years. Nor has the end of the Cold War delivered the peace dividend that was hoped for, while it had (at least until September 2001) meant a decline in military spending overall. That means the benefits of the current international order have not flowed to the poorest persons. What this level of inequality illustrates is not that there is not enough wealth to go around, but that the existing wealth is distributed unequally, and not just unequally, but grossly unequally.

Therefore it ought to be possible to redistribute resources and wealth in order to eradicate severe global poverty; 'with this tremendous upsurge in global inequality comes a dramatic increase in human capabilities to eliminate severe poverty' (Pogge 2002b: 152). Furthermore, many argue it can be done without a devastating or even significant cost to the most developed countries.

However, it is by no means obvious to everyone that the mere existence of inequality, poverty and hunger means that those with the capacity to alleviate them have an obligation to do so. Furthermore, once an obligation has been established, the question then arises of how that obligation can be fulfilled, how far it extends and what it consists of. The next sections explore these questions.

Cosmopolitanism: justice and global poverty

Justice is a term that has many meanings and can be used in many ways. Hedley Bull, in his much discussed 'Hagey Lectures', used it to refer to what is more commonly known as international ethics (Bull 1983). Lawyers use the term to denote conformity with legal rulings and process, in the sense that justice has been done when the law has been followed and upheld. However, for political philosophers, justice is associated with the values of fairness and equality. Justice as a general concept means to treat like cases alike and to treat people according to fair rules. Fairness of this sort is embodied in the value of equality, because to treat people equally means to treat them in a like fashion. Therefore, for political philosophers, justice is usually related to the value of equality of all human beings. Justice occurs when people are treated equally by political, economic and social institutions and laws. Much of political philosophy has been concerned with discussing how people are equal and how this equality should be recognized in law and society. Justice can also be discussed in terms of substantive and procedural justice. Substantive justice refers to the equality of outcomes and the distribution of wealth or power, that is, distributive justice. Procedural justice refers to a fair procedure for deciding who should get what. For example, a world in which there was no poverty might be considered substantively just, but if that situation was arrived at by discriminating against certain categories of people then we might think it was unjust in a procedural sense.

Cosmopolitan responses to the existence of massive and severe poverty on a global scale can be understood as primarily either moral cosmopolitan or global egalitarian. Global egalitarian accounts are dominated by Rawlsian liberals who are concerned with justice as distributive justice. These authors express a technical concern with getting the theory of justice right. Rawls argued that justice begins with the 'basic structure' of society, by which he meant 'the way in which the major social institutions distribute fundamental rights and duties and determine the division of advantages from social cooperation' (Rawls 1972: 7; see chapter 2). Global egalitarianism extends from principles that are internal to this conception of justice.

On the other hand, moral cosmopolitanism responds to the recognition of gross inequality and of certain moral emergencies, such as the existence of massive global poverty. These types of arguments state that there exist responsibilities to act to alleviate suffering. They are motivated by action, what it is right to do, rather than simply with what is right in theory. Kantianism and utilitarianism are both moral cosmopolitan approaches. The most important question raised by these accounts is whether the rich have an obligation to the poor because they are rich, or because they can help, or whether such responsibilities flow from the role the rich may have played in causing or maintaining poverty in poor countries. This contrasts with the global egalitarian account, which focuses on whether distributive justice applies globally, that is, if the conditions of distributive justice are present at the global level. Understanding this difference is helpful in making sense of the sometimes technical nature of the debate and in clarifying what is at stake for different authors.

Of course, there is no clear division between these two approaches and both draw upon each other, while the arguments of the first are certainly made more compelling by the existence of the second. The basic common position here is that the world exhibits inequality and that there are substantive obligations to address this inequality, especially in the case of global poverty. Discussion of this aspect necessarily leads, as we shall see, to discussion of the first type: if there is global inequality, to what extent ought we to design new principles of international political order which will prevent or alleviate it?

In other words, there is an obligation on all those who are able to address and eradicate global poverty and gross inequality. Utilitarians and contractarian deontologists all agree on this point. However, within this, there are substantive disagreements about how these obligations are derived, and how they might be carried out. The question, then, is not merely how to address global poverty. It seems pretty clear a relatively minor shift of wealth from rich to poor could do this. The question is, rather, what principles ought to provide the basis of a global account of justice and the problem of global poverty?

The contractarian account

The liberal cosmopolitan account of global distributive justice, largely inspired by and derived from a broadly Rawlsian account of justice, has been the most comprehensive attempt to deal with this issue in the international realm. Consequently, it has also provoked the most comment and criticism and, as already stated, has provided the focus for the anti-cosmopolitan rejection of cosmopolitanism. This section discusses the liberal claim that a Rawlsian account of justice can be unproblematically globalized, before moving on to the anti-cosmopolitan rejection of this argument.

The basics of the contractarian account of cosmopolitanism were set out in chapter 2. For liberals like Charles Beitz, the requirement to develop an egalitarian global basic structure flows from the account of justice developed by Rawls, and the most common approaches to global justice have, until very recently, been applications of Rawls's theory of justice. Thomas Pogge, Brian Barry and Simon Caney begin with certain Rawlsian presuppositions, even if they do not agree with Rawls's conclusions regarding the composition of a basic structure. What they all agree upon is that any account of justice must be cosmopolitan, in the sense defined by Pogge. In other words, it must be universalist, individualist and impartial. These criteria mean that justice is global or, alternatively, any account of distributive justice that does not address it from a global position is seriously deficient.

For the purposes of this section, there are two components that are relevant here. The Rawlsian approaches argue that the essential features of Rawls's account were universalizable. From this, it follows that cosmopolitans concerned with global justice are predominantly, but not exclusively, concerned with the basic structure of global society, that is, with the ways in which the rules of global order distribute rights, duties and the benefits of social cooperation (i.e., economic activity). For these liberals, Rawls's substantive accounts of justice, as well as his mechanism for arriving at it, provide the criteria for assessing injustice globally and for envisaging a different world order.

Because justice is universal, the difference principle must apply globally to individuals and not states. What ultimately matters is how poor or badly off you are *in the world*, and not just in your own country. Justice requires a system in which all the rules are organized to maximize the outcome of the worst off globally. The basic structure of international relations should be governed, not by inter-state principles, but by cosmopolitan ones that address the inequalities between individuals rather than states. Justice involves 'a just and stable institutional scheme preserving a distribution of basic rights, opportunities and . . . goods that is fair both globally and within each nation' (Pogge 1989: 256). In this regard, liberal Rawlsians agree with Singer and other cosmopolitans 'that we should value equality between societies, and at the global level as much as we value political equality within one society' (Singer 2002: 190). They come to this conclusion by arguing that we must begin with a cosmopolitan original position, not just a national one. There is no need for a second contract between the representatives of peoples because the first 'original' one will necessarily be universally inclusive.

Beitz's argument was that we should consider the world economy a single 'system of social cooperation' in the Rawlsian sense. Therefore, Rawlsian accounts of justice ought to apply to the globe as a whole. As noted in chapter 2, most critics believe that Rawls's conclusions do not follow from his argument and that he is open to much more cosmopolitan interpretations (see chapter 2 and below). According to these authors, there is nothing within the Rawlsian framework that suggests the need to restrict its account of justice to the domestic state. Indeed, there are grounds from within Rawls's approach that lead us to *necessarily* take a cosmopolitan stand, if we accept his other arguments. The Rawlsian account is universalizable for at least two reasons: first because of its account of the nature of the moral person, and, second, because of the economic interdependence of the global system (see chapter 2).

Perhaps the most important aspect of Rawlsian cosmopolitanism is this second claim that it is no longer possible to justify treating states as self-enclosed separate isolated systems. Beitz, Pogge, Moellendorf and most other critics argue that empirically and analytically Rawls's assumptions about enclosed autonomous states simply don't add up. Instead, there is a single global economic network of interdependence. States are intricately interconnected and very few, if any, can claim to be entirely outside the global economic order. For Beitz, once this is recognized, the original position can be globalized. As a result, we can claim that the equivalent of a scheme for mutual gain exists and that 'all that is required [for justice] is that interdependence produce benefits and burdens' (Beitz 1979: 153). Therefore, given that we have an interdependent global economic order that produces benefits and burdens, it follows that the principles of justice apply. More recently, Beitz has emphasized that global inequality and poverty, increasing interdependence, articulation of international institutions and regimes, and the emergence of a global civil society combine to create the condition of a global basic structure (Beitz 1999).

For global egalitarians, Rawlsian method provides the criteria by which the international economic order can be judged and by which global inequality can be interpreted and responsibility for it assigned. From a cosmopolitan Rawlsian position, the basic structure of international society is profoundly unjust and in need of transformation. The existence of massive and severe global poverty represents a failure of the international order to meet standards of justice. Once we accept Rawls's criterion of the difference principle that all inequalities must benefit the position of the worst off, it then follows upon examination that the international order is unjust and in need of reformulation. The second part of Rawls's theory then comes into play here as it provides the basis of that reordering. The structure of international trade and economic interdependence should ensure that, despite an unequal distribution of material resources worldwide, no one should be unable meet their basic requirements; nor should they suffer disproportionately from the lack of material resources. While Beitz, Pogge and Moellendorf have some differences over the exact mechanisms for addressing inequalities, they nonetheless agree that the rules must improve the conditions of the least well-off members of the human race – that is, 'it is the globally least advantaged representative person . . . whose position is to be maximized' (Beitz 1979: 152).

The fundamental insight to be drawn from the Rawlsian cosmopolitan account is that it attempts to provide a single set of criteria by which global inequality, including severe poverty, can be assessed, and an argument that the conditions for meeting those criteria are existent. We can also recall that Rawls stated there is a duty to create a just basic structure. Global egalitarianism does not extend directly from a recognition of the needs of the poorest peoples or any particular moral emergency. At its simplest, it can be understood as a claim that we ought to live in a just world order, followed by a consequent claim about what that order might look like. It is, in a sense, independent of any empirical inequality or injustice in the current system. It is concerned with defining principles that are just in and of themselves, and about defining the principles and procedures for a just community that happens to be global. For cosmopolitan Rawlsians, this means there is a consequent duty to reform the international order and create a just global basic structure. Both of these claims are either rejected or seriously qualified by the communitarian and pluralist arguments.

Anti-cosmopolitan critics of global distributive justice

Simon Caney has identified three types of anti-cosmopolitan position on global distributive justice: the nationalist, the society of states (pluralist) and the realist. For our purposes, it is the nationalist and the pluralist accounts which have most to say about the problem of global poverty. All three, as has already been noted in chapter 3, rely upon broadly speaking communitarian assumptions and therefore reject the broad cosmopolitan claim that morality is necessarily universal, individualist and impartial. Therefore, they also reject the basis for Beitz's claim that global duties of distributive justice exist. In Walzer's terminology, distributive justice involves the imposition of thick moralities and constitutes a too-thick conception of universal morality.

The most important thing to note about the anti-cosmopolitan position on global poverty is that it is almost entirely structured as a response to the Rawlsian accounts of global distributive justice. Indeed, for Miller, cosmopolitanism and global distributive justice are virtually synonymous. For anti-cosmopolitans, the problem of global poverty cannot be met by any single scheme of global distributive justice, and indeed they dispute the idea that there is any substantive global or international responsibility to develop a universal scheme of distributive justice. However, this is not the end of the issue because, they argue, we can still recognize duties to the global starving, such as mutual aid, that come from other less ambitious accounts of morality.

The anti-cosmopolitan position is in part a response to the liberal conception of justice as impartial, universal and individualistic, wherein national or communal allegiances are irrelevant and arbitrary from a moral (impartial) point of view. Thus, starting with an account of cosmopolitanism as an impartial, universal and egalitarian position, Beitz et al. end up with a fairly 'thick' account of justice derived from within the framework of twentieth-century American liberalism. Because they accept the basic principles of Rawlsian liberalism, but reject its limited scope, cosmopolitanism becomes globalized (Rawlsian) liberalism. Their critics, and Rawls himself, identify this project as the universalization of a culturally particular conception of justice with dubious applicability to other societies.

National duties and natural duties

Caney (2001a: 980) argues that common to the 'nationalist' anti-cosmopolitan thesis are three claims: what might be termed the 'national duties' thesis; the 'viability' thesis; and the 'allocation of duty' thesis. These three claim, first, that national compatriots take first priority, and, second, that the conditions necessary for a global account of distributive justice are non-existent (a single global political community or state), therefore the project is not viable, and, third, that the responsibility for meeting justice globally is allocated to individual nation-states and not a world system or world authority. In the national duties thesis, 'individuals bear special obligations of distributive justice to other members of their nation' (Caney 2001a: 980). That is, we owe some things first and foremost to our own nationals and sometimes to the exclusion of outsiders. These duties are generated by, for Miller, shared national culture and history and by a claim that it is primarily within nations that economic exchange occurs and goods are distributed; that is, that nations represent systems of social cooperation in Rawls's model.

The second thesis states that Justice requires a state and/or a shared culture that provide the basic values from which principles are determined. For the critics of global justice, these conditions simply do not apply globally: 'systems of distributive justice, to be feasible, must map onto national communities and hence that global systems of distributive justice are unworkable' (Caney 2001a: 981). In other words, nations provide the conditions of possibility for justice, because they provide the common normative framework and shared social practices that distributive justice requires. Indeed, they are exacerbated by the sheer diversity of different conceptions of the 'good' across the world. Distributive justice can only occur within a single, sovereign state; we may call this the Hobbesian clause, and it is in a sense prior to the viability clause (see Nagel 2005). It is really a condition of possibility clause. Global distributive justice is unviable because there is not and cannot be, or is unlikely to be, any global state or any global political community from which it can be grounded or enforced.

The allocation of duties argument contains two components. The first is that responsibility for distributive justice and addressing poverty is a national responsibility. It is the duty of individual nations to fulfil their obligations to their own members first. David Miller agrees with the claim that individuals have rights – a 'human right to liberty, security and subsistence' (Shue's basic rights), but the responsibility for fulfilling this right lies primarily, in the first instance, with fellow nationals (Miller 2007). For Miller, the primacy of national responsibility also involves the claim that 'we are not in most cases required by justice to intervene to safeguard the human rights of foreigners' (1988: 80). Thus, global justice understood in terms of the recognition of basic rights is best served by national schemes rather than cosmopolitan or global ones. The second significant aspect of the allocation thesis is the recognition of transnational natural duties of 'humanitarianism' or mutual aid. Where there are transborder duties, they are of these limited kinds.

Somewhat ironically, it is Rawls himself who has provided the most stark account of the pluralist (or social liberal) account of global justice in *The Law of Peoples* (1999). Rawls has systematized the general pluralist and 'nationalist' argument against global distributive justice, and in so doing provides a clear account of why these duties do not apply globally and what obligations take their place. The most important thing that Rawls does is to make clear the underlying assumptions of the anti-cosmopolitan position regarding responsibility. Rawls makes it clear that national, not global, societies bear both causal responsibility and curative, or moral, responsibility for poverty.

Rawls and the international

According to Rawls, liberal states have no cosmopolitan duties to globalize their own conception of distributive justice (1999). The Rawlsian theory of justice is based on an assumption about its compatibility with certain values, the reflective equilibrium of values common to liberal, and particularly American, society. As such, it is an account of justice for liberal societies. Rawls's concern in *The Law of Peoples* is not with an account of justice but with the principles that ought to guide a liberal state in its relationships with other 'decent', but not necessarily liberal, states. According to Rawls, a decent liberal state has no duty to globalize its conception of distributive justice or of liberalism itself. Liberal states must accept the fact of reasonable pluralism and acknowledge the possibility that non-liberal accounts of justice might be acceptable.

It follows from this that they have only limited responsibilities to address global poverty. Ultimately, for Rawls, it is not the extent of economic interaction that determines the bounds of moral obligation, but the norms that govern basic institutions. The origins of Rawls's account in a specific liberal tradition which is the heritage of the Western Enlightenment undermines any claim to cross cultural appeal which might allow it to form the basis of a 'thick' global over-lapping consensus. This restriction of his own principle extends from the recognition that the conception of the moral person upon which his theory is based is not uncontested and therefore can only be uni-versalized problematically. Even if economic interdependence existed to the extent claimed by Beitz et al., fundamental cultural differ-ences mean that the Rawlsian account of justice would be unable to resonate at a global level. In other words, not only is there no global political culture, but there is also radical value incommensurability.[3] So, while the parties to the second contracting session of decent socie-ties can agree on some quite substantive values, they are not capable of agreeing on principles of distributive justice.

Equally importantly, Rawls argued that justice is only possible in the presence of a 'system of social cooperation for mutual gain' which produces a surplus product. He argues that the international realm does not resemble a system for mutual advantage. Instead, controversially, he proposes that societies are to be understood in isolation, as if they have only minimal impact upon each other, and are therefore only minimally bound together by webs of interdepend-ence. For Rawls, communities are restricted in their interactions and so restricted in their obligations. The conditions required for global distributive justice are not present. There is no global system of cooperation or any thick global political culture, and no morally significant economic interactions between communities. Therefore, the best that can be hoped for is a 'law of peoples', which covers rules of coexistence between liberal and other decent peoples, such as self-determination, Just War, mutual recognition (sovereignty), non-intervention, mutual aid and human rights (Rawls 1999). *The Law of Peoples* is not concerned with inequalities between societies.

If global distributive justice is inapplicable to the international realm that still leaves open the question of moral responsibility for the current state of global poverty. Rawls rejects the idea that there are significant international or global causes of poverty. Strictly speak-ing, Rawls and anti-cosmopolitans would reject the idea of 'global' poverty as anything other than the sum total of national poverty.

Despite these reservations, Rawls does not wish to suggest that liberal states abandon the poor to their suffering. *The Law of Peoples* does not tolerate severe global poverty because decent states have a duty of mutual aid. In Rawls's case, this extends to a duty to provide humanitarian aid, to assist what he calls burdened societies in becoming decent societies that fulfil basic human rights. A just law of peoples therefore also includes 'a duty to assist other peoples living under unfavourable conditions that prevent their having just or decent political and social regimes' (Rawls 1999: 37). Once a society has become well ordered and decent, then it becomes self-sustaining and no longer needs to be assisted. However, there are no substantive ongoing institutional distributional responsibilities. The duty of assistance is not a commitment to open-ended or permanent transfers of resources in order to achieve global egalitarianism. Kokaz claims that mutual aid is defended by Rawls as a condition of sociability; without it there can be no society, not even a society of peoples (Kokaz 2007). She argues that this principle, along with the inclusion of universal human rights, provides the basis for a global poverty eradication principle from within *The Law of Peoples*.

For Rawls, the principles of mutual aid, human rights and duty of assistance, if fulfilled, would create a world of decent, if not liberal, societies, in which everyone's basic rights were met. This necessarily would be a world without severe hunger, destitution and poverty. As Beitz notes, in the non-ideal world this represents a significant requirement of some form of global distribution of resources on the part of the most well-off states which far outstrips present practices (Beitz 2000). However, it would be a world in which there would still be possibly quite serious inequalities in wealth and which would still therefore be unjust in cosmopolitan Rawlsian terms.

After Rawls, the most sophisticated and thoroughgoing attempt to spell out an alternative to global egalitarianism has been David Miller's account of national responsibility (Miller 2007). Miller's main purpose is to undermine the global egalitarian argument that justice requires global equality of outcome or opportunity. Instead, he argues, like Walzer, that there is and ought to be a wide range of different conceptions and standards of justice between national societies. When it comes to the question of global poverty, Miller's basic contention is that where domestic institutions or practices are the cause of poverty those institutions ought to bear primary responsibility, and outsiders only insofar as they contribute to them (Miller 2007). In other words, there is no cosmopolitan responsibility to achieve global equality; instead, there are different national responsibilities to fulfil their own conception of justice. Here, he seems on pretty safe ground as no one would question this principle in itself, i.e., that nations like individuals must be responsible for the decisions they take and for things they have caused. Thus, like Rawls, Miller places responsibility for poverty alleviation primarily at the feet of nations. In addition, like Rawls, he endorses the empirical claim that it is likely that the domestic level is the most important cause of most famine and poverty (Miller 2007). By this, he means not merely that corruption and so forth are causes of poverty, but also that bad judgement or imprudent economic policies might be morally relevant causes when it comes to remedial justice. In other words, if a country has made bad economic decisions that have led to poverty in its population, then outsiders have little responsibility for fixing this problem.[4] Most importantly, however, he does make it explicit that institutions, like nations and the global institutional order, as well as individuals, must also be responsible for any harms they have caused abroad. Thus, where it can be shown that causes of poverty lie with the international order, a prima facie case exists that the order, or its most powerful states, be held responsible.

As noted, Miller also endorses a conception of global justice which is not egalitarian but which provides a global basic minimum in the form of basic rights. His argument is that, while individual nations have primary responsibility for ensuring that their members have their basic rights met, this obligation shifts to outsiders when they are unable or unwilling to do so. Thus, for instance, in a famine there are minimal cosmopolitan duties of alleviation. Miller also makes a distinction between what he calls humanitarian duties, which are non-binding, non-obligatory (charity), and duties of justice, which are obligatory. Miller rejects Rawls's reliance on mutual aid alone and instead wishes to acknowledge a universal duty to meet basic rights, which he describes as components of an account of global justice that is non-egalitarian. In other words, his account goes beyond recognition of 'natural duties'.

Nonetheless, Miller's account of basic rights is consistent with Rawls's view that the kind of duties required globally are minimal, temporary and remedial, rather than maximal, permanent and curative. Insofar as there are any global principles, they are 'non-distributive in character: they may . . . specify a minimum level of entitlement . . . [or] procedures that should govern relationships between political communities, such as principles of reciprocity or mutual aid' (Miller 2002: 976). Likewise, Walzer recognizes that 'at least one positive moral principle – mutual aid or good samaritanism – extends across political frontiers, specifying duties owed . . . to persons generally' (Walzer 1994: 3). Basic rights, at least in Miller's account, and mutual aid refer to non-distributive principles of assistance and do not address the basic structure.

In keeping with their communitarian starting point, those who reject the liberal solution argue that minimal principles of natural duties or 'natural justice' such as mutual aid are capable of addressing the worst aspects of global inequality and overcoming any failure to nations to fulfil their people's rights. These anti-cosmopolitan accounts tend to associate the term cosmopolitanism with the case for distributive justice and almost exclusively with liberal Rawlsianism or global egalitarianism. For this reason, they tend not to describe 'natural duties' as cosmopolitan duties. However, these duties are clearly, as we have seen, owed to individuals everywhere, impartially, and are therefore cosmopolitan in the strict sense. The anti-cosmopolitan positions on global poverty are therefore best described as minimally cosmopolitan and anti-global egalitarianism.

Ultimately, given both Rawls's and Miller's minimal universalism, the debate between cosmopolitanism and anti-cosmopolitanism in relation to global poverty rests on empirical questions over who can provide the best account of the causes of global poverty. Rawls's picture gets to the disagreement between cosmopolitans and anti-cosmopolitanism, which is between those who see the cause of poverty as ultimately domestic and those who see it as inextricably connected to and caused by, even if only in part, international or global circumstances.

The problems with Rawls's view are many, but, as has been suggested earlier, there are two that are particularly important. The first is that his assumption of, and argument for, a world of autonomous states with only minimal interaction does not reflect the reality of the world as it is; nor does it reflect necessarily a realizable or even desirable utopia. Most importantly, it dismisses the possibility that interactions between communities can both bring benefits and cause morally significant harm, including poverty and starvation. Rawls simply wants to deny the existence of poverty as a *global* problem, conveying poverty as simply the sum total of national failures to successfully manage their economies and natural resources. Thus, as Miller acknowledges, if it can be shown that there are significant external causes of poverty the question of external responsibility is raised as well.

From natural duties to cosmopolitan justice

While many of the criticisms of a global egalitarianism have significant purchase, they do not amount to a case against cosmopolitanism per se, or against more substantive global obligations to help the destitute. At best, they reveal the global egalitarian solution as problematic. There are serious deficiencies as well with the more limited accounts of obligations that anti-cosmopolitans associate with communal autonomy and natural duties.

The following section, rather than examine the limitations of the anti-cosmopolitanism solution and Rawls's assumptions about bounded communities, examines what might follow from a cosmopolitan reading of the concessions that anti-cosmopolitans make to cosmopolitanism on the issue of global distributive justice. In other words, in relation to global poverty, what might natural duties require of us? Doing so reveals that even these limited duties can give rise to substantial cosmopolitan obligations, not only of beneficence but of justice as well. The following sections argue that significant cosmopolitan conclusions flow from the starting assumptions of anti-cosmopolitans when they recognize natural duties or basic rights. This section focuses on the doctrine of human rights, the duty of mutual aid and the duty not to harm or cause unnecessary suffering. It argues that these principles have been used by cosmopolitans to endorse substantial principles of global distributive justice in relation to the existence of global destitution. These duties require substantial efforts to end global poverty but without the drawbacks associated with the cosmopolitan Rawlsianism of Beitz et al. In particular, a number of cosmopolitan positions can be identified which do not have the same failings but which are compatible with anti-cosmopolitan arguments concerning communal autonomy, natural duties and the recognition of basic rights.

Human rights

While anti-cosmopolitans generally are sceptical about moral universalism, they nonetheless have more often than not endorsed a doctrine of basic human rights. For Rawls, respect for human rights was a criterion of a decent society and, as just noted, David Miller explicitly endorses Henry Shue's conception of basic rights as an account of global justice. What does such an endorsement mean when applied to the issue of global poverty? Within cosmopolitanism, we can identify a number of different human rights arguments that often overlap and come to similar conclusions. In these accounts, poverty, inequality and hunger are understood primarily as human rights violations.

If we defend the idea that all human beings have human rights, especially those set out in the Universal Declaration of Human Rights, then it clearly follows that those who suffer from severe poverty are suffering from human rights violations. Thomas Pogge argues poverty can be understood as a violation of human rights as enshrined in Article 28 of the Universal Declaration of Human Rights, which states '[E]veryone is entitled to a social and international order in which the rights and freedoms set forth in the declaration can be fully realized.' The current international economic order constitutes a major violation of human rights because it contributes to the continuation of massive severe poverty. For Pogge (2002b: 164), the current order is clearly failing in this regard because the destitute are unable to realize their basic human rights.

One of the first attempts to spell out the human rights implications of global poverty was Henry Shue's *Basic Rights* where he argued that severe poverty and starvation are violations of basic rights. Basic rights represent 'everyone's minimum reasonable demands upon the rest of humanity' (Shue 1980: 19). These are basic or prior to other rights in the sense that they cannot be fulfilled or enjoyed until basic rights are achieved. According to Shue, there exist two basic rights: a right to security and a right to subsistence. Without a right to physical security or to subsistence, then it is impossible to enjoy any other right. One cannot enjoy a right to political liberty or freedom of expression if one is likely to be murdered or tortured, and has no legal protection from such abuse. Likewise, one cannot enjoy a right to vote if one has to spend all one's time in the search for basic subsistence. It is in this sense that these rights are basic. Basic rights are the condition of enjoyment of other rights. Clearly, severe poverty and starvation constitute violations of basic rights. Massive poverty and hunger on a global scale amount to a failure to meet basic rights to subsistence, which are universal human rights.

More importantly, Shue argues that such rights engender three correlating duties – 'duties to *avoid* depriving, duties to *protect* from deprivation, and duties to *aid* the deprived' (1980: 255). Therefore, there is a universal duty for those who are capable to aid the suffering, and to avoid depriving them of subsistence. This duty falls not just on states but on other actors, including corporations or the IMF. For example, the duty to avoid depriving is universal, and direct. Duties to aid come into place when other agents are unable or unwilling to do so. So, if a state is 'failing', the responsibility falls to outsiders or other agents who are capable of fulfilling it. In addition, Shue argues, 'clearly if duties to avoid depriving people of their last means of subsistence are to be taken seriously some provision must be made for enforcing this duty on behalf of the rest of humanity' (1980: 56). Cosmopolitans clearly argue that human rights generate human duties and that therefore the responsibility to address them is universal. According to Pogge, 'Human rights give persons moral claims not merely on the institutional order of their own societies, which are claims against their fellow citizens, but also on the global institutional order which are claims against their fellow human beings' (2002b: 68).

Nevertheless, in the current international order, it is generally the duties of states to fulfil the rights of their citizens. This would suggest that the anti-cosmopolitans are correct that addressing poverty is a domestic concern. However, this leaves open the question of whose responsibility it is to fulfil those rights when the state in question cannot or will not do so. Does responsibility to uphold human rights extend to the international order or to specific other states?

Under-fulfilment of subsistence rights can have many causes, from bad government to natural disaster and so on, but given that institutional factors can play a part in all of these there is a duty to make sure that the institutions individuals are relying upon do not harm them and enable them to have their basic rights fulfilled. Thus, there is a duty to create an international institutional order that fulfils those rights. It may be that states are the best means for doing so, but if a particular state cannot do so, then the obligation falls on outsiders. It is the responsibility of all of us, therefore, to live up to the principles of international order to end global poverty. According to Shue, 'among the most important duties of individual persons will be indirect duties for the design and creation of positive-duty-performing institutions that do not yet exist and for the modification or transformation of existing institutions that now ignore rights and the positive duties that all rights involve' (1980: 703). In other words, there is something like Rawls's natural duty to create a just institutional basic structure.

Anti-cosmopolitans dispute the liberal cosmopolitan account of who has primary responsibility, but they do not reject international responsibility altogether. As Miller claims, 'we all to some degree share in the responsibility of ensuring that such rights are protected' (1999: 200; see also 2007). Thus, Miller argues that the existence of societies that fail to protect basic rights 'triggers our general obligation to support and aid other human beings regardless of political or cultural boundaries' (Miller 1999: 179). This includes 'injunctions to supply life-preserving resources to those who lack them when it is in your power to do so' (Miller 1999: 199). He also claims that in circumstances where there is absence of an effective political community and the existence of systematic violations of human rights, the obligation shifts directly 'onto the shoulders of outsiders' (Miller 1999: 201). Thus, if the nation-state is incapable or unwilling to uphold basic rights, the responsibility falls to other nation-states or the international community to do so.

Miller endorses the view also that sometimes there must be a universal positive duty to intervene or help uphold the rights of those in other countries and not just a negative duty not to deny those rights. Indeed, as Caney notes, within Miller's scheme there are 'three principles of international distributive justice. These include a principle of human rights, a commitment to non-exploitation and a commitment to provide political communities with enough to be self-determining' (Caney 2001a: 981, citing Miller 2000: 174–8). However, the question for anti-cosmopolitans who do endorse human rights is whether they ought not to endorse the cosmopolitan arguments that extend from it as well.

The recognition of universal human rights complicates the anti-cosmopolitan position and leads to some apparently contradictory claims. In particular, it follows that there are significant global duties to aid the destitute and to create an international order that does not deprive them of their rights. Recognition of basic human rights as universal rights belonging to all people requires at least some commitment to a global distributive account, even if primary duties are allocated to specific sub-units, such as nations. Miller's response to this question is to argue that national responsibility puts limiting conditions upon global or cosmopolitan responsibilities beyond this minimum. Nonetheless, if human rights are indeed universal it follows that at least some universal obligations must also be entailed, otherwise they are by definition not universal rights, to be held against everyone, but only national or particular, to be upheld only against fellow nationals. Miller's position on this question seems to place him much more firmly in the cosmopolitan camp then he would like to admit.

Capabilities approach

An alternative, but also partially derivative, approach, focusing specifically on the problems of the global poor (and in particular on women) in the context of global development, is the so-called capabilities approach (see chapter 2). Moving beyond the basic or subsistence rights approach, focusing on the bare minimum for physical survival, the capabilities approach seeks to extend what it actually means to live a life worth living. The way to do this is to identify a cross-cultural consensus on a list of capabilities common to all humans that when fulfilled allow one to have and enjoy a good life that amounts to truly human functioning, without saying what that good life is or should be for everyone. Severe poverty and starvation clearly represent an obstacle to a fully functioning human life. The truly poor are unable to either enjoy their life or to express their full potential. There is, therefore, an obligation upon everybody to create the conditions whereby successful human functioning can occur.

Nussbaum argues that the expression this sort of thinking takes in Singer-like utilitarianism leads to impractical and unreasonable demands on individuals. Instead, the main responsibility for meeting the entitlements of humans falls to institutions, both global and national, and to other agents like multinational corporations. Institutions must create the conditions in which individuals can realize the entitlements because 'justice is realized in multiple relations, in that responsibilities for promoting human capabilities are assigned to a wide range of distinct global and domestic structures' (Nussbaum 2007: 323).

In this way, Nussbaum is reaching out to Rawlsian ideas about the basic structure and a modified form of the social contract tradition. In her formulation, all those party to and affected by a social contract ought to be included in consideration, and included in such a way that their capabilities are realized. The capabilities approach emphasizes positive duties to meet this aim. According to Nussbaum (2002a), the capabilities approach is an entitlement and outcomes-oriented approach. By focusing on human beings' minimal entitlements it is derivative of rights-based thinking; however, by looking at outcomes it is also not entirely dissimilar to utilitarianism. Indeed, Nussbaum (2002a) claims it also focuses on those to whom harm is done rather than on those who do harm. The state, for instance, has not done enough if it is only committed to negative duties because meeting capabilities criteria requires 'affirmative shaping of the material and social environment . . . to bring all citizens up to the threshold level' (Nussbaum 2002a: 133). The same applies to the international order, which has a duty to promote development policies which aim to meet these criteria. These duties extend across boundaries because our status as human beings means we owe these obligations universally and because we are enmeshed in a global social and economic web of interaction, or global basic structure, which impacts everybody's capacities and which currently denies the poor theirs. The capabilities approach has received some support from anti-cosmopolitans. However, Miller has been explicit in arguing that it has problems extending from its ever extending list of capabilities. He claims that the capabilities approach goes too far beyond the basic requirements of basic rights and ends up describing capabilities that might not be universalizable and that might violate national conceptions of justice.

Mutual aid and global justice: Singer

Without a doubt, the most far-reaching and persuasive, if not controversial, accounts of duties to address global poverty have been provided by the Australian utilitarian philosopher Peter Singer. Singer was also one of the first philosophers in recent times to take the issue of global poverty seriously (Singer 1972). At the core of Singer's case is the not uniquely utilitarian argument that mutual aid, the duty to help another when in need or jeopardy, provided that one can do so without excessive risk or loss to oneself, requires the rich to devote their excess income to relieving poverty in the rest of the world.

Singer argues that in the face of persistent global hunger and dire poverty, which leads to the avoidable death of millions every year, people in affluent countries are in a comparable position to someone watching a child drown in a pond for fear of getting their trousers wet. Singer states, 'if I am walking past a water pond and see a child drowning in it, I ought to wade in and pull the child out. This will mean getting my clothes muddy, but this is insignificant, while the death of the child would presumably be a very bad thing (1972: 231).[5] Therefore, it follows that if we think it wrong to let the child die, then we ought also think it wrong to let millions die from preventable hunger and poverty. In turn, this means, knowing as we do that many people starve, we ought to consider ourselves morally obligated to help those distant foreigners before we help less needy fellow nationals or spend money on ourselves.

What follows from this argument is a prescription for action, stating that individuals and families in well-off countries ought to give all the money left over after paying for necessities to alleviate third world poverty. In this vein, according to Singer, 'each one of us with wealth surplus to his or her essential needs should be giving most of it to help people suffering from poverty so dire as to be life-threatening' (2002: 12). People in affluent countries, and presumably in affluent sections of poor countries, are morally obligated to help those who are in danger of losing their lives, and if they do not they should not consider themselves to be leading morally defensible lives. Singer argues, 'Those who do not meet this standard should be seen as failing to meet their fair share of global responsibility and therefore as doing something that is seriously morally wrong' (2002: 12).

The moral principle that Singer draws from this analogy is mutual aid, though he does not call it such. According to Singer:

> If it is in our power to prevent something bad from happening, without thereby sacrificing anything of comparable moral importance we ought, morally, to do it . . . I mean without causing anything else comparably bad to happen or doing something that is wrong in itself, or failing to promote some moral good, comparable in significance to the bad thing that we can prevent. (1972: 231)

It is also worth noting that the duty to aid others is not affected by anything other than their need. Singer's argument does not draw upon any relation of interdependence or fault, but only upon the premise that there is global poverty and there is global wealth, and there is a capacity for one to end the other. National boundaries, causes and history have no place in his moral reasoning. The Bugatti driver and the man with wet clothes were not related to the children they did or did not save; nor did they know anything about them other than that their life was in peril. Whether the children were Muslim, animist, or even children of terrorists, was completely immaterial. It is only their situation of need, and the observer's capacities to act that were morally relevant. Likewise, whether a child's poverty is a result of some historical legacy is not a morally relevant factor, because the child's need is nonetheless real and to let the child die, say, because perhaps it fell into the pond rather than was pushed, would be wrong. In other words, this is a duty owed to others as people per se without qualification, a natural, though not perfect, duty.

Singer acknowledges that his position might appear too morally demanding but that this does not detract from his moral position. It simply means that it is hard to be moral. As presented, the argument sounds overwhelming in that very extensive obligations fall upon the globally wealthy. This appears even more so when it is remembered that Singer's utilitarianism demands that the wealthy give up to the point of marginal utility. That is, up to the point at which the rich would begin to be harmed, to reduce themselves to a similarly desperate situation. This is not required by utilitarianism, but what is morally prescribed is to give till it is about to hurt. This means in turn that by continuing to spend large amounts of our income on non-essential and luxury items, such as expensive restaurants, upgrading a television set or keeping up with fashions, we are withholding aid to the needy. That is, we could go without, the equivalent of getting our clothes muddy, without incurring a significant harm to ourselves while dramatically increasing the life spans and life chances of hundreds if not thousands of people who otherwise might starve to death. If we are to withhold this money and continue to spend it on luxury items, we then value 'luxury' items above human life.

In the abstract, this does indeed sound demanding and very few people would consider this a just solution (see Arneson 2004). However, it could also be claimed that, given the actual distribution of wealth in the global economy, if the policy were followed it would not take long at all to eradicate poverty. In other words, the rich would only have to surrender a very small amount of their wealth to fulfil their moral duty. This is especially so if it is remembered that Singer's concern is not with global equality but with alleviating destitution and starvation.

However, if we can assume, as Singer does, that most people will not exercise their positive duty to help the poor, then that leaves us with the problem of how global poverty might be ended and whose responsibility it is, and how that responsibility might be met. If we assume that there will not be a large surge in affluent societies' willingness to sacrifice their luxuries, then we must ask what other means are available. Singer, along with many others, also acknowledges that while we as individuals have certain responsibilities, our political institutions and NGOs all have responsibilities as well. There is no inherent contradiction in utilitarianism pursuing this route because utilitarians may be pragmatic regarding the agent of beneficence. Obligations to help the poor fall on whoever can or will do it most efficiently. While we as individuals ought to do whatever we can, this does not relieve states of similar duties. In addition, Singer does not completely deny the importance of causal responsibility, but such responsibility only compounds the duty of mutual aid which exists before any such 'social' relations (Singer 2002).

The most immediate apparent difference between rights approaches and Singer's utilitarianism is in their understanding of what it is about poverty that makes it a moral problem. For utilitarians, it is because poverty is a cause of suffering, whereas, for rights thinkers, poverty is a denial of rights, including a condition whereby individuals can enjoy their higher-order rights. In other words, suffering per se is not the moral motivation; instead, a particular form of harm, the violation of rights, is the source of concern. While measuring or assessing the degree of suffering is a problem for utilitarian theories, an exclusive focus on rights seems also to miss something very important about why poverty should concern us. We do not always think of ourselves first and foremost as rights bearers, but as people capable of suffering, and for most people that is the first thing that strikes us about severe poverty – that people suffer from it, not that their rights have been denied. While rights talk is powerful in legal terms and is increasingly seen as a de facto universal moral language, it has limitations in terms of its capacity to speak to what is perhaps most common to us as humans, which is our capacity to suffer.

One of the most important criticisms of Singer's approach, and indeed of any appeal to mutual aid, is that it has the suggestion of charity about it. Although Singer makes it clear that giving to poverty relief is not optional, but a moral obligation, it still comes across that he is claiming the 'solution' to global poverty is one of individual sacrifice and personal ethics (see Kuper 2002; and Singer's response). One of the problems with his approach, and one reason why many cosmopolitans think the appeal to mutual aid is insufficient, is that it directs attention away from the political and institutional causes of poverty and suffering. Miller also claims that failing to take account of national responsibility would lead to counter-productive policies (Miller 2007: 231). Anti-cosmopolitans, on the whole, as noted above, think this is sufficient at the international level because they choose to believe that poverty is primarily a domestic concern and not a result of the global basic structure. However, there are good reasons for thinking that there are significant global and international causes of global poverty that give rise to significant duties of justice. One way to see this is to begin not with asking whether the international order is inegalitarian, but whether and in what ways it is harmful. That is, with the natural duty to do no harm.

Harm and global poverty

So far, we have discussed the positive duties of mutual aid or beneficence and the idea of basic human rights. The third of Rawls's natural duties is the negative duty to do no harm, including the duty to avoid causing unnecessary suffering. This section presents the argument that the harm principle, in the context of the contemporary global economy, generates a significant duty to eradicate severe global poverty and destitution. The duty to do no harm allows a defence for limiting the harms done to other communities via international economic arrangements, which is consistent with a plurality of conceptions of justice and which would go a long way to meeting the challenge of serious global inequality. According to Linklater, the universality of the harm principle extends from:

> two universal features of human existence: first, all human beings are susceptible to particular (though not identical) forms of mental and physical

pain [. . .] second, shared (though unequal) vulnerability to mental and bodily harm gives all human beings good reason to seek the protection of a harm principle. (2006: 20)

Recognition of the duty to do no harm at its simplest means that 'our' economic well-being cannot come at the expense of the survival or suffering of outsiders. It means we must recognize the possibility that in 'the desire to do the best for our fellow citizens . . . we collude in imposing unacceptable costs on outsiders' (Linklater 2002a: 150). In other words, whatever the condition of our domestic social contract, we cannot consider it legitimate if it imposes unnecessary suffering or harm on those not party to it.

As we noted earlier, for the critics of cosmopolitan justice the question of cause or blame is directly related to responsibility. In this vein, the problems of the poor are not the fault of the rich and therefore there is only a limited, humanitarian, duty to help. Rawls argued that most of the fault lies with corrupt governments, traditional beliefs, civil wars or other problems internal to poor countries.

However, unlike Rawls, both Miller and Walzer accept that the harm principle has some bearing on the questions of global distributive justice, and in particular the question of global poverty. For both these authors, the anti-cosmopolitan or communitarian starting point does not rule out recognition of harm-based obligations in relation to global poverty. This acknowledgement extends potentially from their recognition of the natural duty to do no harm. Thus, implicit in Walzer's position on refugees and membership, is an acknowledgement that states bear responsibility for harm they commit outside their borders. As Jones argues, in relation to Walzer's points, 'global inequalities of wealth resources and living standards are unjust only if those inequalities have been brought about by external intervention in the internal affairs of some otherwise properly self-determining group, nation, or country' (1999: 197). Therefore, it should follow that poverty that can be considered to have been caused by 'outsiders' is a moral concern for those outsiders. It is the responsibility of those outsiders to help address the harms they have caused.

Likewise, Miller (2004a, 2007) suggests that a principle of non-exploitation between countries is compatible with nationalist principles of distribution. It follows, then, that the only objection to a global harm principle that anti-cosmopolitans can make is to claim that only morally significant causes of poverty are domestic. However this is an empirical claim and not a normative/ethical one. As Beitz argues, 'if the determinants of a society's level of well-being are internal and non-economic, then concern about the international distribution . . . might appear to be pointless' (1999: 524).[6] However, if it can be shown the wealthy states are collectively responsible for an economic order which harms the poor by causing or perpetuating their poverty, then there are no reasons from a communitarian starting point for rejecting obligations to reform this order.

Clearly, in order to make this case, it must first be demonstrated how and in what ways the rich harm the poor. The most important question, then, is to examine this empirical claim and to see what ethical considerations follow from it. In this manner, an account of global justice that is going to be persuasive beyond an appeal to mutual aid might need to establish some causal relationship between 'their poverty' and our 'affluence'. This section discusses how the harm principle is employed by Thomas Pogge in the context of global poverty to demonstrate that the rich and powerful countries of the world owe a significant duty of global justice to the poorest.

According to Pogge, regardless of the lack of a common culture or 'global society', there are relationships of dominance, dependence and inequality present in the international sphere that are unjust to perpetuate. The wealthiest states in the world have imposed and continue to impose an economic order that disadvantages the poorest: 'there is an injustice in the economic scheme, which it would be wrong for more affluent participants to perpetuate. And that is so quite independently of whether we and the starving are united by a communal bond or committed to sharing resources with one another' (2001a: 97). Unlike Beitz, Pogge does not assume that the international order can be characterized as a system of mutual advantage. In particular, Pogge argues, we participate in common institutional structures such as the WTO, IMF and World Bank. Furthermore, the global economy is not a system for mutual advantage, but rather it is one of domination whereby certain practices are imposed by some on others. It is the nature of the relationship that creates the circumstances of justice via a negative duty.

The main point is that we have duties to others regardless of whether we are engaged in an activity of mutual advantage: we have (natural) negative duties not to impose harms and to redress the harms we have inflicted. This generates a negative duty on the part of the rich to cease harming the poor. Even if we disagree upon what a just world order would look like, we can agree that the present international order is unjust, and that there is a responsibility to make it more just.

Whose fault is it?

So, in what ways are the rich engaged in a causally negative relationship with the poor? According to Pogge, the question concerns not only simple causation but a number of contributory factors and 'morally relevant' connections between the rich and poor.

Pogge identifies three such connections which are not simply causal but which nonetheless contribute to the existence and persistence of poverty:

> First, their social starting positions and ours have emerged from single historical process that was pervaded by massive grievous wrongs. The same historical injustices including genocide, colonialism, and slavery, play a role in explaining both their poverty and our affluence. Second, they and we depend on a single natural resource base, from the benefits of which they are largely, and without compensation, excluded. The affluent countries and the elites of the developing world divided these resources on mutually agreeable terms, without leaving 'enough and as good' for the remaining majority of humankind. Third they and we coexist within a single global economic order that has a strong tendency to perpetuate and even to aggravate global economy inequality. (2001b: 14)

The legacy of the past is to have left former colonies worse off than they might have been and left former colonial powers better off. The rich have benefited from past crimes and continue to do so, while the poor have suffered as a result and continue to do so. In that sense, there is an obligation to repair or at least to address the damage done and to acknowledge a debt that has been accrued. In addition, the current international inequality is not disconnected from the past but is in fact a direct result of former policies that favoured the wealthy and powerful. According to Pogge, 'most of the existing international inequality in standards of living was built up in the colonial period when today's affluent countries ruled today's poor regions of the world: trading their people like cattle, destroying their political institutions and cultures and taking their natural resources' (2001b: 9). Thus, past exploitation and injustice have a direct bearing upon the present conditions, and obligations are owed to either, at least, repair the damage done or to compensate for the unequal 'starting point'. Pogge concludes that under a negative duties conception 'upholding a radical inequality counts as harming the worse-off when the historical path on this inequality arose is pervaded by grievous wrongs' (2001b: 10). In defending the status quo we are causing a harm, and this is aggravated by our privileged position in the status quo which is the result of past wrongs.

This essentially cosmopolitan point is not inconsistent with the accounts of justice given by Miller and Walzer who endorse the principle that past injustices do raise duties of responsibility. Miller argues that exploitation is a form of unjustifiable harm and that 'many existing inequalities are likely to be the result of past exploitation of the poor countries by rich countries . . . so they will be unjust' (1999: 207). Walzer, for instance, states that the past practices may provide the basis for a global effort to address poverty and that 'a strong critique of global inequalities and a persuasive claim that we are obligated to help the poorest countries can be derived from an historical account of how the world economy developed' (2003b). In making this recognition, they both go further than Rawls who seems to maintain that past injustices are irrelevant, or do not exist. However, where they agree with Rawls is in their rejection of global egalitarianism as providing the criteria and means of addressing injustice.

While historical contributions may be less controversial, the extent to which the current global economic order causes greater inequality is a matter of some debate.[7] Many argue that the poor are benefiting under globalization and some anti-cosmopolitans argue that even under 'globalization', responsibility for causing and addressing poverty remains primarily domestic.

However, against the explanatory nationalism of Rawls and Miller, Pogge identifies two ways in which the current international order contributes to global destitution. The first is direct and the second indirect. The direct contribution is the degree to which the global order directs resources and wealth away from the poor and prevents them from accessing it. The second is the degree to which the global political economic order reinforces corrupt practices and governments. Pogge makes a case that the two are intimately connected. Rather than promoting free trade across the board, the WTO is geared in favour of the rich countries by imposing unfair protectionist measures that discriminate against the poorest countries. Pogge's argument is that the WTO has made things worse for very many people:

> In the WTO negotiations, the affluent countries insisted on continued and asymmetrical protections of their markets through tariffs, quotas, anti-dumping duties, export credits, and subsidies to domestic producers, greatly impairing the export opportunities of even the very poorest countries. These protections cost developing countries hundreds of billions of dollars in lost export revenues . . . and certainly account for a sizable fraction of the 270 million poverty related deaths since 1989. (2002a: 21)

The rich countries could have chosen a different set of rules that didn't actively discriminate against the poor. So, even if the old regime was bad, the new regime is also bad and is worse than it ought to have been. Under the WTO regimes, quotas and protectionist measures were lower between the rich countries than between the rich and poorer countries. As a result, Pogge (2002a: 18) argues that 'Millions who would have lived had the old regime continued have in fact died from poverty related causes. These people were killed, and others harmed in other ways, by the change over to the new regime.' The point is that this harm was avoidable and that rich countries could have agreed to less 'burdensome' rules for the rest of the world.

Under the current system, the poor are not doing well enough, and they would do better under a feasible alternative system. Therefore, even if the poor are better off, they are not better off enough because they remain in avoidable poverty. Even though global institutions may not directly be the major cause, they can nonetheless play a major role in alleviating the problem. Therefore, given that something like the duty of mutual aid demands that if we can help another without significant cost to ourselves then we ought to, the rules of global trade can be changed to help the poor escape their poverty and there is a duty on the part of those with the power to do so. Pogge is not necessarily claiming that the institutional order is the *main* cause of world poverty, but that most severe poverty worldwide 'was and is avoidable through global institutional reforms' (2002a: 19).

As we have seen, Rawls argues that third world poverty must be attributed to national level decisions and determinants. This can include everything from domestic corruption to poor management. However, Pogge shows that this is not the end of the story because the international system or rules of international order, and especially rules of international finance, provide incentives to undemocratic and corrupt governments. Whatever domestic causes there may be for poverty and starvation, they cannot be understood in the absence of the global institutional scheme in which they sit. In the words of Pogge, 'an adequate explanation of persistent global poverty must not merely adduce the prevalence of flawed institutional regimes and of corrupt, oppressive, incompetent elites in the poor countries, but must also provide an explanation for this prevalence' (2001b: 45). That is, it must establish the reason why there are so many poorly run, corrupt, non-accountable governments in the world and the extent to which the international order permits, encourages or does not seek to prevent the emergence of these governments.

Pogge (2002a) identifies two institutional supports that the international order provides corrupt and undemocratic states, including international resources and international borrowing privileges. The first of these refers to the right of states, once they are deemed sovereign, to sell natural assets on the world market. In the case of non-democratic regimes, this is the equivalent of selling stolen property and provides an incentive to corrupt or tyrannical actors to seize control of the state so that they can acquire the benefits of selling that property. This sort of action is perfectly legal in the international realm while illegal domestically.

Likewise, the borrowing privilege refers to the right of any sovereign government to borrow against its natural assets. This effectively allows access to global economic resources, regardless of the nature of the regimes. Again, this provides an incentive to corrupt or non-democratic actors to seize control of the state. The point here is that in both these practices the international order provides a condition of possibility and does not punish behaviour that encourages corruption and is therefore a contributing factor to global poverty.

Pogge's account of poverty is an institutional account rather than an interactional one. The interactional account says moral cosmopolitanism flows from our understanding of what is owed to persons qua persons. Singer's utilitarian argument is an interactional account, as it does not rely logically and morally on any causal connection or institutional relationship between the affluence of some parts of the world and the poverty of others. On the other hand, the institutional account emphasizes that justice is an institutional practice and we owe duties of justice to those we affect through our institutional relationships. In this way, Pogge's approach is Rawlsian because it looks at the effects of the basic institutional structure in relationships between states, without relying upon a claim about mutual advantage.

In this context, Pogge emphasizes the *harmful* relationship between the wealth of the rich and the poverty of the poor. The rich have a duty to help the poor because the international order, which they largely created, is a major cause of world poverty. Such a duty is 'not . . . a merely positive responsibility . . ., like Rawls's duty of assistance, but a negative responsibility to stop imposing the existing global order and to prevent and mitigate the harms it continually causes for the world's poorest populations' (2001b: 22). The rich countries are collectively responsible for about 18 million deaths from poverty annually: 'the citizens and governments of the wealthy societies, by imposing the present global economic order, significantly contribute to the persistence of severe poverty and thus share institutional moral responsibility for it' (2001b: 57). The rules of the system, and the basic structure of international society, actively damage or disadvantage certain sectors of the economy, thereby directly contradicting Rawlsian principles of justice. Thus, Pogge claims:

> because we are . . . implicated . . . in shaping and enforcing the social institutions that produce these deprivations, and are . . . benefiting from the enormous inequalities these unjust institutions reproduce, we have . . . stringent duties to seek to reform these social institutions and to do our fair share toward mitigating the harms they cause. (2002a: 7)

Therefore, given that an international economic order which causes harms exists now, there are good reasons to accept that certain universal rules ought to be devised to limit, redress, alleviate or eradicate such harm and to prevent it in the future.

This latter point is important because it suggests that, even if the current order is not entirely to blame for persistent starvation, it still has to justify the contribution it does make and why any alternative is not feasible (Pogge 2002a: 44). Again, Miller endorses such an approach when he condemns exploitation and unfair terms of trade and asks 'how an international economic order can be created in which opportunities for exploitation be minimized and . . . that constrains the actions of potential exploiters' (1999: 208). On this point, Miller only disagrees with Pogge over the extent of the international obligation but not over its presence (Miller 2007: 240–50).

There is, then, a minimal obligation on the rich to engineer a global international order that improves, or at least does not harm, the worst off. The current international order, which is largely the creation of the most powerful and wealthy states, actively disadvantages and harms the poor and prevents the eradication of poverty. Those who gain most from the current economic order have an obligation to change it in such a way that the most needy benefit. First and foremost, the current rules of international trade discriminate against the poor and, given its inequalities, there is a duty to reform the existing rules of international trade. The current rules of international trade discriminate against the poor by subsidizing the rich and blocking access to imports from the poorest countries. Global justice demands that rich countries, such as Australia, should open their markets to the poorer countries. Pogge (2005a: 197) also argues that they can do so without causing disproportionate harm to the rich. The resource rights and global lending rights should be withdrawn from illegitimate governments, and a natural resources dividend paid to the poor.

Pogge's argument demonstrates that the 'do no harm' principle, when applied to relationships between political communities and globally, reveals the current world economic order to be very harmful indeed to many. The 'do no harm' principle, when seen through a cosmopolitanism lens, reveals poverty to be never just a national problem but a global one also. There is, then, even on 'anti-cosmopolitan' grounds, a significant duty to cease harming the global poor that requires significant reform of the international order. In other words, there are significant cosmopolitanism responsibilities for global justice that flow from the natural duty of 'do no harm'.

Pogge's institutional account, while persuasive, is also incomplete because it only addresses the issue of institutional harm and suggests that there is little or no role for individual beneficence. While it is clearly incumbent upon the rich to reform the world economic order, this may take some time and in the meantime millions will die. As Pogge himself notes, this is a morally horrific situation. For any cosmopolitan response, simply letting millions die while waiting for structural reform neglects those people's status as ends. How, then, should we understand the relationship between justice and beneficence, or mutual aid? The following section makes it clear that these two principles should never have been separated, and instead when understood from a Kantian position are the basis of a coherent cosmopolitan approach to global poverty.

Kant: from beneficence to justice and back again

In contrast to rights-based and utilitarian positions, Onora O'Neill (1986) argues that a Kantian ethic of universal obligations based on a principle of non-coercion provides both a more effective and also a more just means of addressing the moral problem of hunger and starvation. Rights-based and contractarian approaches have two major flaws, according to her. Contractarianism, by which she means Rawlsianism, is based on too idealized a conception of agency. Rawls's social contract, based on the hypothetical original position, requires an account of human beings that robs them of essential human qualities. The peoples situated behind a veil of ignorance are unrecognizable as real people and are simply 'types'. The Rawlsian conclusion, therefore, will be too abstract and unpersuasive to those who do not understand or share this view. Its level of abstraction from recognizable human beings (i.e., those not situated behind a veil of ignorance) precludes its accessibility to real human beings.

Rights-based approaches are criticized for also having an unnecessarily idealized concept of agency and a bias towards the claimants of rights, and not enough to say about who has the obligation to fulfil those rights. In terms of those with the power and ability to effect change, according to O'Neill, 'rights discourse often carries only a vague message to those whose action is needed to secure respect for rights' (1986: 117). Rights, in other words, are only half the story. They provide an incomplete moral framework and are inadequate for both practical and ethical reasons as a means of addressing global hunger.

Utilitarianism, on the other hand, while speaking the everyday language of suffering, suffers from making mutual aid the entirety of justice. Under Singer's conception, mutual aid as the individual's duty to help becomes the entire solution to poverty and hunger. This is also a mistake because it does not understand the relationship between beneficence and justice. This relationship is best understood by Kant and articulated in the Kantian tradition. The Kantian approach understands that the duty of mutual aid arises in part because of failings of justice. An unjust world will have more call for mutual aid. However, this is no substitute for 'the institutional conditions which systemically meet material needs and guarantee the absence of coercion and deception' (O'Neill 1986: 146). In other words, mutual aid is no substitute for a just basic structure.

O'Neill argues that what is needed is a (non-utilitarian) theory of human obligations, a theory of fundamental morality which designates whose responsibility it is to address the problems of hunger and starvation and which understands the relationship between the duty to aid and the duty of justice. Thus, O'Neill argues, Kant provides the best response to the problems of global poverty. The CI, we recall, declares that our primary moral obligation is to treat others as ends in themselves. For O'Neill, this means to recognize their capacity of morally autonomous agency, rather than, say, guaranteeing a share of material wealth, though material needs must be met in order to realize our agency. Ultimately, the existence of starvation and hunger are grievous breaches of this obligation.

O'Neill argues that there are at least two maxims which fulfil the criteria of the categorical imperative and they give rise to both perfect and imperfect duties, duties of justice and duties of beneficence. The duty of beneficence, as we have already noted, requires that if others are in need, or need help in order to achieve effective autonomy, then there exists an obligation on the part of those without need to help and develop the talents needed to actualize autonomy in others. As we have seen, for Kant, mutual aid was required in cases where a person's moral capacity to act was impaired by undue suffering or deprivation such as poverty or destitution. As Herman states, 'respecting the humanity of others involves acknowledging the duty of mutual aid: one must be prepared to support the conditions of the rationality of others [their capacity to set and act for ends] when they are unable to do so without help' (1984: 597). This means there are both positive and negative duties to aid those whose agency is not being actualized and to refrain from coercion and deception in relations with others. In the words of O'Neill, 'Kantian beneficence supplies help needed if they are unable to act . . . Kantian development of talents supplies skills and capacities . . . that are needed for autonomous action' (1986: 146).

Beneficence, however, is not justice. The other rule to be taken from the CI is a more public rule of non-coercion and non-deception. According to O'Neill, the 'central demand of Kantian justice is negative: that actions, policies and situations not be based on or confirm to fundamental principles of coercion or deception' (1986: 146). In other words, do no harm. Coercion and deceit are violations of the agency of others and therefore constitute a denial of the others as ends in themselves. For O'Neill, 'Justice is embodied in public institutions and policies which secure freedom from deep forms of coercion and deception' (1986: 146). The Kantian response to poverty and hunger 'would begin with ways of organizing both production and distribution to meet needs, including material needs, which destroy capacities or power to act autonomously' (O'Neill 1986: 149).

As Pogge powerfully demonstrates, the current political order rests on structures of interaction which do rely on inequality, coercion and deception: 'The present international economic order is patently an institutional structure whose normal operation does not eliminate coercion of deception but often institutionalize them. It also standardly fails to respect, or to provide the help or development of talents needed for lives that can include autonomous action' (O'Neill 1986: 145). The application of a Kantian ethic would necessarily require a large-scale and thorough transformation of existing social-economic arrangements across the globe, 'a just global economic and political order would then have to be one designed to meet material needs . . . It would be embodied in economic and political structures which do not institutionalize coercion or deception and so respect rationality and autonomy in the vulnerable forms in which they are actually found' (O'Neill 1986: 149).

Not much has been said in this chapter about the foundational problem of global pluralism identified in the introduction. However, it is possible to identify and somewhat substantiate the claim made earlier that the Kantian approach overcomes the objections to cosmopolitanism on the ground of global pluralism. Put simply, there is little in the Kantian account that suggests the solution to global poverty requires the imposition of a single determinant version of distributive justice or the good. Instead, it requires only that the political institutions of the day do not systemically harm those affected by them and that aid be given to those who need help when they are harmed or otherwise in need.

The significance of the Kantian approach is that it demonstrates that the 'natural duties' of no harm and mutual aid actually generate and are core parts of a cosmopolitan account of global justice. This account is neither Rawlsian nor utilitarian, but Kantian, and as such has significant advantages over them.

For instance, any solution to global poverty – including any rewriting of the rules of international order – must be agreeable to those affected by it. In that fashion, there is a responsibility on the part of the rich not only to cease the current harms but also to prevent future harms or problems that might arise in the redrafting of the rules of international economic life. Furthermore, they must not compound their harms by excluding the interests and arguments of the poor. Therefore, the solution must not be imposed without the consultation and agreement of the poorest people and their representatives.

Nowhere in this solution is the prospect of imposing a particular account of the good upon others raised as an option. Instead, the opposite is true: the rich have an obligation to cease imposing an unjust institutional order on the poor. It should also be noted that the dialogic component of harm avoidance helps to overcome the objections that not all harms trigger obligations, in particular, that some suffering is 'self-incurred' or purely a domestic responsibility (Miller), or that lines of causation are too diffuse or hard to determine. The cosmopolitan harm principle begins with the harms that states have imposed, that is, harms which have not been consented to by those who are harmed.

Corresponding to the duty to not harm is a positive duty to consult outsiders about any issue which may have harmful effects upon them, in order to assess whether it does constitute a harm, whether it is acceptable or not, and where responsibility lies. As Pogge's arguments about the role played by the global economic order in contributing to global poverty demonstrate, there are very few instances where responsibility is purely domestic because all domestic policy is conducted within a global context as well. So, for instance, if a population in one country experiences hunger or severe poverty it may be due to any number of factors, including domestic mismanagement (or worse), or it may be due largely to external factors attributable to one or a diffuse range of sources. Under these circumstances, there is a good case that before responsibility for harm can be determined all parties who may reasonably be thought to be contributing to the situation in some measure have a responsibility to consult each other to assess the lines of causation and the proportion of responsibility born by each. While this is a morally demanding implication of the harm principle, it is one that buttresses the rights of independent communities, even while limiting their absolute freedom of action.

Conclusion

This chapter began by arguing that the most important issue raised by global poverty is that of moral responsibility. It was also claimed that global poverty presented a fundamental challenge to anti-cosmopolitanism. At the same time, it was argued that cosmopolitan approaches to poverty had been dominated by considerations of distributive justice and global egalitarianism, based on Rawls.

However, while some important differences exist, there is significant agreement over the responsibility for global hunger and starvation. The arguments above suggest an agreement that there are both 'national' or particular responsibilities, as well as global institutional and individual or universal responsibilities for ending global poverty. As Pogge's arguments about the role played by the global economic order in contributing to global poverty demonstrate, there are very few instances where responsibility is purely domestic, because all domestic policy is conducted within a global context as well.

In addition, the chapter showed that, when it comes to addressing the problem of global poverty, cosmopolitan positions and anti-cosmopolitan positions also agree about the following things:

- Global poverty is a significant moral problem.
- There are global duties of mutual aid to address severe poverty and destitution.
- These duties are owed to individuals and extend from what we owe to each other as persons.
- These duties may be mediated by a variety of institutions including states.
- Under certain circumstances if states or local institutions are unable to fulfil these duties then the international community or other states have responsibility to fulfil them.
- Obligations to the poor also extend from harms which may have arisen in specific causal relationships both historically and in the past. That is, there is a duty to redress harm that extends across borders.

- There is also a duty to significantly reform the current international order which extends from the harm that it does to the poorest.

What the areas of agreement demonstrate is that once the idea of natural duties has been accepted and it is clear that national or communal loyalties do not override natural duties, then differences can be understood as disagreement about the nature and extent of cosmopolitan principles but not on their desirability. In addition, the implication of this argument is that cosmopolitan solutions, understood in the broad sense, to global poverty do not require the type of homogenous political community envisaged by the anti-cosmopolitans, and can be reconciled with a world formally divided into separate political communities so long as those communities understand themselves to be bound by both national and cosmopolitan duties owed to humanity.

In sum, the chapter has argued that the specific problem of global poverty, or destitution, rather than of inequality, is amenable to other cosmopolitan solutions. In particular, it has argued that the most persuasive accounts of cosmopolitanism, which do not suffer the limitations of global Rawlsianism, are in fact extensions of the natural duties of mutual aid and do no harm. There are two implications of this argument. The first is that the anti-cosmopolitanism argument against global egalitarianism does not undermine the cosmopolitan position per se. The second is that it confirms the cosmopolitan presuppositions of the anti-cosmopolitan appeal to natural duties. Third, natural duties themselves generate significant duties of global distributive justice in the context of global poverty.

8

Conclusion

This book began by asking a number of significant questions which lie at the heart of international ethics as a field of study – in particular, whether outsiders ought to be treated according to the same ethical principles that insiders are. In other words, ought outsiders to be treated as moral equals, what might those principles be, and how do we interpret them? The book has focused on the theoretical answers rather than relying on a detailed case study approach. The purpose has been to elucidate the basic philosophical responses to these questions. Elucidation of this type is the first step towards arriving at well-thought through and defensible responses to the wide variety of ethical issues that confront today's global citizens.

The book has identified the distinction between cosmopolitan and anti-cosmopolitan traditions as reflecting commonly held assumptions and beliefs that are widely represented throughout the world today, and which condition most responses to the ethical issues arising in a globalized world. Cosmopolitanism appeals to the awareness of global interconnection and belongingness to humanity, while anti-cosmopolitanism appeals to the fact of belonging to and interconnection with local and specific sub-groups of humanity. However, despite such differences, this book has shown that cosmopolitanism and communitarianism represent positions on a spectrum that rests on universalist assumptions, and the significant differences between them appear only in relation to the extent and content of that universalism.

I have aimed to discuss and evaluate this distinction in a number of issue areas, as well as at a philosophical level, and have demonstrated that the most consistent distinction in international ethics is between those who argue for extensive universal principles of equality, broadly speaking principles of justice, and those who defend minimal, natural duties such as mutual aid. However, in evaluating these arguments, the conclusion is that, contrary to the claims of anti-cosmopolitans, a commitment to the idea of natural duties gives rise to significant cosmopolitan obligations of mutual aid and harm avoidance. Both of these views are cosmopolitan in origin and scope. In other words, once it has been acknowledged that all individuals should be treated with equal moral worth and that this requires certain specific things such as mutual aid and the commitment not to harm others, then the core threshold into a cosmopolitan position has already been crossed. The conclusion to be drawn from this observation is not that there are no significant differences between natural duties and global egalitarianism, but rather that the distinction between them is one that occurs within a cosmopolitanism frame.

Furthermore, there are real difficulties in maintaining a strict distinction between natural duties and duties of justice. Once the argument for natural duties is accepted, then the onus of proof or argument rests on those who wish to restrict us to these duties only. While we may begin with natural duties, we very quickly find that in the context of contemporary international politics fulfilling natural duties can lead to extensive cosmopolitan duties and arrangements. In a globalized world, communities are challenged to develop new principles or refine old ones to govern the increased interactions between individuals, communities and nation-states. The occasions and ability to provide mutual aid, and the opportunities for harm and suffering, have increased so greatly that even the fulfilment of natural duties requires extensive commitments of time and resources, and brings radically different cultures and ethical codes in touch with each other. Under these conditions, even natural duties end up demanding a cosmopolitan response. The 'do no harm' principle, which is a natural duty, gives rise to significant cosmopolitan duties when interactions increase.

This book has also suggested that there are serious limitations accompanying the account of cosmopolitanism derived from John Rawls, which understands ethics as derived from distributive justice. Rawlsian liberalism, with few exceptions, is unable to adequately address the concerns of anti-cosmopolitans regarding cultural differences because its account of justice does not sufficiently recognize the risk of liberal imperialism. This fault extends from the reduction of all questions of ethics to those of justice.

In contrast, the Kantian approach provides a better interpretation of the relationship between these two realms. The Kantian account should be privileged over the Rawlsian account because of its emphasis on the pursuit of the categorical imperative rather than substantive principles of global justice. For this reason, a Kantian ethics is better suited for the ethical tasks that concern the application and interpretation of morality in specific circumstances that focus on the question of what one ought to do here and now, as well as in the future. One of the aims of this book has been to demonstrate that by directing cosmopolitan thinking to basic principles such as humanitarianism and harm, and away from more substantive ones such as Rawls's difference principle or equality of opportunity, it is also possible to forestall and overcome some of the common criticisms of cosmopolitanism made by anti-cosmopolitans.

Because cosmopolitanism exceeds the framework of liberalism, and in particular of Rawlsian distributive justice, it is possible to argue that the insights of the anti-cosmopolitan position have only limited purchase. In particular, the equating of cosmopolitanism with liberal schemes for global egalitarianism, or the implied political centralization it requires (Walzer 2004), diverts attention from more fundamental principles that might be more consistent with and amenable to anti-cosmopolitan sensitivities. That cosmopolitan universalism 'points to the nightmare vision of ethical principles . . . that are inevitably and relentlessly blind to human differences and mandate rigid uniformity' (O'Neill 1996: 77) does not necessarily follow from the recognition of duties owed to all human beings.

If it can be demonstrated that cosmopolitanism could be reconciled with an extensive range of human differences (and indeed that the recognition of difference is itself a cosmopolitan principle), then much of the communitarian critique no longer stands. In other words, if cosmopolitanism can accommodate communitarian concerns about difference and communal autonomy, then the grounds for anti-cosmopolitan arguments fall away. The Kantian approach outlined here not only overcomes these concerns, but does so by elaborating on the 'natural duties' endorsed by anti-cosmopolitans.

The ethical challenge that this book has addressed takes the form of the question of 'how to treat everybody as ends in themselves in a world which is not a "kingdom of ends".' That is, how do those who wish to defend universalism act as cosmopolitans in a non-cosmopolitan world, in which most people give moral priority to their local or national community and in so doing make themselves the enemy of humankind? The argument has been that cosmopolitanism requires only the following: friendship towards the rest of the human race; support for the Kantian notion of respect for persons, or some equivalent notion of the equality of all human beings; and the conviction that there ought to be harm conventions (Linklater 2001: 264).

Throughout, one of the aims has been to elaborate on the meaning of these three components: friendship, respect of persons, and harm conventions. This is best understood through the Kantian account of the relationship between justice and beneficence. This provides at least a minimal account of what cosmopolitanism entails for those persuaded by the basic principle of human equality. Humans are situated in both the community of their birth (or adoption) and the community of humankind, but being so situated requires that neither realm be exclusive of the other nor exhaust our moral responsibilities. Cosmopolitanism means that obligations to friends and neighbours – our fellow countrymen – must be balanced with obligations to strangers and to humanity, and that at times humanity must be given first priority. This book has presented a case for an account of moral duties to humankind that can be reconciled with particularist duties to compatriots.

Notes

Chapter 2 Cosmopolitanism

1 The concept of generality is more accurately represented by the idea of impartiality. Though not identical, it serves largely the same function, that is, to provide a transcendent perspective that is above any individual/partial perspective.

2 Utility in this sense refers to welfare, which is understood as happiness, which in turn is understood as the presence of pleasure and the absence of pain.

3 For our purposes, one of the interesting things about Rawls's account of justice is that it is also based on a version of the Kantian CI. The veil of ignorance is meant to ensure that all parties to the contract treat each other as ends in themselves because each individual could occupy the place of each other individual; therefore, they must come up with a set of rules that everyone could reasonably agree to.

4 The recognition that different cultures and people may interpret harm differently could be said to reinforce the opposition to cosmopolitan universalism. However, this would be so only if one accepts a radical incommensurability thesis regarding the impossibility of translation and interpretation (see Shapcott 1994). Such a reading would render the possibility of translating the concept of harm beyond our reach. It would make it impossible to identify any circumstances where our actions 'harm' others, by their standards.

5 This chapter has focused on the dominant versions of liberal cosmopolitanism. Cosmopolitanism is not exhausted by a predominate conception of liberal cosmopolitanism, focusing on rights or deontological justice. A growing literature on ethics is informed by continental traditions of thought, which do not rely on the same ontological and

epistemological assumption of liberalism. Rather than drawing on the resources and the form of Kantian universalism, informed as it is by transcendental and foundational claims about right and wrong, anti-foundational authors such as David Campbell wish to reject any claims to absolute truth or a truth that can be used to enforce one particular view of ethics of morality, be it cosmopolitan or communitarian. Nonetheless, anti-foundationalist authors are cosmopolitan in scope, that is, in terms of where they extend the realm of the ethical, even if they understand the grounds for alternative applications of this, while the nature of their understanding of the ethical radically differs from that of liberals and communitarians. Broadly speaking, the anti-foundationalist approaches can be identified as poststructuralist. Of the two, critical theory is explicitly Kantian in its origins, taking the lead not only from Kant's moral philosophy but from his critical philosophy as well. In contrast, the anti-foundationalists take their leads from a variety of sources, including twentieth-century philosophers such as Jacques Derrida and Emmanuel Levinas. Indeed, at times, anti-foundationalism rejects cosmopolitanism along similar grounds to those of communitarian writers. However, for the most part, anti-foundationalists promote ethics of openness and inclusion, which is compatible with core cosmopolitan arguments.

Chapter 3 Anti-cosmopolitanism

1   Indeed, as Morgenthau noted, realism is a 'subversive' approach because it questions all claims to possess 'the truth' or a universal truth, as realism recognizes that all such claims are inextricably linked with power and interest.
2   This view is dramatically articulated in the film *A few Good Men* by the character Col Jessop's (Jack Nicholson) defence of his decision to order a 'code red'. That decision, which results in the death of a US marine at the hands of his comrades, is ultimately justified on the grounds that it was necessary in a world of 'walls patrolled by men with guns'.
3   I have discussed the significance of this aspect in more detail in my 2001.

Chapter 4 Hospitality: Entry and Membership

1   Carens (1980: 260) observes the only reason that could be used to restrict movement is that of extreme emergencies, such as threats to public order, and this reason could only be used 'at that level of restriction essential to maintain public order'. Public order is necessary only to guarantee the liberty of all. Therefore, it is only in the interests of liberty itself that movement can be restricted.

2 In another context, Carens acknowledges and explores this issue in more depth (1996, 1999).
3 Australia has a not entirely dissimilar policy today – see '"Pom invasion" hitting Down Under'. Available at: <http://news.bbc.co.uk/go/em/fr//2/hi/uk_news/6972076.stm>.
4 The UNHCR, on the other hand, distinguishes between refugees and asylum seekers as different stages in the process. A person begins as an asylum seeker, claims asylum, and then is declared a refugee when that claim is accepted (UNHCR 2008).
5 Thus, Australia's policy requires cooperation with other states and impacts upon them. It has also involved the demarcation of a migrant exclusion zone whereby certain islands are no longer deemed to be part of the Australian territory from an asylum perspective. Therefore, when asylum seekers make it to these islands they are not considered to have reached Australian shores and so are not subject to international or Australian laws (Gelber and McDonald 2006).
6 South Africa received more asylum seekers than any other country, with 53,400 new asylum claims, followed by the United States (50,800), Kenya (37,300), France (30,800), the United Kingdom (27,800), Sweden (24,300) and Canada (22,900). However, the largest refugee flows were from Afghanistan (2.1 million), and Iraq (1.2 million) into neighbouring countries (UNHCR 2009).
7 In a later interview on the subject, Walzer seems to blur the two categories (Walzer 2003).

Chapter 5 Humanitarianism and Mutual Aid

1 Bellamy (2006) argues that the popular perception is wrong and that deportations started before the NATO bombing campaign.

Chapter 6 The Ethics of Harm: Violence and Just War

1 The core doctrines relate to the treatment of non-combatants, who are entitled to respect for their lives and for their physical and mental integrity. They must be protected and treated humanely in all circumstances with no adverse distinction. The rule of non-combatant immunity states that it is forbidden to kill or wound an enemy who surrenders or is unable to fight; medical personnel, supplies, hospitals and ambulances must all be protected; injured soldiers and civilians and prisoners of war must be protected; the sick and wounded must be collected and cared for by the party in whose power they find themselves; and prisoners of war must be guaranteed the provision of food, shelter and medical care, and the right to exchange messages with their families (ICRC website).

2   That is a concept whose definition is contested in its essentials; there is no possibility of a single authoritative definition.

3   This is especially difficult with regard to the intentions of a statesperson or politician who can reasonably be thought to have several motives, not all of which are virtuous.

4   Though this is not always easily ascertained, as in the case where revolutionary activity is funded by criminal activity such as the drugs trade.

5   Bellamy claims that British military planners developed saturation bombing before the war began. In addition, the campaigns lasted well beyond the immediate danger to Britain's survival. So it is clear that civilian deaths were both anticipated and planned as part of a war-fighting strategy. According to Bellamy (2004: 842), the emergency 'presented itself in the terms it did because, at least twenty years earlier, the RAF leadership had taken the moral decision that it was legitimate to target non combatants to make a psychological and economic impact upon the enemy. "Fateful choices" are similarly constructed in other supreme emergencies.'

Chapter 7 Impermissible Harms: Global Poverty and Global Justice

1   For convenience, I have used Pogge's 2001 statistics. More recent reports from the World Bank and UNDP suggest that up to 2005 some shift occurred in these figures in favour of an overall reduction in poverty, as a percentage but not in absolute numbers. This reduction is also geographically weighted, with China's rapid economic growth accounting for a significant proportion and the situation largely unchanged in sub-Saharan Africa. This situation is likely to change again with the advent of the global financial crisis of 2008. All indicators are that the global financial crisis will lead to an increase in poverty in the poorest countries.

2   However, even within this range, the concentration of wealth among the few is startling. According to the UNDP Human Development Reports: 'The world's 200 richest people more than doubled their net worth in the four years to 1998, to more than US$1 trillion. The assets of the top three billionaires are more than the combined GNP of all least developed countries and their 600 million people' (Pogge 2004: 19).

3   For a further account of this problem, see Shapcott (1994), 'Conversation and Coexistence, Gadamer and the Interpretation of International Society', *Millennium* 23/1: 57–83; and Chris Brown (1988), 'The Modern Requirement?: Reflections on Normative International Theory in a Post-Western World', *Millennium* 17/2: 339–48.

4   In making this claim, these authors re-emphasize communitarian priorities; it is the nation as whole that is being held responsible both

causatively and curatively. This argument is clearly unacceptable from the cosmopolitan position because justice is owed to individuals and not collectivities. To hold the worse-off victims of mismanagement responsible for the failings of their leaders verges on a form of collective punishment. The point of the cosmopolitan objection is that responsibility is owed to individuals who are starving, not to nations or peoples.

5 A similar analogy is made by Peter Unger, the case of Bob's Bugatti. Bob is close to retirement. He has invested most of his savings in a very rare and valuable old car, a Bugatti, which he has not been able to insure. The Bugatti is his pride and joy. In addition to the pleasure he gets from driving and caring for his car, Bob knows that its rising market value means that he will always be able to sell it and live comfortably after retirement. One day, when Bob is out for a drive, he parks the Bugatti near the end of a railway siding and goes for a walk up the track. As he does so, he sees that a runaway train, with no one aboard, is running down the railway track. Looking farther down the track, he sees the small figure of a child very likely to be killed by the runaway train. He can't stop the train and the child is too far away to warn of the danger, but he can throw a switch that will divert the train down the siding where his Bugatti is parked. Then nobody will be killed – but the train will destroy his Bugatti. Thinking of his joy in owning the car and the financial security it represents, Bob decides not to throw the switch. The child is killed. For many years to come, Bob enjoys owning his Bugatti and the financial security it represents. Bob's conduct, most of us will immediately respond, was gravely wrong. Unger agrees. But then he reminds us that we, too, have opportunities to save the lives of children. We can give to organizations like UNICEF or Oxfam America (Unger, qtd in Singer 2002).

6 For Singer, this is immaterial because capacity to help is important. But, as we have seen, Singer's approach is not convincing to all and, more importantly, is very demanding and reliant on individual altruism, despite its argument for obligations. One response to Singer's approach might also be that to give money only makes matters worse by encouraging inefficiency and corruption, by developing a welfare culture of dependency and by removing any incentive to address internal causes of poverty and hardship, not to mention the possibility that aid might go to corrupt officials.

7 Even Peter Singer (2002: 100), in a very balanced assessment of the effects of globalization, states: 'No evidence I have found enable me to form a clear view about the overall impact of economic globalisation on the poor. Most likely it has helped some to escape poverty and thrown others deeper into it. But whether it has helped more people than it has harmed, and whether is has caused more good to those it has helped than it has brought misery to those it has harmed is something that, without better data, we just cannot know.'

Bibliography

Amstutz, M. R. (1999) *International Ethics*. New York: Rowman & Littlefield.

Anderson, M. (1999) *Do No Harm: How Aid Can Support Peace – Or War*. Boulder, CO: Lynne Rienner.

Anderson, M. B. (1998) 'You Save My Life Today, but for What Tomorrow?', in J. Moore, *Hard Choices: Moral Dilemmas in Humanitarian Intervention*. New York: Rowman & Littlefield.

Anderson-Gold, S. (2001) *Cosmopolitanism and Human Rights*. Cardiff: University of Wales Press.

Archibugi, D., ed. (2003) *Debating Cosmopolitics*. London: Verso.

Archibugi, D. (2004) 'Cosmopolitan Guidelines for Humanitarian Intervention', *Alternatives* 29/1 (January–February): 1–21.

Arendt, H. ([1951] 1967) *The Origins of Totalitarianism*. New York: Harcourt.

Arendt, H. (1968) *Imperialism* (part two of *The Origins of Totalitarianism*). New York: Harcourt.

Aristotle (1980) *Nicomachean Ethics*. Oxford: Oxford University Press.

Arneson, R. J. (2004) 'Moral Limits on the Demands of Beneficence?', in D. K. Chatterjee, ed., *The Ethics of Assistance*.

Australian Refugee Rights Alliance (ARRA) (2007) *Tackling Refoulement*. Available at: <http://www.crr.unsw.edu.au/documents/Tackling%20refoulement.pdf>.

Avineri, S., and de-Shalit, A., eds (1992) *Communitarianism and Individualism*. Oxford: Oxford University Press.

Baldry, H. C. (1965) *The Unity of Mankind in Greek Thought*, Cambridge: Cambridge University Press.

Barnett, M. (2005) 'Humanitarianism Transformed', *Perspectives on Politics* 3/4 (December): 723–40.

Barry, B. (1989) *A Treatise on Social Justice*. Berkeley, CA: University of California Press.

Barry, B. (1992) 'The Quest for Consistency: A Sceptical View', in B. Barry and R. E. Goodin, eds, *Free Movement*.

Barry, B. (1995) *Justice as Impartiality*. Oxford: Oxford University Press.

Barry, B. (1998) 'International Society from a Cosmopolitan Perspective', in D. Mapel and T. Nardin, eds, *International Society: Diverse Ethical Perspectives*. Princeton, NJ: Princeton University Press, 144–63.

Barry, B. (1999) 'Statism and Nationalism: A Cosmopolitan Critique', in I. Shapiro and L. Brilmayer, eds, *Nomos Global Justice*. New York: New York University Press, 12–66.

Barry, B., and Goodin, R. E., eds (1992) *Free Movement: Ethical Issues in the Transnational Migration of People and of Money*. Hemel Hempstead: Harvester Wheatsheaf; University Park, PA: Pennsylvania State University Press.

Bauer, J., and Bell, D. A., eds (1999) *The East Asian Challenge for Human Rights*. Cambridge: Cambridge University Press.

Beitz, C. (1979) *Political Theory and International Relations*. Princeton, NJ: Princeton University Press.

Beitz, C. R. (1983) 'Cosmopolitan Ideals and National Sentiment', *Journal of Philosophy* 80/10 (October): 591–600.

Beitz, C. ed. (1985) *International Ethics*. Princeton, NJ: Princeton University Press.

Beitz, C. (1991) 'Sovereignty and Morality in International Affairs', in D. Held, ed., *Political Theory Today*.

Beitz, C. (1992) 'Cosmopolitanism and Sovereignty', *Ethics* 103: 48–75.

Beitz, C. (1994) 'Cosmopolitan Liberalism and the States System', in C. Brown, ed., *Political Restructuring in Europe: Ethical Perspectives*, 123–36.

Beitz, C. (1999) 'Social and Cosmopolitan Liberalism', *International Affairs* 75/3: 512–99.

Beitz, C. (2000) 'Rawls's Law of Peoples', *Ethics* 110/4 (July): 669–6.

Bell, D., and Carens, J. (2004) 'The Ethical Dilemmas of International Human Rights and Humanitarian NGOs: Reflections on a Dialogue between Practitioners and Theorists', *Human Rights Quarterly* 26/2: 300–29

Bellamy, A. (2004) 'Supreme Emergencies and the Protection of Non-combatants in War', *International Affairs* 80/5: 829–50.

Bellamy, A. (2006) *Just Wars*. Cambridge: Polity.

Bellamy, A. (2008) *Responsibility to Protect*. Cambridge: Polity.

Benhabib, S. (1992), *Situating the Self*. Oxford: Blackwell.

Benhabib, S. (1995) 'Cultural Complexity, Moral Interdependence and the Global Dialogical Community', in M. Nussbaum and Glover, eds, *Women, Culture and Development*. Oxford: Oxford University Press.

Benhabib, S. (2004) *The Rights of Others: Aliens, Residents and Citizens*. Cambridge: Cambridge University Press.

Bentham, J. ([1789] 1970) *An Introduction to the Principles of Morals and Legislation*, ed. J. Burns and H. L. A. Hart. London: Athlone Press.

Blake, M. (2003) 'Immigration', in R. G. Frey and C. H. Wellman, eds, *A Companion to Applied Ethics*, 224–37.

Booth, K., and Dunne, T., eds (2002) *Worlds in Collision: Terror and the Future of Global Order*. London: Palgrave Macmillan.

Boucher, D. (1998) *Political Theories of International Relations: From Thucydides to the Present*. Oxford: Oxford University Press.

Brooks, T. (2002), 'Cosmopolitanism and Distributing Responsibilities', *Critical Review of International Social and Political Philosophy* 5/3 (autumn): 92–7.

Brown, C. (1992) *International Relations Theory: New Normative Approaches*. New York: Columbia University Press.

Brown, C., ed. (1994) *Political Restructuring in Europe: Ethical Perspectives*. London: Routledge.

Brown, C. (1998) 'Ethics of Coexistence: The International Theory of Terry Nardin', *Review of International Studies* 14: 213–22.

Brown, C. (1999) 'Universal Human Rights: A Critique', in N. Wheeler, ed., *Human Rights in Global Politics*, 103–27.

Brown, C. (2002) *Sovereignty, Rights and Justice: International Political Theory Today*. Cambridge: Polity.

Brown, M. A. (2002) *Human Rights and the Borders of Suffering: The Promotion of Human Rights in International Politics*. Manchester: Manchester University Press.

Brown, P. G., and Shue, H. (1981) *Boundaries: National Autonomy and its Limits*. New Jersey: Rowman & Littlefield.

Buchanan, A. E. (1989) 'Assessing the Communitarian Critique of Liberalism', *Ethics* 99/4: 852–82.

Buchanan, A. (2000) 'Rawls's Law of the Peoples: Rules for a Vanished Westphalian World', *Ethics* 110/4: 697–721.

Buchanan, A., and Keohane, R. (2004) 'The Preventive Use of Force: A Cosmopolitan Institutional Proposal', *Ethics and International Affairs* 18/1: 1–22.

Bull, H. (1966) 'The Grotian Conception of International Society', in Herbert Butterfield and Martin Wight, eds. *Diplomatic Investigations*, 51–73.

Bull, H. (1967) 'Society and Anarchy in International Affairs', in M. Wight and H. Butterfield, eds, *Diplomatic Investigations*. London: Allen & Unwin.

Bull, H. (1977) *The Anarchical Society: A Study of Order in World Politics*. New York: Columbia University Press.

Bull, H. (1979) 'Recapturing the Just War for Political Theory', *World Politics* 31/4: 588–99.

Bull, H. (1983) *Justice in International Relations* (The Hagey Lectures). Ontario, Canada: University of Waterloo.

Burke, A. (2004) 'Just War or Ethical Peace? Moral Discourses of Strategic Violence after 9/11', *International Affairs* 80/2: 329–53.

Burke, A. (2007) *Beyond Security, Ethics and Violence: War Against the Other*. London: Routledge.

Butterfield, Herbert, and Wight, Martin, eds (1966) *Diplomatic Investigations*. London: Allen and Unwin.

Buzan, B. (2002) 'Who May We Bomb?', in K. Booth and T. Dunne, eds, *Worlds in Collision: Terror and the Future of Global Order*, 85–94.

Cabrera, L. (2004). *Political Theory of Global Justice: A Cosmopolitan Case for the World State*. New York: Routledge.

Calhoun, C. (2003) 'The Class Consciousness of Frequent Travellers: Towards a Critique of Actually Existing Cosmopolitanism', in D. Archibugi, ed., *Debating Cosmopolitics*, 86–116.

Campbell, D. (1998) 'Why Fight? Humanitarianism, Principles, and Post-Structuralism', *Millennium* 27/3: 497–521.

Caney, S. (2001a) 'International Distributive Justice (review article)', *Political Studies* 49: 974–97.

Caney, S. (2001b) 'Cosmopolitan Justice and Equalising Opportunities', *Metaphilosophy* 32/1–2 (January): 113–34.

Caney, S. (2005) *Justice Beyond Borders: A Global Political Theory*. New York: Oxford University Press.

Carens, J. (1980) 'Aliens and Citizens: The Case for Open Borders', *The Review of Politics* 49: 251–73.

Carens, J. (1992a) 'Refugees and the Limits of Obligation', *Public Affairs Quarterly* 6/1: 31–44.

Carens, J. (1992b) 'Migration and Morality: A Liberal Egalitarian Perspective', in Barry and Goodin, eds, *Free Movement*, 25–47.

Carens, J. (1996) 'Realistic and Idealistic Approaches to the Ethics of Migration', *International Migration Review* 30/1. *Special Issue: Ethics, Migration, and Global Stewardship* (spring): 156–70.

Carens, J. (1997) 'The Philosopher and the Policymaker: Two Perspectives on the Ethics of Immigration with Special Attention to the Problem of Restricting Asylum', in Kay Hailbronner, David A. Martin and Hiroshi Motomura, *Immigration Admissions: The Search for Workable Policies in Germany and the United States*. New York: Berghahn Books, 3–50.

Carens, J. (1999) 'A Reply to Meilaender: Reconsidering Open Borders', *International Migration Review* 33/4 (winter): 1082–97.

Carens, J. (2000) *Culture Citizenship and Community. A Contextual Exploration of Justice as Even-handedness*. Oxford: Oxford University Press.

Carens, J. (2003) 'Who Should Get In? The Ethics of Immigration Admissions', *Ethics and International Affairs* 17/1: 95–110.

Carr, E. H. (1939) *The Twenty Years' Crisis*. London: Routledge.

Ceadal, M. (1989) *Thinking about Peace and War*. Oxford: Oxford University Press.

Chandler, D. (2001) 'The Road to Military Humanitarianism: How the Human Rights NGOs Shaped a New Humanitarian Agenda', *Human Rights Quarterly* 23: 678–700.

Charny, J. R. (2004) 'Upholding Humanitarian Principles in an Effective Integrated Response', *Ethics and International Affairs* 18/2: 13–20.

Charvet, J. (2001) 'The Possibility of Cosmopolitan Ethical Order Based on the Idea of Universal Human Rights', in H. Sekinelgin and H. Shinoda, *Ethics and International Relations*, London: Palgrave, 8–29.

Chatterjee, D. K., ed. (2004) *The Ethics of Assistance: Morality and the Distant Needy*. Cambridge: Cambridge University Press.

Clapp, J. (2005) 'The Political Economy of Food Aid in an Era of Agricultural Biotechnology', *Global Governance* 11: 467–85.

Coates, A. J. (1997) *The Ethics of War*. Manchester: Manchester University Press.

Coates, A. J. (2000) 'Just War in the Persian Gulf', in A. Valls, ed., *Ethics in International Affairs*, 33–48.

Coady, C. A. J. (2004) 'Terrorism, Morality, and Supreme Emergency', *Ethics* 114 (July): 772–89.

Cochran, M. (1999) *Normative Theory in International Relations*. Cambridge: Cambridge University Press.

Cole, P. (2000) *Philosophies of Exclusion: Liberal Political Theory and Immigration*. Edinburgh: Edinburgh University Press.

Cooper, D. E., ed. (1998) *Ethics: The Classic Readings*. Oxford: Blackwell.

David, S. R., and Stein, Y. (2003) 'Debate on Israel's Policy of Targeted Killing', *Ethics and International Affairs* 17/1: 111–26.

De Greiff, P., and Cronin, C., eds (2002) *Global Justice and Transnational Politics*. Cambridge, MA: MIT Press.

De Torrente, N. (2004) 'Humanitarianism Sacrificed, Integration's False Promise', *Ethics and International Affairs* 18/2): 3–12.

Derrida, J. (2001) *On Cosmopolitanism and Forgiveness*. London: Routledge.

Devetak, Richard (2007) 'Between Kant and Pufendorf: Humanitarian Intervention, Statist Anti-cosmopolitanism and Critical International Theory', *Review of International Studies* 33: 151–74.

Donaldson, T. (1990) 'Kant's Global Rationalism', in Nardin and Mapel, *Traditions of International Ethics*, 136–57.

Donini, A. (2004) 'An Elusive Quest: Integration in Response to the Afghan Crisis', *Ethics and International Affairs* 18/2: 21–7.

Donini, A. (2007) *How Compatible Are UN Coherence and Humanitarian Partnership?* Medford, MA: Feinstein International Center, Tufts University. Available at: <https://wikis.uit.tufts.edu/confluence/

download/attachments/14553621/Donini-How+Compatible+Are+UN +Coherence+and+Humanitarian+Partnership.pdf?version=1>.

Donnelly, J. (1989) *Universal Human Rights in Theory and Practice.* Ithaca, NY: Cornell University Press.

Donnelly, J. (1999a) *International Human Rights.* Boulder, CO: Westview Press.

Donnelly, J. (1999b) 'Human Rights and Asian Values: A Defence of "Western" Universalism', in J. Bauer and D. Bell, eds, *The East Asian Challenge for Human Rights*, 60–87.

Dower, N. (1998) *World Ethics: The New Agenda.* Edinburgh: Edinburgh University Press.

Dower, N. (2009) *The Ethics of War and Peace.* Cambridge: Polity.

Dummett, A. (1992) 'The Transnational Migration of People and Money Seen within a Natural Law Tradition', in Brian Barry and Robert E. Goodin, eds, *Free Movement*, 169–80.

Dummett, M. (2001) *On Immigration and Refugees.* London: Routledge.

Eckert, A. E. (2008) 'Obligations beyond National Borders: International Institutions and Distributive Justice', *Journal of Global Ethics* 4/1: 67–78.

Edkins, J. (1996) 'Legality with a Vengeance: Famines and Humanitarian Relief in "Complex Emergencies"', *Millennium: Journal of International Studies* 25/3: 547–75.

Edkins, J. (2003) 'Humanitarianism, Humanity, Human', *Journal of Human Rights* 2/2 (June): 253–8.

Ellis, A. (1992) 'Utilitarianism', in Nardin and Mapel, *Traditions of International Ethics*, 158–70.

Elshtain, J. (1992) *Just War Theory.* New York: New York University Press.

Elshtain, J. (2003) *Just War Against Terror: The Burden of American Power in a Violent World.* New York: Basic Books.

Elshtain, J. (2005) 'Against The New Utopianism', *Ethics and International Affairs* 19/2: 91–5.

Erskine, T. (2001) 'Assigning Responsibilities to Institutional Moral Agents: The Case of States and Quasi -States', *Ethics and International Affairs* 15/2: 67–85.

Erskine, T. (2002) '"Citizen of Nowhere" or "the Point where Circles Intersect"? Impartialist and Embedded Cosmopolitanisms', *Review of International Studies* (2002) 28: 457–78.

Etzioni, A. (2004) *From Empire to Community: A New Approach to International Relations.* New York: Palgrave Macmillan.

Fabre, C. (2007) *Justice in a Changing World.* Cambridge: Polity.

Favez, J-C. (1999) *The Red Cross and the Holocaust*, ed. and trans. John and Beryl Fletcher; originally published as *Une mission impossible?* (1988). Cambridge: Cambridge University Press.

Feinberg, J. (1984) *Harm to Others: The Moral Limits of the Criminal Law.* Oxford: Oxford University Press.

Finnis, J. (1996) 'The Ethics of War and Peace in the Catholic Natural Law Tradition', in Nardin, ed., *The Ethics of War and Peace*, 15–39.

Fixdal, M., and Smith, D. (1998) 'Humanitarian Intervention and Just War', *Mershon International Studies Review* 42: 283–312.

Fox, F. (2001) 'New Humanitarianism: Does It Provide a Moral Banner for the 21st Century?', *Disasters* 25/4: 275–89.

Franceshet, A. (2002) *Kant and Liberal Internationalism*. London: Palgrave.

Frazer, E., and Lacey, N. (1993) *The Politics of Community: A Feminist Critique of the Liberal–Communitarian Debate*. New York and London: Harvester Wheatsheaf.

Frey, R. G., and Wellman, C. H., eds (2003) *A Companion to Applied Ethics*. Oxford: Blackwell.

Frost, M. (1996) *Ethics in International Relations: A Constitutive Theory*. Cambridge: Cambridge University Press.

Frost, M. (1998) 'Migrants, Civil Society, and Sovereign States: Investigating an Ethical Hierarchy', *Political Studies* 46/5 (December): 871.

Frost, M. (2002) *Constituting Human Rights: Global Civil Society and the Society of Democratic States*. London and New York: Routledge.

Gall, J., and O'Hagan, J. (2003) 'Humanitarianism in International Society: A Genealogy', paper presented to Ethics and Australian Foreign Policy Symposium, University of Queensland.

Gallie, W. B. (1978) *Philosophers of Peace and War*. Cambridge: Cambridge University Press.

Gardiner, S. (2004) 'The Global Warming Tragedy and the Dangerous Illusion of the Kyoto Protocol', *Ethics and International Affairs* 18/1: 23–39.

Gardiner, S. (2004) 'Ethics and Global Climate Change', *Ethics* 114 (April): 555–600.

Gelb, L. H., and. Rosenthal, J. A. (2003) 'The Rise of Ethics in Foreign Policy: Reaching a Values Consensus', *Foreign Affairs* 82/3 (May/June): 2–7.

Gelber, K., and McDonald, M. (2006) 'Ethics and Exclusion: Australia's Approach to Asylum Seekers', *Review of International Studies* 32/2 (April): 269–89.

Gibney, M. J. (1999) 'Liberal Democratic States and Responsibilities to Refugees', *American Political Science Review* 93/1 (March): 169.

Gibney, M. J. (2004) *The Ethics and Politics of Asylum: Liberal Democracy and the Response to Refugees*. Cambridge: Cambridge University Press.

Goodin, R. E. (1988) 'What is So Special About Our Fellow Countrymen?', *Ethics* 98/4 (July): 663–86.

Goodin, R. E. (1992) 'If People Were Money', in Barry and Goodin, eds, *Free Movement*, 6–22.

Gordon, J. (1999) 'The Ethics of Economic Sanctions', in *Ethics and International Affairs* 13: 123–42.

Gray, C. S. (2000) 'No Good Deed Shall Go Unpunished', *International Journal of Human Rights* 4/3–4 (autumn–winter): 302–6.

Grossrieder, P. (2002). 'Humanitarian Action in the 21st Century: The Danger of a Setback', *Refugee Survey Quarterly* 21/3: 23–32.

Grubb, M. (1995) 'Seeking Fair Weather: Ethics and the International Debate on Climate Change', *International Affairs* 71/3: 463–96.

Gunnell, J. (1974) *Political Theory, Tradition and Interpretation*. Cambridge, MA: Winthrop, Inc.

Guyer, P. (2007) *Kant's 'Groundwork for the Metaphysics of Morals'*. London: Continuum.

Gvosdev, N. K. (2005) 'Communitarian Realism', *American Behavioural Scientist* 48/12 (August): 1591–1606.

Habermas, J. (1990) *Moral Consciousness and Communicative Action*. Cambridge: Polity.

Habermas, J. (1992, 2008) 'Citizenship and National Identity: Some Reflections on the Future of Europe', in T. Pogge and K. Horton, eds, *Global Justice*, 285–310.

Habermas, J. (1999) 'Between Bestiality and Humanity: A War on the Border between Legality and Morality', *Constellations* 6/3: 263–74.

Habermas, J. (2003) 'Interpreting the Fall of a Monument', *Constellations* 10/3: 364–70.

Hailbronner, K., Martin, D., and Motomura, H., eds, (1997) *Immigration Admissions: The Search for Workable Policies in Germany and the United States*. New York: Berghahn Books.

Harbour, F. V. (1998) *Thinking about International Ethics*. Boulder, CO: Westview Press.

Harris, P. G. (2001) *International Equity and Global Environmental Politics*. Aldershot: Ashgate.

Hashmi, S. H., ed. (2002a) *Islamic Political Ethics*, Princeton, NJ: Princeton University Press.

Hashmi, S. H. (2002b) 'Interpreting the Islamic Ethics of War and Peace', in Nardin ed., *The Ethics of War and Peace*, 146–66.

Hashmi, S. (2003) 'Is there an Islamic Ethics of Humanitarianism Intervention?', in Lang, Jr, Anthony, F., *Just Intervention*. Washington, DC: Georgetown University Press, 62–83.

Hayden, P. (2005) *Cosmopolitan Global Politics*. Aldershot: Ashgate.

Hayter, T. (2000) *Open Borders, the Case against Immigration Controls*. London: Pluto Press.

Held, D. (1997) 'Cosmopolitan Democracy and the Global Order', in J. Bohman and Lutz-Bachman, eds, *Perpetual Peace*. Cambridge, MA: MIT Press, 235–52.

Held, D. ed. (1991) *Political Theory Today*. Cambridge: Polity.

Held, D., and Archibugi, D. (1995) *Cosmopolitan Democracy*. Cambridge: Polity.

Held, V. (2006) *The Ethics of Care*. Oxford: Oxford University Press.

Hendrickson, D. (1992) 'Migration in Law and Ethics: A Realist Perspective', in Barry and Goodin, eds, *Free Movement*, 213–31.

Herman, B. (1984) 'Mutual Aid and Respect for Persons', *Ethics* 94/4 (JulY): 577–602.

Herman, B. (2001) 'The Scope of Moral Requirement', *Philosophy and Public Affairs* 30/3 (summer): 227–56.

Herman, B. (2008) 'Morality Unbounded', *Philosophy and Public Affairs* 36/4: 323–58.

Hoffman, S. (1981) *Duties Beyond Borders*. Syracuse, NY: Syracuse University Press.

Hoffmann, S. (1995–6) 'The Politics and Ethics of Military Intervention', *Survival* 37/4: 29–51.

Hopgood, S. (2000) 'Reading the Small Print in Global Civil Society: The Inexorable Hegemony of the Liberal Self', *Millennium: Journal of International Studies* 29/1: 1–25.

Howard, M. (1994) 'Constraints on Warfare', in M. Howard, G. J. Andreopoulos and M. R. Shulman, eds, *The Laws of War: Constraints on Warfare in the Western World*. New Haven, CT: Yale University Press, 12–26.

Hurrell. A. (2007) *On Global Order, Power Values and the Constitution of International Society*. Oxford: Oxford University Press.

Hutchings, K. (1999) *International Political Theory*. London: Sage.

Ignatieff, M. (2000) *Virtual War*. London: Chatto & Windus.

International Commission on Intervention and State Sovereignty (ICISS) (2001) Available at: <http://www.iciss-ciise.gc.ca/>.

International Committee of the Red Cross (ICRC) (2007) Available at: <http://www.icrc.org>.

Jackson, R. H. (2000) *The Global Covenant*. Oxford: Oxford University Press.

Jackson, R. H. (2005) *Classical and Modern Thought on International Relations*. New York: Palgrave.

Jamieson, D. (1997–8) 'Global Responsibilities: Ethics, Public Health, and Global Environmental Change', *Global Legal Studies* 99: 99–119.

Jochnick, C., and. Normand, R. (1994) 'The Legitimation of Violence: A Critical History of the Laws of War', *Harvard International Law Journal* 49: 49–95.

Johnson, J. T. (1997) *The Holy War Idea in Western and Islamic Traditions*. Pennsylvania, PA: Pennsylvania State University Press.

Johnson, J. T. (2002) 'Jihad and Just War', *First Things* 124/12 (June–July): 14.

Johnson, J. T., and Kelsay, J., eds (1991) *Just War and Jihad: Historical and Theoretical Perspectives on War and Peace in Western and Islamic Traditions*. Westport, CT: Greenwood Press.

Jones, C. (1999) *Global Justice: Defending Cosmopolitanism*. Oxford: Oxford University Press.

Jones, P. (2000) 'Global Distributive Justice', in Valls, ed., *Ethics in International Affairs*, 169–84.

Jordan, B., and Duvell, F. (2003) *Migration: The Boundaries of Equality and Justice*. Cambridge: Polity.

Kant, I. ([1795] 1983) *Perpetual Peace and Other Essays*, trans. Ted Humphrey. Indianapolis, IN: Hackett.

Kant, I. (1998) 'Fundamental Principle of the Metaphysic of Morals', in D. E. Cooper, ed., *Ethics: The Classic Readings*. Oxford: Blackwell, 166–80.

Kant, I. ([1785] 2002) *Groundwork for the Metaphysics of Morals*, in Focus series, ed. L. Pasternak. London: Routledge.

Kapur, D., and McHale, J. (2006) 'Should a Cosmopolitan Worry about the Brain Drain?', *Ethics and International Affairs* 20/3: 305–20.

Kelsay, J. (1993) *Islam and War: A Study in Comparative Ethics*: Louisville, KY: Westminster, John Knox Press.

Kennan, G. (1986) 'Morality and Foreign Policy', *Foreign Affairs* 64: 205–18.

Khadduri, M. (1955) *War and Peace in the Law of Islam*. Baltimore, MD: Johns Hopkins Press.

Klosko, G. (2004) 'Multiple Principles of Political Obligation', *Political Theory* 32: 801.

Kokaz, N. (2007) 'Poverty and Global Justice', *Ethics and International Affairs* 21/3: 317–36.

Kung, H. (1990) *Global Responsibility: In Search of a New World Ethic*. London: SCM Press.

Kuper, A. (2002) 'More than Charity: Cosmopolitan Alternatives to the "Singer Solution"', *Ethics and International Affairs* 16/1: 107–20.

Kymlicka, W. (2001) *Politics in the Vernacular: Nationalism, Multiculturalism, and Citizenship*. Oxford: Oxford University Press.

Kymlicka, W., and Opalski, M., eds (2001b) *Can Liberal Pluralism Be Exported?: Western Political Theory and Ethnic Relations in Eastern Europe*. Oxford: Oxford University Press.

Last, D. (2000) 'Reflections from the Field: Ethical Challenges in Peacekeeping and Humanitarian Interventions', *Fletcher Forum of World Affairs* 24/1: 73–86.

Lebow, R. N. (2003) *The Tragic Vision of Politics: Ethics Interests and Orders*. Cambridge: Cambridge University Press.

Lieven, A., and Hulsman, J. (2006) *Ethical Realism: A Vision for America's Role in the World*. New York: Pantheon.

Linklater, A. (1990a) 'The Problem of Community in International Relations', *Alternatives* 15: 135–53.

Linklater, A. (1990b), *Men and Citizens in the Theory of International Relations*, 2nd edn. London: Macmillan.

Linklater, A. (1990c) *Beyond Realism and Marxism: Critical Theory and International Relations*. London: Macmillan.

Linklater, A. (1992) 'The Question of the Next Stage in International

Relations: A Critical Theoretical Point of View', *Millennium* 21/1 (spring): 77–100.

Linklater, A. (1998) *The Transformation of Political Community: Ethical Foundations of the Post-Westphalian Era.* Cambridge: Polity.

Linklater, A. (1999) 'The Evolving Spheres of International Justice', *International Affairs* 75/3: 473–82.

Linklater, A. (2000) 'The Good International Citizen and the Crisis in Kosovo', in A. Schnabel and R. C. Thakur, eds, *Kosovo and the Challenge of Humanitarian Intervention: Selective Indignation.* Tokyo: United Nations University Press, 482–95.

Linklater, A. (2001) 'Citizenship, Humanity and Cosmopolitan Harm Conventions', *International Political Science Review*, special issue, 22/3: 261–77.

Linklater, A. (2002a) 'Cosmopolitan Political Communities in International Relations', *International Relations* 16/1: 135–50.

Linklater, A. (2002b) 'Cosmopolitan Harm Conventions', in S. Verkovec and R. Cohen, eds, *Conceiving Cosmopolitanism: Theory, Context and Practice.* Oxford: Oxford University Press, 254–67.

Linklater, A. (2002c) 'Unnecessary Suffering', in K. Booth and T. Dunne, eds, *Worlds in Collision: Terror and the Future of Global Order.* London: Palgrave, 303–12.

Linklater, A. (2002d) 'The Problem of Harm in World Politics: Implications for the Sociology of States-Systems', *International Affairs* 78/2: 319–38.

Linklater, A. (2004) 'Emotions and World Politics', *Aberystwyth Journal of World Affairs* (December).

Linklater, A. (2005a) 'Discourse Ethics and the Civilizing Process', *Review of International Studies* 31/1 (January): 145–54.

Linklater, A. (2005b) 'Global Ethics', in J. A. Scholte and R. Robertson, eds, *An Encyclopaedia of Globalisation.* London: Routledge.

Linklater, A. (2005c) 'The Harm Principle and Global Ethics', *Global Society* 20/3 (July): 329–43.

Linklater, A. (2006) 'Cosmopolitanism', in A. Dobson and R. Eckersley, eds, *Political Theory and the Ecological Challenge*, Cambridge: Cambridge University Press, 109–28.

Lu, C. (2000) 'The One and Many Faces of Cosmopolitanism', *Journal of Political Philosophy* 8/2: 244–67.

Luban, D. (1980) 'Just War and Human Rights', *Philosophy and Public Affairs* 9: 160–81.

Luban, D. (2002) 'Intervention and Civilisation: Some Unhappy Lessons of the Kosovo War', in Pablo de Greiff and Ciaran Cronin, *Global Justice and Transnational Politics.* Cambridge, MA: MIT Press, 79–116.

Lynch, M. (2000) 'The Dialogue of Civilisations and International Public Spheres', *Millennium* 29/2: 307–30.

MacIntyre, A. (1966) *A Short History of Ethics.* London: Routledge.

MacIntyre, A. (1999) 'Is Patriotism a Virtue?', in M. Rosen and Jonathan Wolff, eds, *The Oxford Reader in Political Thought*. Oxford: Oxford University Press, 269–84.

Make Poverty History. 2000– . High-profile public campaign to end poverty. Available at: <www.makepovertyhistory.org>,

Mapel, D., and Nardin, T., eds (1998) *International Society: Diverse Ethical Perspectives*. Princeton, NJ: Princeton University Press.

Mapel, D. R. (1996) 'Realism and the Ethics of War and Peace', in Nardin, ed., *The Ethics of War and Peace*. Princeton, NJ: Princeton University Press, 54–77.

Martin, R., and Reidy, D. A., eds (2006) *Rawls's Law of Peoples: A Realistic Utopia*. Oxford: Blackwell.

Martone, G. (2002) 'Relentless Humanitarianism', *Global Governance* 8/2: 149–54.

Mearsheimer, J. (2001) *The Tragedy of Great Power Politics*. New York and London: W.W. Norton & Co.

Mearsheimer, J., and Walt. S. (2003) 'An Unnecessary War', *Foreign Policy* (January/February): 51–3.

Médecins Sans Frontières (MSF) (no date) Online source. Available at: <www.msf.org>.

Meilaender, P. (1999) 'Liberalism and Open Borders: The Argument of Joseph Carens', *International Migration Review* 33/4 (winter): 1062–81.

Meilaender, P. (2001) *Toward a Theory of Immigration*. New York: Palgrave.

Mill, J. S. (1960) '*Utilitarianism; Liberty; Representative Government*', Everyman Edition. London: J. M. Dent.

Mill, J. S. (2002) 'A Few Words on Non-Intervention', in C. Brown, T. Nardin, and N. J. R. Rengger, *International Relations in Political Thought*. Cambridge: Cambridge University Press, 486–93.

Miller, D. (1988) 'The Ethical Significance of Nationality', *Ethics* 98/4 (July): 647–62.

Miller, D. (1995) *On Nationality*. Oxford: Clarendon Press.

Miller, D. (1999) 'Justice and Inequality', in N. Woods and A. Hurrell, eds, *Inequality, Globalisation and World Politics*. Oxford: Oxford University Press, 187–210.

Miller, D. (2000) 'National Self-Determination and Global Justice', in D. Miller, ed., *Citizenship and National Identity*. Cambridge: Polity, 161–79.

Miller, D. (2001a) 'Distributing Responsibilities', *Journal of Political Philosophy* 9/4: 453.

Miller, D. (2001b) 'Two Ways to Think about Justice', *Politics, Philosophy and Economics* 1: 5–28.

Miller, D. (2002) 'Caney's "International Distributive Justice"': A Response', *Political Studies* 50: 974–7.

Miller, D. (2004a) 'Holding Nations Responsible', *Ethics* 114: 240–68.

Miller, D. (2004b) 'National Responsibility and International Justice', in D. K. Chatterjee, The *Ethics of Assistance*. Cambridge: Cambridge University Press, 123–76.

Miller, D. (2005) 'Immigration: The Case for Limits', in A. I. Cohen and C. H. Wellman, eds, *Contemporary Debates in Applied Ethics*. Oxford: Blackwell, 193–206.

Miller, D. (2007) *National Responsibility and Global Justice*. Oxford: Oxford University Press. Oxford Scholarship Online. Oxford University Press. 30 July 2009: <http://dx.doi.org/10.1093/acprof:oso/9780199235056.001.0001>.

Miller, D. (2008) 'National Responsibility and Global Justice', *Critical Review of International Social and Political Philosophy* 11/4: 383–99.

Miller, D., and Walzer, M., eds (1995) *Pluralism, Justice and Equality*. Oxford: Oxford University Press.

Miller, L. H. (1964) 'The Contemporary Significance of the Doctrine of Just War', *World Politics* 16/2 (January): 254–86.

Miller, S. (2005) 'Need, Care and Obligation', *Royal Institute of Philosophy Supplement* 80: 137–60.

Moellendorf, D. (2002) *Cosmopolitan Justice*. Boulder, CO: Westview.

Morgenthau, H. (1952) *American Foreign Policy: A Critical Examination* (also published as *In Defence of the National Interest*). London: Methuen.

Morgenthau H. ([1948] 1960) *Politics among Nations*, 3rd edn. New York: Knopf.

Moses, J. W. (2006) *International Migration: Globalization's Last Frontier*. London: Zed Books.

Mouffev, C. (2005) 'The Limits of John Rawls's Pluralism', *Politics, Philosophy & Economics* 4/2: 221–31.

Murray, A. (1996) 'The Moral Politics of Hans Morgenthau', *Review of Politics* 19: 81–107.

Nafziger, E., Wayne, F. S., and Väyrynen, R., eds (2000) *War, Hunger, and Displacement: The Origins of Humanitarian Emergencies*. Oxford: Oxford University Press.

Nagel, T. (2005) 'The Problem of Global Justice', *Philosophy and Public Affairs* 33/2: 112–47.

Nandy, A. (2002) 'The Beautiful Expanding Future of Poverty: Popular Economics as a Psychological Defense', *International Studies Review* 4/2 (summer): 107–22.

Nardin, T. (1983) *Law, Morality and the Relations of States*. Princeton, NJ: Princeton University Press.

Nardin, T. (1992) 'Ethical Traditions in International Affairs', in T. Nardin and D. Mapel, eds, *Traditions of International Ethics*, 1–22.

Nardin, T. (1996) 'The Comparative Ethics of War and Peace', in *The Ethics of War and Peace: Religious and Secular Perspectives*, 245–64.

Nardin, T. ed. (2002a) *The Ethics of War and Peace: Religious and Secular Perspectives*. Princeton, NJ: Princeton University Press.

Nardin, T. (2002b) 'The Moral Basis of Humanitarian Intervention', *Ethics and International Affairs* 16/1: 57–70.

Nardin, T., and Mapel, D., eds (1992) *Traditions of International Ethics*. Cambridge: Cambridge University Press.

Nash, K. (2003) 'Cosmopolitan Political Community: Why Does It Feel So Right?', *Constellations* 10/4 (December): 506–18.

Neumayer, E. (2005) 'Is the Allocation of Food Aid Free from Donor Interest Bias?', *Journal of Development Studies* 41/3: 394–411.

Nussbaum, M. (1995) 'Human Capabilities, Female Human Beings', in M. Nussbaum and J. Glover, *Women, Culture and Development*. Oxford: Oxford University Press, 61–104.

Nussbaum, M. (1996) 'Patriotism and Cosmopolitanism', in M. Nussbaum et al., *For Love of Country; Debating the Limits of Patriotism*. Boston, MA: Beacon Press, 2–20.

Nussbaum, M. (2002a) 'Capabilities and Human Rights', in P. De Greiff and C. Cronin, eds, *Global Justice and Transnational Politics*.

Nussbaum, M. (2002b) 'Capabilities and Social Justice', *International Studies Review* 4/2: 123–35.

Nussbaum, M. (2007) *Frontiers of Justice, Disability, Nationality and Species Membership*. Cambridge, MA: Belknap Press, Harvard.

Nussbaum, M., and Glover, J. (1995) *Women, Culture and Development: A Study of Human Capabilities*. Oxford: Oxford University Press.

OCHA (2008) Available at: <http://ochaonline.un.org/AboutOCHA/>.

O'Neill, O. (1986) *Faces of Hunger*. London: Allen & Unwin.

O'Neill, O. (1988) 'Ethical Reasoning and Ideological Pluralism', *Ethics* 98/4 (July): 705–22.

O'Neill, O. (1990) 'Transnational Justice', in D. Held, ed., *Political Theory Today*. Cambridge: Polity, 276–304.

O'Neill, O. (1996) *Beyond Justice and Virtue*. Cambridge: Cambridge University Press.

O'Neill, O. (2000) *Bounds of Justice*, Cambridge: Cambridge University Press.

Orend, B. (1999) 'Crisis in Kosovo: A Just Use of Force?' *Politics* 19/3: 125–30.

Orend, B. (2000) 'Jus Post Bellum', *Journal of Social Philosophy* 31/1: 117–37.

Orend, B. (2002) 'Justice After War', *Ethics and International Affairs* 16/1: 43–56.

Orend, B. (2005) 'War', *Stanford Encyclopaedia of Philosophy*. Available at: <http://plato.stanford.edu/entries/war>.

Pécoud, A., Paul, F., and Guchteneire, A., eds (2007) *Migration Without Borders*. Berghahn and Unesco.

Penz, P. (2000) 'Ethical Reflections on the Institution of Asylum', *Refuge: Canada's Periodical on Refugees* 19/3 (December): 44–53.

Pictet, J. (1979) 'The Fundamental Principles of the Red Cross: Commentary'. Available at: <www.icrc.org>.

Pittaway, E., and Pittaway, E. (2004) '"Refugee Woman": A Dangerous Label', *Australian Journal of Human Rights* 20. Available at: <http://www.austlii.edu.au/au/journals/AJHR/2004/20.html>.

Pogge, T. (1989) *Realizing Rawls*. Ithaca, NY: Cornell University Press.

Pogge, T. (1994) 'Cosmopolitanism and Sovereignty', in C. Brown, *Political Restructuring in Europe*, 89–122.

Pogge, T. (1997) 'Migration and Poverty', in M. Veit-Bader, ed., *Citizenship and Exclusion*. Houndmills: Macmillan, 12–27; reprinted in R. Goodin and P. Pettit, eds (2005), *Contemporary Political Philosophy: An Anthology*. Oxford: Blackwell, 710–20.

Pogge, T. (1998) 'The Bounds of Nationalism', in J. Couture et al., eds, *Rethinking Nationalism Canadian Journal of Philosophy Supplementary Volume 22*: 463–504. Calgary: University of Calgary Press.

Pogge, T (2001a) 'Moral Universalism and Global Economic Justice', *Politics Philosophy and Economics* 1/1: 29.

Pogge, T. (2001b) 'Priorities of Global Justice', *Metaphilosophy* 32/1–2 (January) (Special Issue on Global Justice): 6–24.

Pogge, T. (2001c) 'Achieving Democracy', *Ethics and International Affairs* 15: 3–23.

Pogge, T. (2001d) 'Eradicating Systemic Poverty: Brief for a Global Resources Dividend', *Journal of Human Development* 2: 59–77.

Pogge, T. (2001e) 'Rawls on International Justice', *Philosophical Quarterly* 51: 246–53.

Pogge, T. (2002a) *World Poverty and Human Rights: Cosmopolitan Responsibilities and Reforms*. Cambridge: Polity.

Pogge, T. (2002b) 'Human Rights and Responsibilities', in De Greiff and Cronin, *Global Justice and Transnational Politics*, 151–96.

Pogge, T. (2002c) 'Cosmopolitanism: A Defence', *Critical Review of International Social and Political Philosophy* 5/3: 86–91.

Pogge, T. (2004) 'The First United Nations Millennium Development Goal: A Cause for Celebration?', *Journal of Human Development* 5/3 (November): 377–97.

Pogge, T. (2005a) 'World Poverty and Human Rights', *Ethics and International Affairs* 19/1: 1–8.

Pogge, T. (2005b) 'Recognized and Violated by International Law: The Human Rights of the Global Poor', *Leiden Journal of International Law* 18: 717–45.

Pogge, T. (ed) (2007) *Freedom from Poverty as a Human Right*. Oxford: Oxford University Press.

Pogge, T., and Horton, K. (2008) *Global Ethics: Seminal Essays*. St Paul, MN: Paragon House.

Pogge, T., and Moellendorf, D., eds (2008) *Global Justice: Seminal Essays*. St Paul, MN: Paragon House.

Ramsbotham, O., and Woodhouse, T. (1996) *Humanitarian Intervention in Contemporary Conflict*. Cambridge: Polity.

Rawls, J. (1972) *A Theory of Justice*. Oxford: Oxford University Press.

Rawls, J. (1996) *Political Liberalism*. Columbia: Columbia University Press.

Rawls, J. (1999) *The Law of Peoples*. Cambridge, MA: Harvard University Press.

Rengger, N. (2002) 'On the Just War Tradition in the Twenty-first Century', *International Affairs* 78/2: 353–63.

Reus-Smit, C. (2005) 'Liberal Hierarchy and the License to Use Force', *Review of International Studies* 31 (December): 71–92.

Robinson, F. (1999). *Globalizing Care: Toward a Politics of Peace*. Boston, MA: Beacon Press.

Robinson, F. (2008) 'The Importance of Care in the Theory and Practice of Human Security', *Journal of International Political Theory* 4/2: 167–88.

Rousseau, J. J. (1968) *The Social Contract*. London: Penguin.

Sandel, M. (1982) *Liberalism and the limits of Justice*. Cambridge: Cambridge University Press.

Seckinelgin, H. (2004) 'Between Aspirations and Assimilations: The World's Poor Meet the Cosmopolitans', *Alternatives* 29/1 (January–February): 69–88.

Seglow, J. (2005) 'The Ethics of Immigration', *Political Studies Review* 3: 317–34.

Sen, A. (1998) 'Justice across Borders', in De Greiff and Cronin, *Global Justice and Transnational Politics*, 37–52.

Shapcott, R. (2001) *Justice, Community and Dialogue in International Relations*. Cambridge: Cambridge University Press.

Shapcott, R. (2007) 'Global Justice and Cosmopolitan Democracy', in R. Devetak, A. Burke and J. George, eds, *An Introduction to International Relations: Australian Perspectives*. Cambridge: Cambridge University Press, 109–19.

Shapcott, R. (2008a) 'Anti-Cosmopolitanism, Pluralism and the Cosmopolitan Harm Principle', *Review of International Studies* 34 (April): 185–205.

Shapcott, R. (2008b) 'International Ethics', in S. Smith, J. Baylis and P. Owens, eds, *The Globalization of World Politics*, 4th edn. Oxford: Oxford University Press, 192–206.

Shapiro, I., and Brilmayer, L., eds (1999) *Nomos: Global Justice*. New York: New York University Press.

Shue, H. (1980) *Basic Rights*. Princeton, NJ: Princeton University Press.

Shue, H. (1981) 'Exporting Hazards', in P. G. Brown and H. Shue, eds, *Boundaries: National Autonomy and its Limits*. New York: Rowman & Littlefield, 24–40.

Shue, H. (1983) 'The Burdens of Justice', *The Journal of Philosophy* 80/10 (Part 1): 600–8.

Shue, H. (1992) 'The Unavoidability of Justice', in Hurrell and Kingsbury, *The International Politics of the Environment*. Oxford: Clarendon Press, 373–97.

Shue, H. (1996) 'Environmental Changes and the Varieties of Justice,' in Fen Osler Hampson and Judith Reppy, eds, *Earthly Goods Environmental Change and Social Justice*. Ithaca, NY: Cornell University Press, 9–29.

Shue, H. (2008) 'Subsistence Emissions and Luxury Emissions', in T. Pogge and K. Horton, *Global Ethics*, 207–32.

Simmons, A. J. (2001) *Justification and Legitimacy: Essays on Rights and Obligations*. Cambridge: Cambridge University Press.

Singer, P. (1972) 'Famine Affluence, Morality', *Philosophy and Public Affairs* 1/3 (spring): 229–43.

Singer, P., ed. (1990) *A Companion to Ethics*. Oxford: Blackwell.

Singer, P. (2000) 'About Ethics' (from *Practical Ethics*), in *Writings on an Ethical Life*. New York: HarperCollins, 7–20.

Singer, P. (2002) *One World: The Ethics of Globalisation*. Melbourne: Text Publishing.

Singer, P., and Gregg, T. (2004) *How Ethical is Australia?* Melbourne: Australian Collaboration Black Inc.

Sinnott-Armstrong, W. (2006) 'Consequentialism', *Stanford Encyclopedia of Philosophy Online*. Available at: < http://plato.stanford.edu>.

Sjoberg, L. (2006) 'Gendered Realities of the Immunity Principle: Why Gender Analysis Needs Feminism', *ISQ* 50/4 (December): 889–910.

Slim, H. (1997) 'Relief Agencies and Moral Standing in War: Principles of Humanity, Neutrality, Impartiality and Solidarity', *Development in Practice* 7/4: 342–52.

Slim, H. (1998) 'Sharing a Universal Ethic: The Principle of Humanity in War', *International Journal of Human Rights* 2/4 (winter): 28–48.

Slim, H. (2002) 'Not Philanthropy But Rights: The Proper Politicisation of Humanitarian Philosophy,' *The International Journal of Human Rights* 6/2: 1–22.

Slim. H. (2003) 'Why Protect Civilians? Innocence, Immunity and Enmity in War', *International Affairs* 79/3: 481–501.

Soforonio, E. (2000) '"Humanitarianism that Harms": A Critique of NGO Charity in Southern Sudan', *Civil Wars* 3/3 (autumn): 45–73.

Sommaruga, C. (1999) 'Humanity: Our Priority Now and Always: Response to "Principles, Politics, and Humanitarian Action"', *Ethics and International Affairs* 13/1: 23–8.

The Sphere Project and the Humanitarian Charter (1996) *Sphere Handbook*. Available at: <http://www.sphereproject.org>.

Stanford Encyclopaedia of Philosophy. Available at: <http://plato.stanford.edu/ contents.html>.

Sterba, J. P. (2005) *The Triumph of Practice Over Theory in Ethics*. Oxford: Oxford University Press.

Stockton, N. (2002) 'The Failure of International Humanitarian Action in Afghanistan', *Global Governance* 8: 265–71.

Sutch, P. (2001) *Ethics, Justice and International Relations*. London: Routledge.

Tan, K. C. (2000) *Toleration, Diversity and Global Justice*. Pennsylvania: Pennsylvania State University Press.

Tanguy, J., and Terry, F. (1999) 'Humanitarian Responsibility and Committed Action', *Ethics and International Affairs* 13: 29–34.

Terry, F. (2002) *Condemned to Repeat?: The Paradox of Humanitarian Action*. Ithaca, NY, and London: Cornell University Press.

Thucydides [427 BC] (1972) *The History of the Peloponnesian War*. Harmondsworth: Penguin.

Thompson, Janna (1992) *Justice and World Order: A Philosophical Enquiry*. London: Routledge.

Tibi, B. (2002) 'War and Peace in Islam', in S. H. Hashmi, ed., *Islamic Political Ethics*, Princeton, NJ: Princeton University Press, 175–93.

Timmons, M. (2002) *Moral Theory: An Introduction*. Lanham, MD: Rowman & Littlefield.

Unger, Peter (1996) *Living High and Letting Die: Our Illusion of Innocence*. New York: New York University Press.

UNHCR (1951) United Nations Convention Relating to the Status of Refugees. Available at: <http://www.unhcr.org>.

UNHCR (2007) 'Global Trends: Refugees, Asylum-seekers, Returnees, Internally Displaced and Stateless Persons'. Available at: <http://www.unhcr.org/statistics>

UNHCR (2007–9) Protecting Refugees, the Role of the UNHCR. Available at: <http://www.unhcr.org>.

Valls, A. ed. (2000) *Ethics in International Affairs: Theories and Cases*. Lanham, MD: Rowman & Littlefield.

Vincent, R. J. (1986) *Human Rights in International Relations*, Cambridge: Cambridge University Press.

Vincent, R. J. (1992) 'The Idea of Human Rights in International Ethics', in T. Nardin and D. Mapel, eds, *Traditions of International Ethics*. Cambridge: Cambridge University Press, 250–65.

Walzer, M. (1977) *Just and Unjust Wars*. Harmondsworth and New York: Penguin.

Walzer, M. (1981) 'The Distribution of Membership', in P. G. Brown and H. Shue, eds, *Boundaries: National Autonomy and its Limits*, 24–40.

Walzer, Michael (1983) *Spheres of Justice*. Oxford: Blackwell.

Walzer, M. (1994) *Thick and Thin: Moral Argument at Home and Abroad*. Notre Dame, IN: University of Notre Dame Press.

Walzer, M. (1997) *On Toleration*. New Haven, CT: Yale University Press.

Walzer, M. (2003a) '(interview) Universalism, Equality, and Immigration', in Herlinde Pauer-struder, ed., *Constructions of Practical Reason: Interviews on Moral and Political Philosophy*. Stanford, CA: Stanford University Press, 194–213.

Walzer, M. (2003b) 'Interview', *Imprints: A Journal of Analytical Socialism* 7/1. Online content. Available at: <http://eis.bris.ac.uk/~plcdib/imprints/michaelwalzerinterview.html>.

Walzer, M. (2004) *Arguing about War*. New Haven, CT: Yale University Press.

Warner, D. (1999) 'Searching for Responsibility/Community in International Relations', in D. Campbell and M. Shapiro, eds, *Moral Spaces: Rethinking Ethics and World Politics*. Minneapolis, MN: University of Minnesota Press, 1–28.

Weiner, M. (1996) 'Ethics, National Sovereignty and the Control of Immigration', *The International Migration Review* 30/1 (spring): 171–97.

Weiss, T. (1999) 'The Humanitarian Identity Crisis', *Ethics and International Affairs* 13: 1–22.

Weissman, F., ed. (2004) *In the Shadow of 'Just Wars': Violence, Politics and Humanitarian Action*. Ithaca, NY: Cornell University Press.

Weithman, P. J. (1992) 'Natural Law, Solidarity, and International Justice', in Brian Barry and Robert E. Goodin, eds, *Free Movement*, 181–202.

Wenar, L. (2006) 'Why Rawls is Not a Cosmopolitan Egalitarian', in R. Martin and D. A. Reidy, eds, *Rawls's Law of Peoples*, 95–114.

Wenar. L, (2007) 'Responsibility and Severe Poverty', in T. Pogge, ed., *Freedom from Poverty as a Human Right*, 255–74.

Wesley, M. (2005) 'Towards a Realist Ethics of Intervention', *Ethics and International Affairs* 19/2: 55–72.

Wheeler, N. J. (2000) *Saving Strangers*. Oxford: Oxford University Press.

Wheeler, N., ed., (1999) *Human Rights in Global Politics*. Cambridge: Cambridge University Press.

Wheeler, N., and Dunne, T. (1996) 'Hedley Bull's Pluralism of the Intellect and Solidarism of the Will', *International Affairs* 72: 1–17.

Wight, M. (1991) *International Theory: The Three Traditions*. Leicester: Leicester University Press.

Williams, B. (1973) 'A Critique of Utilitarianism', in J. J. C. Smart and B. Williams, *Utilitarianism: For and Against*. Cambridge: Cambridge University Press, 77–150.

Williams, B. (1985) *Ethics and the Limits of Philosophy*. London: Fontana.

Williams, M. C. (2005) *The Realist Tradition and the Limits of International Relations*. Cambridge: Cambridge University Press.

Williams, R. E., and Caldwell, D. (2006) 'Jus Post Bellum: Just War Theory and the Principles of Just Peace', *International Studies Perspectives* 7: 309–20.

Woods, N., and Hurrell, A., eds (2000) *Inequality, Globalisation and World Politics*, Oxford: Oxford University Press.

Young, I. M. (1990) *Justice and the Politics of Difference*. Princeton, NJ: Princeton University Press.

Index